Winning America's
Second Civil War

Winning America's Second Civil War

Progressivism's Authoritarian Threat,
Where It Came From, and How to Defeat It

JEFFREY E. PAUL

New York • London

First American edition published in 2023 by Encounter Books,
an activity of Encounter for Culture and Education, Inc.,
a nonprofit, tax-exempt corporation.
Encounter Books website address: www.encounterbooks.com

Manufactured in the United States and printed on
acid-free paper. The paper used in this publication meets
the minimum requirements of ANSI/NISO Z39.48–1992
(R 1997) (*Permanence of Paper*).

FIRST AMERICAN EDITION

LIBRARY OF CONGRESS CATALOGING-IN-PUBLICATION DATA IS AVAILABLE
Information for this title can be found at the Library of Congress
website under the following ISBN 9781641773799 and LCCN 2023054388.

This book is dedicated to Herbert Tuttle, who was Cornell University's highly esteemed historian of Germany. In the August 1883 issue of the *Atlantic Monthly*, Tuttle warned that an influx of Americans who were earning doctoral degrees in German universities and attaining appointments at American universities in the humanities and social sciences could have a disastrous effect on higher education. The theory of government they learned abroad, he explained, was the opposite of this country's founding ideals; it "assumes as postulates the ignorance of the individual and the omniscience of the government," a government, moreover, "removed as far as possible from" the influence of elected legislatures and public opinion. If America's academic "pilgrims are faithful disciples of their masters," Tuttle concluded, they will be "advocates of a political system, which, if adopted and literally carried out, would wholly change the spirit of our institutions, and destroy all that is oldest and noblest in our natural life."

CONTENTS

PREFACE

In 18th-century colonial America, two irreconcilable institutions and their justifications clashed—slavery, which had existed from the beginning of recorded human history, and the universal human right of self-ownership. The latter derived from John Locke's *Second Treatise of Civil Government*, initially published in England in 1690, thereafter making its way to America. By the time of the Declaration of Independence, the belief that all individuals have natural rights had become the dominant view among imminent revolutionaries like George Mason, John and Samuel Adams, and Thomas Jefferson. From the Lockean view that all persons have an exclusive right of ownership over themselves, and, therefore, to their liberty, it followed that the product of an individual's labor would be his or her exclusive property. Governments do not "create" these rights; instead, they exist to protect them and surely not to violate them.

And yet the governments of the colonies that adopted this view through their Declaration were openly engaged in violating the rights that they claimed to be absolute and universal. This contradiction went unresolved (though several of the former colonies, now states, went on to abolish slavery) until the Civil War and the subsequent adoption of the Thirteenth, Fourteenth, and Fifteenth Amendments to the Constitution.

It is, therefore, remarkable that after the deaths of hundreds of thousands of Americans in a war that freed the slaves, higher education's most influential university and college professors,

◆

calling themselves progressives, would turn against the rights that freed them. Having more in common with the social and political outlook of the defeated Confederacy (and its subsequent Jim Crow laws) than with the republican principles of the victorious Union, these academics became the growing enemy of this country's founding principles, with deleterious consequences in primary and secondary education, law, the judiciary, journalism, and politics. How this happened and what can be done to transcend its adverse consequences for American political culture and institutions is the subject of this book.

◆

CHAPTER 1

TWO AMERICAN CIVIL WARS
Human Rights and Their Domestic Enemies

This book is an account of the preface to two American civil wars. The first, waged from 1861 to 1865, was ultimately the result of an irreconcilable disagreement about slavery—an obvious violation of the individual's right to liberty that American revolutionaries invoked to justify their break from Great Britain. The second emerged in 2016, when members of the outgoing administration, along with others inside and outside of the government, used their powers illicitly in an attempt to determine the results of a presidential election in order to impose an outcome that reflected their own preferences.[1]

This second civil war is ultimately the result of an irreconcilable disagreement over the central principle that animated the first. And both were preceded by sharp philosophical disputes that began slightly more than a century before the outbreak of each conflict.

The philosophical dispute that led to the first civil war is well-known and thoroughly documented, though I will summarize it. The second philosophical dispute is not well-known and began slightly more than a decade after the defeat of the Confederacy. Its unlikely origins were in Germany, where most of the first generation of this country's doctoral faculty were educated.

◆

This group seeded the graduate programs initiated by American universities in the 1870s, 1880s, and 1890s.

The American college students and graduates who studied in Germany returned with an opposition to this country's founding principles—specifically, the natural rights of the individual—as virulent and inflexible as that embraced by the defenders of slavery several decades earlier. They sought to reconstruct and replace America's governmental and economic institutions in the image of Germany's autocratic government and oligarchical society. The graduate programs they established and led would appoint their successors in American universities, who would appoint, in turn, *their* successors. The cumulative impact on education, law, journalism, and political culture over seven generations cannot be overstated. The effect of their efforts amounted to a new American founding—or more precisely, a counter-founding—by the turn of the 20th century based on principles antithetical to the first. An increasingly common view that this country's transformation was set in motion by the rise of the New Left in the 1960s, in other words, is off—by almost 90 years.

NATURAL RIGHTS: A HISTORICAL SINGULARITY

What were those two sets of opposed principles that led to both civil wars? The first, invoked by America's Founders and their predecessors in essays and pamphlets that appeared before the Declaration of Independence, were drawn principally from one particular work published in 1690 and written by the English philosopher John Locke. Locke's *Second Treatise of Government* argued that

> every man has a property in his own person; this nobody has a right to but himself. The labor of his body and the work of his

hands, we may say, are properly his. Whatsoever then he removes out of that state that nature has provided and left it in, he has mixed his labor with, and joined to it something that is his own, and thereby makes it his property. It being by him removed from the common state nature has placed it in, it has by this labor something annexed to it that excludes the common right of other men.[2]

Among the early Americans to defend this universal human right of self-ownership was the Massachusetts attorney James Otis. In his 1764 essay *The Rights of the British Colonies Asserted and Proved*, he wrote that "there is nothing more evident, says Mr. Locke, than 'that creatures of the same species and rank, promiscuously born to all the same advantages of nature and the use of the same faculties, should also be equal one among another.'"[3] "The natural liberty of man," Otis continued, quoting Locke, "'is to be free from any superior power on earth, and not to be under the will or legislative authority of man, but only to have the law of nature for his rule.'"[4]

Otis also said, "The Colonists are by the law of nature free born, as indeed all men are, white or black." He warned of the "cruel slavery exercised over the poor Ethiopians; which threatens one day to reduce both Europe and America to the ignorance and barbarity of the darkest ages."[5] He was joined by Samuel Adams, a member of the Massachusetts House of Representatives. "Among the natural Rights of the Colonists," Adams wrote in 1772, "are these: *First*, a Right to Life; *Secondly*, to Liberty; *Thirdly*, to Property; together with the right to support and defend them in the best manner they can."[6]

These views were hardly exceptional: Locke's understanding of natural rights based on self-ownership was widely espoused in the colonies. To take one example, a 1775 pamphlet, *America's Appeal to the Impartial World*, by Connecticut minister Moses Mather declared

◆

that man hath an absolute property in, and right of dominion over himself, his powers and faculties; with self-love to stimulate, and reason to guide him, in the free use and exercise of them, independent of, and uncontrol[l]able by any but him, who created and gave them. And whatever is acquired by the use, and application of a man's faculties, is equally the property of that man, as the faculties by which the acquisitions are made.[7]

The appeal to natural rights that would justify the American Revolution could have easily been replaced by a justification strictly in terms of the absence of representation in the British Parliament, which was taxing and regulating the colonies. While this appeal was made in the Declaration of Independence,[8] it was only one complaint in a long list headlined by the invocation of universal human rights. And of course, invoking these rights placed many of the Founders in a position of gross hypocrisy (and their subsequent government arguably in a position of illegitimacy, given that the component states of the new nation allowed slavery at the outset of the revolution).[9]

Nevertheless, the First Continental Congress declared on October 14, 1774, that "by the immutable laws of nature," the inhabitants of the colonies of North America "are entitled to life, liberty, and property."[10] And in his draft Declaration of Independence, Thomas Jefferson stated that "We hold these truths to be self-evident: that all men are created equal; that they are endowed by their creator with [certain] inherent and self-evident rights; that among these are life, liberty and the pursuit of happiness."[11]

Jefferson understood the contradiction between the revolutionaries' moral justification for their revolution and the stark reality of slavery. He added a paragraph to the draft— subsequently deleted by the Second Continental Congress at the particular insistence of South Carolina and Georgia—that sought to shift the blame.

The "present King of Great Britain," according to Jefferson, "has waged cruel war against human nature itself, violating its most sacred rights of life and liberty in the persons of a distant people who never offended him, captivating & carrying them into slavery in another hemisphere or to incur miserable death in their transportation thither." And, he added, "Determined to keep open a market where *Men* should be bought & sold, he has prostituted his negative for suppressing every legislative attempt to prohibit or to restrain this execrable commerce."[12] Having attempted this exculpation of the slaveholders' crimes, a ban on slavery was included in Section 14, Article 6 of the Northwest Ordinance passed in 1787 by the Confederation Congress. Ultimately, the U.S. Constitution did not outlaw slavery, but as Princeton historian Sean Wilentz has recently emphasized, the document drafted in 1787 carefully avoided statements that would validate the principle that there could be a property right held by one person in another.[13]

Locke's concept of natural rights would exercise a lasting influence in this country. As the founder and first rector of the University of Virginia, for instance, Jefferson would have a resolution passed that required all students in the law school to read Locke's *Second Treatise of Government*.[14] And as the contradiction between liberty and slavery became more glaring in the decades following the revolution, antislavery advocates grew ever more vociferous, especially about a human being's self-ownership, the concept pioneered by Locke. As one abolitionist leader, Theodore Dwight Weld, put it in 1838, "if justice adjudges the slave to be 'private property,' it adjudges him to be *his own* property, since the right to *one's-self* is the first right—the source of all others—the original stock by which they are accumulated—the principal, of which they are the interest."[15]

◆

Another vigorous opponent of slavery was Francis Wayland (1796–1865), the president of Brown University and a professor of moral philosophy.[16] His widely influential treatise *The Elements of Moral Science*, first published in 1835, would sell more than 200,000 copies in the 19th century.[17] Wayland distinguished between "society" and "government," noting that "Government is merely the instrument by which it [society] accomplishes its purposes. Government is the *agent*. Society is the *principal*."[18] And the individuals who make up society all have the fundamental right of self-ownership:

> Thus a man has an entire right to use his own *body* as he will, provided he do[es] not so use it as to interfere with the rights of his neighbor. He may go where he will and stay where he please; he may work or be idle; he may pursue one occupation or another or no occupation at all; and it is the concern of no one else, if he leave[s] inviolate the rights of every one else.[19]

Frederick Douglass, a former slave and famous abolitionist leader, also emphasized that "Every man is the *original, natural, rightful* and *absolute* owner of his own body...and can only part from *his* self-ownership, by the commission of [a] crime."[20] To his former owner, Douglass wrote:

> I am myself; you are yourself; we are two distinct persons, equal persons. What you are I am....God created both, and made us separate beings. I am not by nature bound by you, or you to me. Nature does not make your existence depend upon me, or mine to depend upon yours.[21]

Natural rights and self-ownership as conceived by Douglass, Wayland, Jefferson, and Locke before them, pertained to the relationship between man and society. Their larger framework was the theistic worldview shared by most Americans (and Englishmen)—though many, like Locke, saw nature as God's creation so that His intentions could be inferred directly from it.

Others, then and now, base these rights simply on the observed facts of nature. My own view is that every living animal has a body and a neurological system to regulate its movements and provide for its awareness of its physical environment. The human species is unique in that its members have the mental capacity to recognize and understand abstractly what they are and what they exclusively possess. Members of the human species, therefore, unlike those of other animal species, are capable of claiming that they have a body and brain and are able, in addition, to make agreements with other members of their species to respect what each owns. Some political and moral philosophers would explicitly or tacitly argue that having a body does not imply that one should own it. One alternative, of course, is that it should be owned by someone who has the privilege of self-ownership and the privilege of ownership of others. The other alternative is that no one owns his or her body or that of anyone else. We will examine some of these claims later in this book.

For most of history, some human beings have claimed an entitlement not only to what nature has given them but to what nature has given others. From Egyptian pharaohs to communist dictators, tyrants have either implicitly or explicitly claimed ownership of everyone else; and personal slavery has existed, and continues to exist, in various societies. The justifications have ranged from divine selection to paternalistic superiority, in which the governed or the slave is supposed to be the beneficiary of the wisdom of the master. Pretexts aside, nature has given to each living thing a single body and life, and to humans the capacity to understand what he or she has been given and, therefore, owns.

◆

To be sure, in cases where mental impairment makes it difficult to conduct one's affairs, civilized societies create the legal means of providing a guardianship or conservatorship for specific instances of such impairment. Human infants will acquire that capacity, unlike the infants of other species, and are, therefore, treated as adults with respect to the right of self-ownership, though under the guardianship of their parents. But the claims made by any number of aspiring dictators, autocrats, paternalists, and predators to a privilege of self-ownership not enjoyed by others are groundless deceptions ending typically in catastrophe for the subjects of their rule.

The Lockean conception of a right of self-ownership universally possessed by all members of the human species was remarkable not only for its singularity in American history but also for its singularity in human history. It replaced the ownership of one human by another—whether a monarch, emperor, tyrant, majority of his fellows, the nation, or some race—with universal self-ownership, and by doing so, restricted the principal role of governments to the protection of that right and others implied by it.

LIBERTY A "PRIVILEGE" NOT A RIGHT?

Nevertheless, the concept of natural rights that are prelegal—that are prior to, and the purpose of, government, and are written into the Declaration of Independence and the Constitution's Bill of Rights[22]—would soon come under a mounting and sustained attack. The most famous opponent in the first half of 19th-century America was John C. Calhoun, a vice president of the United States under two presidents, the sixteenth secretary of state, the tenth secretary of war, a congressman and then a senator from South Carolina, as well as a slave owner and fierce

♦

defender of slavery. In a speech on the floor of the U.S. Senate, Calhoun argued that it had been unnecessary for Jefferson to have inserted the phrase that "all men are created equal" in the Declaration of Independence to justify the American Revolution, as the "lawless encroachment[s] on our acknowledged and well-established rights by the parent country, were the real causes" of the colonies' separation.[23]

"The state of nature has a law of nature to govern it," Locke wrote, that "obliges every one; and reason, which is that law, teaches all mankind who will but consult it that, being all equal and independent, no one ought to harm another in his life, health, liberty, or possessions."[24] Calhoun rejected Locke's reasoning. He denied that all men are born "either free or equal, as if those high qualities belonged to man without effort to acquire them, and to all equally alike, regardless of their intellectual and moral condition." Liberty and equality were not *intrinsic* to being human: instead, Calhoun claimed, they were a grant by the government, "high prizes to be won," he said, "the highest reward that can be bestowed on our race, but the most difficult to be won—and when won, the most difficult to be preserved."[25] Jefferson, according to Calhoun, had "an utterly false view of the subordinate relation of the black to the white race in the South; and to hold, in consequence, that the former, though utterly unqualified to possess liberty, were as fully entitled to both liberty and equality as the latter; and that to deprive them of it was unjust and immoral."[26]

The crucial point here is that Calhoun, like his fellow defenders of slavery, finds that, first, he must deny that *all* members of the human species are uniquely endowed by nature with a property right in themselves, and second, he must argue that governments, therefore, possess autocratic discretion to invent and assign "rights" as privileges—a fundamental position that effectively renders political institutions unbounded in their powers. Calhoun, in

◆

short, defended political institutions that it had been the purpose of America's natural-rights revolutionaries to escape.

Calhoun's denial that all individuals had natural rights to life, liberty, and the pursuit of happiness was echoed by other defenders of slavery. Some, like John Fletcher in his 637-page *Study on Slavery in Easy Lessons* (1852), cited biblical evidence of God's sanctioning of slavery.[27] Fletcher's principal adversaries were Brown University's Francis Wayland and William Ellery Channing, a Unitarian minister and abolitionist in Boston, Massachusetts.[28]

Another defender of slavery—Albert Taylor Bledsoe, a professor of mathematics at the University of Virginia—acknowledged that human beings have natural rights, but such rights are superseded by a higher principle: "The general good is the sole and sufficient consideration which justifies the state in taking the life or liberty of its subjects."[29] The general good, he went on to claim, is served by assigning those undeserving of liberty to a subservient status. Again, the argument is that *rights are ultimately the creation of political institutions*—they are not antecedent to government and do not set boundaries on the government. Whatever "unalienable rights" can be plausibly claimed by human beings may be overridden by the government when assessing their contribution to, or detraction from, the general good in particular cases.

Perhaps the most unqualified defense of American slavery before the Civil War was presented by George Fitzhugh in two books, *Sociology for the South: Or the Failure of Free Society* (1854) and *Cannibals All! Or Slaves without Masters* (1857). What makes Fitzhugh's arguments striking is that they anticipated much of the criticism that German-trained American academics and their students would make of this country's founding institutions.

Fitzhugh not only denounced natural rights as fictitious inventions. He also claimed that it was the employees of private

◆

businesses, rather than the South's slaves, who were the victims of exploitation. It was the capitalist society of the North, not slavery in the South, that needed to be replaced, and replaced by socialism, which, like slavery, would tend to the needs of those unsuited, in Fitzhugh's view, to fend for themselves.

The putative natural right to oneself and the fruits of one's labor, as Fitzhugh would have it, was a pretext invented by those who were aspiring exploiters of the weak and whose principal motivation was greed. Fitzhugh disputed the contention that capitalist economies and free trade maximized the standard of living of both employers and their employees. Socialism and limitations on foreign trade, he believed, were economically superior to their alternatives.

"Liberty and free competition," Fitzhugh claimed, "is especially injurious to the poorer class; for besides the labor necessary to support the family, the poor man is burdened with the care of finding a home, and procuring employment, and attending to all domestic wants and concerns." Thus, he announced,

> slavery relieves our slaves of these cares altogether, and slavery is a form, and the very best form, of socialism.... The association of labor properly carried out under a common head or ruler, would render labor more efficient, relieve the laborer of many of the cares of household affairs, and protect and support him in sickness and old age, besides preventing the too great reduction of wages by redundancy of labor and free competition. Slavery attains all these results.[30]

To the abolitionist claim that "Man ought not to have property in man," Fitzhugh responded that "the great truth which lies at the foundation of all society" is *that every man has property in his fellow-man!* It is because that adequate provision is not made properly to enforce this great truth in free society, that men are

◆

driven to the necessity of attempting to remedy the defects of government by voluntary associations, that carry into definite and practical operation this great and glorious truth."[31]

The conclusion Fitzhugh drew was that "Socialism is already slavery in all save the master. It had as well adopt that feature at once, as come to that it must to make its schemes at once humane and efficient." The "only quarrel" he had "with Socialism is, that it will not honestly admit that it owes its recent revival to the failure of universal liberty, and is seeking to bring about slavery again in some form."[32]

Thankfully, the proposal on offer from Fitzhugh was rejected in this country. It would of course be attempted in 20th-century Russia, China, Cuba, Cambodia, North Korea, North Vietnam, and Eastern Europe, with catastrophic results for the living standards of their inhabitants, as well as costing millions of lives.[33] By contrast, this country's capitalist economy fostered a plenitude that all manner of commentators have recognized.

"From a comparative perspective," as law professor Ajay K. Mehrotra observed, "the United States by the 1880s had per capita real income levels that were among the highest in the world. Although American prosperity was astonishingly disparate, the general standard of living in the United States outpaced many countries, including leading European imperial powers."[34] In his authoritative study; Johns Hopkins economist Clarence D. Long concluded that "Daily wages and annual earnings in manufacturing both increased about 50% between 1860 and 1890."[35] Princeton economist Thomas C. Leonard nicely summarized America's extraordinary economic growth in this period:

> In 1870, the last of the Civil War amendments to the US Constitution was ratified. Thirty-five years later, the US economy had *quadrupled* in size. American living standards had doubled. US

economic output surpassed each of the German, French, and Japanese empires in the 1870s. It overtook the nineteenth century's global colossus, the British Empire, in 1916.[36]

These modern scholars were preceded a century earlier by Werner Sombart, a German Marxian socialist at the time, who sought to answer the question posed in the title of his famous 1906 book, *Why Is There No Socialism in the United States?* "This much is certain," Sombart concluded; "the American worker lives in comfortable circumstances."[37] He drew this conclusion from a meticulous comparison of American and German living standards (based on official records of both countries). Industry by industry—including clothing, wood, iron and steel, textiles, and chemicals—the average annual wages of American workers were double, even triple that of their German counterparts.[38] "We ought never to forget," Sombart added, "the continuous progress that 'economic prosperity' in the United States has made, apart from short interruptions, in the last two generations, during which time one would have thought that Socialism could not have failed to take root. Evidently this prosperity was not in spite of capitalism but because of it."[39]

In the decades following the American Revolution, the conflict between natural rights and slavery was ultimately resolved by a civil war to free a population from Fitzhugh's socialist heaven and promulgate constitutional amendments intended to secure legal equality for the emancipated slaves.[40] Yet this civil war turned out to be the last chapter of the American Revolution rather than the prelude to a new chapter. Instead, a counterrevolution began silently and out of public view that would, over time, set the stage for a second civil war.

◆

CHAPTER 2

COUNTERREVOLUTION

A fter 1865, the philosophy of natural rights—pioneered by John Locke, written into the Declaration of Independence, and reaffirmed by constitutional amendments following the Revolutionary and Civil Wars—would have seemed to be a settled statement about the fundamental relationship between the individual and the government. Yet less than four decades later, Charles Edward Merriam—the founder of the political science department at the University of Chicago and a major proponent of progressivism—concluded that the consensus among his academic peers had taken a radically different turn. The "individualistic ideas of the 'natural right' school of political theory, [e]ndorsed in the Revolution," he wrote in *A History of American Political Theories* (1903), have been "discredited and repudiated."[1] Instead, as an example of the then-current view, he quoted John W. Burgess, the founder of Columbia University's doctoral program, that "the state is the source of individual liberty."[2]

With natural rights repudiated, so too was equality before the law. "Liberty," Merriam declared, "is not a right equally enjoyed by all. It is dependent upon the degree of civilization reached by the given people, and increases as this advances." From this premise, Merriam claimed first that "the Teutonic nations are particularly endowed with political capacity," and thus "in a state composed of several nationalities, the Teutonic element should never surrender

◆

15

the balance of power to the others." Internationally, he added, "the Teutonic races must civilize the politically uncivilized" and "barbaric races, if incapable, may be swept away." Such action, Merriam wrote approvingly, again quoting Burgess, "violates no rights of these populations which are not petty and trifling in comparison with its [the Teutonic races'] transcendent right and duty to establish political and legal order everywhere."[3] This sort of unblinking ethnocentrism/racism was not uncommon among the early progressives, and added credibility to their claim, with John C. Calhoun, that rights are to be assigned by governments on the basis of race.[4]

In addition to rescinding natural rights and restoring racial privileges, Merriam favored a limited degree of socialism. The functions of the state, according to Merriam, are two. First are those that governments must perform because otherwise they would be performed by no one. Second are those, like communication and transportation, that *would* be performed through private initiative but *should not* be. Railways, telephone, and telegraphs, he suggested, might best operate as government monopolies, as "socialistic" functions.[5] "The new position," Merriam wrote, "is a mean between Socialism and extreme individualism."[6]

Another academic progressive, Woodrow Wilson—a professor of history and political science, president of Princeton University, and governor of New Jersey—was elected president of the United States in 1912. He too dismissed natural rights[7] and equality before the law. Once in office, Wilson quietly approved segregation in the federal civil service, which had been integrated after the Civil War. This included separate bathrooms, offices, and lunchrooms, dismissing black supervisors, and requiring photographs for anyone applying for a job.[8] At a tense meeting in the White House, Wilson dismissed the protests of black leader William Monroe

◆

Trotter, claiming that the issue had nothing to do with "intrinsic equality." According to the president, it involved "economic equality—whether the Negro can do the same things with equal efficiency." Once that was proven, "a lot of things are going to solve themselves."[9] (Years earlier, however, after Wilson became president of Princeton, historian Henry Blumenthal noted that "all Negroes were successfully encouraged to withdraw their applications for admission."[10])

How a country that had fought a revolution and a civil war on behalf of natural rights came to establish research universities in the late 19th century whose doctoral faculties held the views of men such as Merriam and Burgess and Wilson—and what effect it has had on American society—is the major subject of this book. It is a question, the introductory answer to which has three parts. The first is the European opposition to natural rights, especially by German academics. The second is an explanation of why American colleges felt impelled to import faculty trained at German universities. The third is the unintended effect of that importation.

CONTRA LOCKE: ROUSSEAU, BENTHAM, AND THE GERMANS

Opponents of natural rights surfaced early in 18th-century Europe. The first of them was Jean-Jacques Rousseau (1712–1778). Locke had claimed for members of the human species a right of self-ownership that implied a right to one's liberty and to one's labor and its fruits. These rights, Locke asserted, could either be personally protected by their holders or secured by employing a provider of such protection. One of the possible means of doing so was by coalescing with others to create an instrument to provide protection for the rights of the coalition, i.e., a government. That government, with the consent and financial support of the governed, could provide rules or laws and the means of their execution.

Rousseau did not acknowledge the existence of such rights but assumed that conditions had become such that the preservation of human life and liberty without an aggregate defense was no longer feasible. The problem was to "find a form of association which may defend and protect the person and property of every associate, and by means of which each, coalescing with all, may nevertheless obey only himself and remain as free as before."[11] But for Rousseau, unlike for Locke, while the members of the association may be moved to coalesce to protect their persons and property, *they have no prelegal rights to either.* Instead, he insisted that in such a compact the individual surrenders himself and all he owns to the collective: "Each of us puts in common his person and his whole power under the supreme direction of the general will; and in return we receive every member as an indivisible part of the whole."[12]

The act of association, Rousseau asserted, "produces a moral and collective body, which is composed of as many members as the assembly has voices, and which receive from this act its unity, its common self (*moi*), its life, and its will."[13] Moreover, "the State, with regard to its members, is owner of all their property by the social contract."[14] Once what Rousseau called "the General Will" of the association is exercised, it directs "the forces of the State according to the object of its institution, which is the common good."[15]

But the General Will of the people and what Rousseau called the "will of all," i.e., their expressed elective preferences, may not be the same. When they differ, the general will, which is the exclusive means to the common good, must prevail and the electoral preferences of the voters are ignored or changed. To direct their preferences toward an expression of the general will, Rousseau insisted, requires a person of exceptional genius and power, whom he called "the Legislator."[16] This person must "speak to the vulgar in their own language instead of a popular way that will not be understood."[17]

Ultimately, Rousseau wrote, the legislator needs to rely on some other authority to compel obedience "without violence and persuade without convincing," and "it is this which in all ages has constrained the founders of nations to resort to the intervention of heaven." The legislator puts "into the mouths of the immortals that sublime reason which soars beyond the reach of common men, in order that he may win over by divine authority those whom human prudence could not move."[18]

The stark contrast between Locke's natural-rights republic and Rousseau's pseudomajoritarian dictatorship—concealed ineffectually by the latter's use of a social compact as the pretext for one-man rule—led, unsurprisingly, to a disparity in the revolutions produced by each. The French Revolution led to the Jacobin dictatorship and terror of Maximilien Robespierre, who repeatedly cited Rousseau to justify his tyranny,[19] followed a few years later by the Napoleonic Empire.

Locke's principal critic in England was Jeremy Bentham (1748–1832), for whom the concept of natural rights as antecedent to government and its laws was empty. The statement of these rights in the Declaration of Independence he called a "cloud of words," "absurd and visionary," and the "opinions of the modern Americans on Government, like those of their good ancestors on witchcraft, would be too ridiculous to deserve any notice, if like them too, contemptible and extravagant as they be, they had not led to the most serious evils."[20] In another famous passage, Bentham wrote that "natural rights is simple nonsense: natural and imprescriptible rights, rhetorical nonsense,—nonsense upon stilts."[21]

◆

Bentham erroneously attributed to Lockeans a mistaken equation of possession of rights and their enforcement by government. But Locke claimed that the right of self-ownership is a part of human nature and is, therefore, prior to its enforcement by any government.[22] Human beings can claim entitlement to themselves, a claim that lower species are incapable of making. Human governments can protect what each human being has (or is), or not, and claim entitlement to other human beings. Only the former entitlement, for Locke, is just. The latter is unjust because it gives to the governors something *that is not their own.*

Having dismissed the existence of an entitlement to oneself, Bentham goes on to claim that since all humans seek pleasure and attempt to avoid pain, the former must be good and the latter evil.[23] Moreover, according to Bentham's most prominent disciple, John Stuart Mill, each person seeks his own happiness as a good, and therefore, he said, people collectively should seek to maximize the happiness of their greatest number.[24] Bentham and Mill called this the utilitarian principle. And governments, then, should legislate to secure the utilitarian principle.

The defects of utilitarianism are apparent. If the happiness of any individual is good in itself regardless of its source, then the pleasure of the rapist is morally indistinguishable from the pleasure of a surgeon who saves someone's life. If in order to circumvent this equation, one introduces some measure to distinguish good from bad pleasures, then the utilitarian enterprise collapses, *since that measure overrides the utilitarian principle.*

Moreover, how does it follow from the claim that the maximization of any individual's happiness is good for him, that the greatest happiness of the greatest number of people is the highest good? The fulfillment of the greatest happiness of the greatest number may require the pain of some, which Bentham said is

♦

evil. Which is it? Bentham has endorsed two different ends that can be mutually exclusive.

For both Bentham and Rousseau, individual self-ownership and liberty can only be instrumentally good if they secure the General Will (for Rousseau) or the greatest happiness of the greatest number (for Bentham). For Locke, by contrast, self-ownership is a right the protection of which is the *purpose* of any legitimate government, not simply a means to secure some other end.

This brings us to Germany, where a tradition of unbending opposition to natural rights can be traced to Johann Gottlieb Fichte (1762–1814), who taught philosophy at the Universities of Jena and Berlin. Like Rousseau, he viewed the union of individual wills by social compact as having produced a General Will embodied in the state. Lockean rights do not exist. Individual liberty is only to be protected when it is a means of securing the General Will of the state. (In the 20th century, the Nazis would cite Fichte as a source of their views.)

Fichte was succeeded by Georg Wilhelm Friedrich Hegel (1770–1831), who taught at the University of Berlin. For Hegel, the state is like an organism, and its inhabitants are like cells within it. The "real" will of each inhabitant is to secure what is in the interests of the state, for its interests advance the collective interests of its inhabitants. Individual "freedom" for Hegel consists in obedience to the commands of the state when individual inclinations are to oppose it, because, like Rousseau, the individual's "real will" is never opposed to the commands of the state, which always accord with the real interests of all. And human history as embodied in states follows a trajectory in which superior states succeed inferior ones, frequently by means of armed conquests. Human history, in this way, is driven by an internal *telos* of progressive improvement. Hegel's philosophy decisively influenced his German academic successors in philosophy, history, political

◆

science, and economics in the latter half of the 19th century and for much of the 20th century (including nonacademic philosophers like Karl Marx).

Examples of such successors included Johann Kaspar Bluntschli (1808–1881), a professor of political science at the University of Heidelberg, who would influence the thinking of several American progressive academics.[25] "If the ancient philosophers did not sufficiently regard the rights of individuals," Bluntschli argued, "the modern have committed the opposite error so much as to ignore the significance of the State as a whole."[26] In summarizing the superiority of Hegel to the natural-rights theorists, Bluntschli described him as having "emphasized the moral significance of the State, and in opposition to the wretched idea that it was only a necessary evil, he praised it, as the highest and noblest realization of the idea of Right."[27] Bluntschli concluded from this that "we are justified, then, in speaking of a national spirit and a national will which is something more than the mere sum of the spirit and will of individuals composing the Nation."[28] He added that "nations, moreover, are organic beings, and as such are subject to the natural laws of organic life."[29]

As for the relationship of the prince to the state, Bluntschli wrote that in "the sovereignty of the State and the sovereignty of the prince there is the same harmony as between the whole man and his head."[30] With respect to human equality, he claimed concerning "the Aryan family of nations, whose language is the richest in forms and in thought holds first place in the history of States," that "it is here that their manly genius for politics has unfolded and matured."[31]

Bluntschli was exceeded in prestige and influence only by Heinrich von Treitschke (1834–1896), who taught politics, political theory, and history at the University of Berlin. Treitschke was a monarchist and a fervid antisemite. "Without roots in the German soil," as biographer Andreas Dorpalen explained Treitschke's

◆

prejudice, "Jews had been the carriers of such un-German doc-trines as rationalism and Manchesterism [i.e., England's liberal free-market economics] and had helped to infect the German body politic with that hateful bourgeois-economic spirit which was so alarming a sign of the times."[32] Treitschke admitted that American democracy yielded extraordinary economic benefits but exhibited only contempt for its political institutions. The sole American institution that he admired was the vanquished "aristocracy of slaveholders," which he found "infinitely superior to the Democracy of the North."[33]

Treitschke and Bluntschli were not exceptional; two other influential German historians, Theodor Mommsen and Johann Gustav Droysen, had similar views.

WHY GERMANY?

The first American doctoral programs were founded by men whose views were the antithesis of the ones that animated the American Revolution and Civil War. Yet this dramatic change was a historical accident, the by-product of an attempt to transform American colleges and universities—which (like elementary and secondary schools) had been principally pedagogical, not research, institutions—into institutions that would also encourage research to *advance knowledge* in the various disciplines offered by them. In mathematics, the empirical natural sciences, engineering, and medicine, this transformation was largely, and successfully, achieved. But in disciplines where *moral values either explicitly or implicitly inform the conclusions of its faculties*, the results were reactionary with respect to the purpose of America's revolution: the protection of universal natural rights.

American colleges before the Civil War tended to have a fixed curriculum for all students, with little opportunity to specialize or elect concentrations in a course of study focusing on a particular discipline. Pedagogy in these institutions depended largely upon recitation and memorization, not the development of analytical, deductive, and inductive capacities. Furthermore, faculty members tended to teach a variety of distinct disciplines and, in this respect, resembled instructors in precollegiate institutions. Without the expertise of the specialist, American college faculties could offer a curriculum dominated by introductory courses, not advanced ones. This characteristic was in marked contrast to the curriculum, disciplinary expertise, and sophisticated pedagogical skills that Americans observed when visiting foreign, specifically German, universities in the first half of the 19th century.

What Americans encountered in these institutions was, in large part, due to reforms that had begun in the first decade of the century. The universities of the various German states, of which Prussia was the largest, were principally *state-owned*, *state-funded*, and *state-controlled*. In Prussia, for example, the sovereign appointed all "ordinary" professors—ordinary, or "with a chair," being the highest-ranking permanent faculty position. The minister of education appointed all "extraordinary" professors (lower-ranked, without a "chair").[34] While the faculty could make three recommendations when a vacancy occurred, the government was not bound to make its appointments from that list and could ignore and, indeed, frequently did ignore faculty recommendations. For a newly created position, the faculty had no right at all to recommend their preferred appointee to the government.[35]

Moreover, all professors, whether ordinary or extraordinary, were state officials and governed by a code that applied to all civil servants.[36] Appointments were permanent, and upon retirement the professor continued to be paid his salary. Friedrich Paulsen, a professor of philosophy at the University of Berlin, contrasted the German university with its American counterparts, which,

◆

he said, were "for the most part still purely private corporations, founded by private individuals and wholly independent of the state in the administration of their internal and external affairs."[37]

Government ownership of education in the German states (the country was not unified until 1871) had several effects. First, in the early 19th century, Prussia, for example, could dramatically expand existing institutions and create new ones in Berlin and Bonn by autocratic decisions and public finance. Initially, the funds were used to expand faculties in philosophy, philology, history, language, and medicine.[38] In the 1830s, the natural sciences began a period of dramatic growth both in the numbers of their faculty and in their erudition, research, and scientific discoveries. By 1880, the university sciences in Germany had become world-famous.[39] Beginning at the University of Königsberg, with Franz Neumann and C. G. J. Jacobi's seminar in mathematics and physics, the trajectory of German scientific research followed a path that by 1880 led to its eminence in Euro-American tertiary education.

Because the content of disciplines such as mathematics, physics, chemistry, and astronomy exceeded the knowledge of state authorities, they deferred to the faculty in making appointments. The conclusions and prescriptions of philosophers and historians, however, could be understood by the state and its officials, initially with Chancellor Otto von Bismarck at the helm after the country's unification. In the case of offensive views, the state had the prerogative of withholding appointments. It is difficult to imagine, for example, a German John Locke gaining an appointment as Fichte's or Hegel's successor at the University of Berlin.

Quite the contrary: by the latter decades of the 19th century, the faculties in Germany, particularly in history, political science, and economics, shared neither the views of John Locke as to the

◆

appropriate role of government nor of Adam Smith, the 18th-century free-market economist, and his English followers as to the appropriate extent of government protection of property rights.

By the last third of the 19th century German universities, unlike their American counterparts, had graduate training that consisted not only of a doctoral degree but of a "habilitation," which required an additional three years of work beyond the doctorate leading to the lowest faculty rank of privatdozent (a lecturer or teacher). Colleges in this country, by contrast, had no separate graduate schools, and only one, Yale, had awarded its first doctoral degrees in 1861. And the doctoral degree had been a feature of German universities for two centuries. This was in stark contrast to their American counterparts.

American colleges were disparaged by critics as being equivalent to German college preparatory high schools (called *Gymnasien*) rather than to their universities. In response, a handful of college officials and trustees in this country pressed for a transformation by emulating German universities. And these universities became the models for American collegiate reform, which was accomplished in two steps. The first was to staff these schools either with Americans who had earned doctoral degrees from German universities or German faculty willing to move to American institutions. The second was to create a separate graduate school within each institution that could provide PhDs. This formula was followed assiduously throughout the last quarter of the 19th century (supplemented by recruiting some Oxford- and Cambridge-trained faculty and Americans who had been trained by other Americans holding German doctorates).

Doctoral degrees in the United States after the Civil War were awarded at the University of Pennsylvania in 1871, Cornell in 1872, Harvard in 1873, and Columbia and Princeton in 1879. Nevertheless, according to historian James Axtell, "all of these colleges had added postgraduate students to their undergraduate departments without organizing full-fledged graduate schools to serve them."[40] Schools of science had been founded at Harvard in 1846 and Yale in 1852, followed by a graduate department at Harvard in 1873, but the first full-scale graduate school in America was not created until 1876. The Johns Hopkins University in Baltimore, founded in emulation of the University of Berlin, was an institution dedicated principally but not exclusively to graduate education, culminating in the PhD degree. The majority of graduate students there were either in the disciplines now comprising the arts and sciences, or in medicine. Graduate students from 1876 to 1903 outnumbered undergraduates at Johns Hopkins, typically by a factor of two to one. Of the 69 doctorates awarded by Johns Hopkins in the arts and sciences between 1876 and 1886, 56 obtained positions on college and university faculties.[41] "By 1891," Axtell noted, "184 of its 212 PhDs—who outnumbered Harvard's and Yale's combined totals—were teaching, the great majority in colleges and universities."[42]

By the 1890s, with the addition of the University of Chicago, Stanford University, and Clark University, graduate education in the United States was gaining in stature. In 1900, the presidents of 14 universities met to form the Association of American Universities. Its members were Harvard, Johns Hopkins, Columbia, University of Chicago, University of California at Berkeley, Clark, Cornell, Catholic University, University of Michigan, Stanford, University of Wisconsin, University of Pennsylvania, Princeton, and Yale. While the production of PhDs from these institutions was growing rapidly, Germany remained a major source of America's new graduate faculty since university training in that country was the standard by which the American institutions measured their progress. "The numerical peak of American study in Germany was reached in 1895–96," according to the late historian Laurence R. Veysey, "when 517 Americans were officially matriculated at German institutions." By 1900, he added, the PhD had become mandatory for an appointment to the faculty of every prominent American collegiate or graduate institution.[43]

The transformation of American higher education in the last quarter of the 19th century provided a foundation for remarkable achievements in the natural sciences, engineering, and medicine in the next century. But these achievements were in empirical and/or mathematical disciplines. In what were called the social sciences and some of the humanities, the record was, at best, ambiguous. Nevertheless, political science, history, sociology, and economics in the late 19th century eagerly claimed a stature for themselves equal to the prestigious natural sciences. Yet these disciplines—unlike their counterparts in the natural sciences—either tacitly or explicitly combined empirical and moral elements, so that their conclusions blended the two. The normative or moral prism employed by their practitioners frequently undercut their claims of empirical neutrality.

Because they were trained either by professors at German institutions or by Americans awarded doctorates by those institutions, the political scientists, historians, sociologists, and (many) economists shared the same moral prism. And so, two decades after the comment by Charles Merriam (who studied in Berlin) about the tendencies in his *History of American Political Theories*, the eminent Harvard economist Frank W. Taussig echoed his view:

> The theory that property rests on labor, and therefore on what is conceived to be the "natural" right of each man to that which he has produced, has gone into the lumber room of discarded doctrines. It was elaborated by Locke, accepted more or less through the 18th century, and used freely by the English economists of

the first half of the 19th century. But it plays little part in modern discussion. "Natural" rights have quite gone out of fashion.[44]

A genuine *empirical* scientist does not appeal to *moral fashion* in reaching conclusions in his discipline—and the claim of faculty outside of the natural sciences and mathematics to a scientific objectivity that was the equal of a physicist or chemist was patently disingenuous. Nevertheless, the historians, political scientists, and economists mentored by Germans wanted to be treated as the equals of empirical scientists while indulging in political advocacy and moral assessment. Their assessments were profoundly at odds with those that animated the American Founding. And so, ironically, the moral debates that had originated in antebellum America were settled twice. First, in favor of natural human rights by military triumph in the Revolutionary and Civil Wars, and second, against those rights, by accidentally awarding to the German academy a lock on the moral opinions of America's first generation of PhDs.

What is remarkable is how a tiny number of faculty in a handful of universities, having created what amounted to a monopoly in the training and appointment of all subsequent faculty—first in the universities and colleges, then in the high schools and primary schools, and finally in the legal and journalistic professions—would ultimately change American culture. The contempt for natural rights evinced by Calhoun, Fitzhugh, and other defenders of slavery was echoed with virtual unanimity by the first generations of American doctoral faculty. Ironically, these men characterized themselves as "progressive"—the term itself borrowed from Germany's Progress Party.

The first faculties in what can be dubbed "empirical cum normative" disciplines were a small group, located principally at Johns Hopkins and Columbia. Because they wanted to be treated

◆

as equal in stature to their colleagues in the natural sciences, they had to portray themselves as empirical, objective scientists *while propagating their moral convictions.* These were irreconcilable ambitions, and so they relied on the naivete of the funders and trustees of their institutions as well as the (sometimes naive) collaboration of their presidents to treat them as if they were scientists embarking on purely empirical investigations.

To be sure, if these faculty were on a par with the chemists, physicists, mathematicians, astronomers, biologists, and physicians, it would have made sense that they should—like the specialists engaged in scientific investigation, research, and discovery—train the next generation in the newly established graduate schools. But if they were merely moral disputants—much like Edward Gibbon, David Hume, John Stuart Mill, Karl Marx, George Bancroft, and Herbert Spencer, none of whom held university appointments—they should not. Treating academic disciplines such as political science, history, political philosophy, and sociology as if they were sciences was the equivalent of founding a department of religious studies and staffing it with orthodox theologians of one religion. And by filling these departments with only the opponents of natural rights and simultaneously portraying their disciplines as purely empirical sciences, this is exactly what they did. In doing so, they quietly, out of public view, began to overturn the results of America's Revolution and Civil War.

CHAPTER 3

COLUMBIA UNIVERSITY

During the years he taught at what is now Columbia University, John William Burgess was a towering figure in American political science. In 1880, he established the School of Political Science—the country's first major doctoral programs in political science, history, and economics. Six years later he founded the venerable academic journal *Political Science Quarterly*. He published books on comparative constitutional law and American history. Along with other influential academics of the late 19th century, Burgess studied at a number of German universities, especially the University of Berlin, where he received a doctorate.

In Berlin, Burgess was mentored to some extent by many of the pedagogical giants of German higher education, studying Roman history under Theodor Mommsen, for example, and German history under Heinrich von Treitschke. Among these men and others, Burgess singled out "Rudolph von Gneist, the chief professor of public law and counsel to Bismarck on all legal matters." Gneist, he wrote, "led me in the line of work to which my subsequent professional life was chiefly devoted."[1] Like many of his contemporaries who imbibed political theory from the Germans, Burgess dismissed natural rights. "I defined sovereignty," he wrote of his steadfast view, "to be the original, underived, unlimited power to command for disobedience." Among outsiders to the academy, Burgess's position on this fundamental position

◆

was anathema. "The natural rights school of political philosophy saw in this quality, so defined, the apotheosis of tyranny, and as this was the prevailing school everywhere, I was denounced as the monster of political philosophy."[2]

He denied, vehemently, that this was so; he always professed his commitment to the U.S. Constitution as written, including its limits on federal authority, its careful separation of legislative, executive, and judicial powers, and the liberties it accorded with respect to one's person and property. Burgess did not believe that his devotion to the rights in the Constitution, *while rejecting the moral foundation of those rights*, was a contradiction. He bridged the difference by pointing to the history of Anglo-European governments, culminating in the independence of the American colonies and their adoption of a constitution that produced an increasing propensity for expanding the immunities of citizens.

This evolution, in short, was what Burgess relied on to protect the liberties of Americans from the otherwise limitless power of the government—and not "mere ideas" that "had their origin outside of political society and limited the State in its power over its subjects."[3] History had a civilizing trajectory, he insisted, and each sovereign state would improve upon the achievements of its predecessors with respect to its protections for individual liberty. This view of history was embodied in the political philosophy he taught to his students. Unfortunately, two of his prized faculty appointments to the School of Political Science would help move the evolutionary needle of American political institutions in the opposite direction.

INCOME TAXATION WITHOUT LIMITATION

Edwin Robert Anderson (E. R. A.) Seligman went to college at Columbia and then at the Universities of Berlin, Heidelberg, and

Geneva. He received his PhD from Columbia in 1885 and joined the faculty in political economy the same year. Seligman's father and uncle were members of a wealthy New York City banking family and donors to Burgess's political science graduate program. Seligman's major work as an economist was in making the case for a federal progressive income tax.

Throughout the 19th century, the federal government was largely funded by tariffs and "sin taxes" on goods like alcohol. But other than during the Civil War, when a temporary income tax was enacted, it did relatively little and thus needed very little revenue. The combined government spending and revenue on the state and local levels outstripped federal spending in the early decades of the 19th century and, as historian W. Elliott Brownlee writes, "beginning in the 1840s, local governments collectively spent and taxed on a scale that almost equaled that of the federal government."[4]

State and local governments raised the revenue they needed overwhelmingly from what was called a "general property tax," i.e., a proportional tax on all tangible property (land, houses, etc.) and intangible property (stocks, bonds, the value of a private business, etc.) minus debt. Proponents of natural rights such as Brown University's Francis Wayland justified this by noting that each taxpayer was paying the government for the protection of his life and rightful property, which would be measured by his net worth, not his income. The tax, in other words, was justified by the *benefit the taxpayer received.*

Seligman rejected the "benefits principle" of taxation because he rejected natural rights and believed there should be no fixed moral boundaries to government powers. Instead, along with the swelling number of young men who studied abroad after the Civil War, Seligman acquired a striking outlook—that the highly educated were a new class entitled to formulate the rules by which the rest of society should live.

◆

Above all, they acquired these convictions from German academics of the late 19th and early 20th centuries. This class has been aptly characterized by the late historian Fritz K. Ringer[5] as "mandarins"—a self-anointed elite class entitled, like Plato's Guardians, to educate and regulate the affairs of their "inferiors" due to their unique insights into what social arrangements would most benefit those whom they, through government bureaucracies, would rule. To describe the position and role of these mandarins, Ringer noted how the University of Berlin's Friedrich Paulsen described university graduates as "a kind of intellectual aristocracy," indeed, "a kind of official nobility, and as a matter of fact, they all really take part in the government and administration." Indeed, without a university education, that level of social status was unattainable to an individual, regardless of his "wealth and noble birth."[6]

Burgess believed in the rights to liberty and property that happened to have evolved in this country over time. Of course, times change, and as Seligman opined, moral principles have no permanence but rather evolve historically to accommodate new circumstances. "Modern jurisprudence and political philosophy," Seligman claimed,

> however, have incontestably proved the mistake underlying this assumption of natural law or natural rights. They have shown that natural law is simply the idea of particular thinkers of a particular age of what ought to be law. These particular thinkers, indeed, often influence the social consciousness, as they in turn are influenced by it, so that natural law may be called law in the making. But at any given time it represents simply an ideal. Whether that ideal will approve itself to society depends on a variety of circumstances, but chiefly on the question whether society is prepared for the change. Just as the modern method of

◆

jurisprudence is the historical method, so also the modern theory
of property may be called the social utility theory.[7]

Seligman wrote vaguely that "just as all law, all order and all
justice are the direct outgrowths of social causes, and just as
private ethics is nothing but the consequence of social ethics, so
private property is to be justified simply by the fact it…came
to be recognized as tending on the whole to further the welfare
of the entire community."[8] How does one define the welfare of
the entire community, and who decides when an institution or
practice does or does not further it? Seligman didn't say, although
the direction of his thinking is not hard to see:

> What phrases are more common to-day than the obligation of
> wealth—the public trusteeship of property, and the like. How long
> will it be before we tread the same path that has been opened up
> in the fiscal domain, where voluntary contributions have been
> transmuted into compulsory payments, and where the moral
> duty is now converted into a legal obligation. With the advance
> of society the individual element in the justification and in the
> content of private property recedes, and the social element comes
> to the fore.[9]

Having severed taxation from its natural-rights moorings, Seligman believed that he had severed it as well from the benefits
theory. He argued that for government expenditures either on a
war of national defense or on local police, "it cannot be claimed
that any one individual receives a measurable special benefit."[10]
But, of course, that is not what Wayland claimed; his point was,
instead, that what is protected in both examples *is* measured by
what the individual owns—himself and his property. Homeown-
ers insurance, for example, requires that premiums are correlated

◆

with the monetary value of the property; taxes that protect all of an individual's property should be similarly correlated.

Seligman, however, believed that it is the community rather than the individual that benefits from government expenditures and that, therefore, there is no way of measuring the benefits accruing to an individual from such state actions. From this argument, he leaped to the conclusion that "when payment is made for these general expenditures—and such payment is called a tax—the principle of contribution is no longer that of benefits or of give and take, but of ability, faculty, capacity. Every man must support the government to the full extent of his ability to pay."[11] It seems that Seligman believed the government had capacious duties beyond those required by natural-rights theory and, therefore, not measurable by the objects secured by those rights and thus, should tax its citizens according to their respective capacities to pay. And yet, since that capacity is most accurately measured by an individual's wealth or net worth, the type of tax, i.e., a property or net worth tax, would be the same as that implied by the benefits theory. Income, being only a portion of one's net worth, would not reflect that capacity.

To this sort of argument, Seligman responded that the benefit theory assumes every individual has a clear and distinct entitlement to what he has produced or to what another has produced that he has acquired by purchase or by a gift from its rightful owner. This, he argued, was wrong: no one has the right to anything because no one has "produced anything in civilized society":

Take, for example, the workman fashioning a chair. The wood has not been produced by him; it is the gift of nature. The tools that he uses are the result of the contributions of others; the house in which he works, the clothes he wears, the food he eats (all of which are necessary in civilized society to the making of

◆

a chair), are the result of the contributions of the community. His safety from robbery and pillage—nay, his very existence—is dependent on the ceaseless co-operation of the society about him. How can it be said, in the face of all this, that his own individual labor wholly creates anything? If it be maintained that he pays for his tools, his clothing and his protection, it may be answered that the landowner also pays for the land. Nothing is wholly the result of unaided individual labor. No one has a right to say: This belongs absolutely and completely to me, because I alone have produced it. Society, from this point of view, holds a mortgage on everything that is produced. The socialists have been in this respect more logical.[12]

Of course, if natural resources belong to no one because no human being created them, then what would follow logically is that no one is entitled to use or own them. Society being composed of individual human beings collectively considered is similarly not entitled to own or "hold a mortgage" on any natural resource, having collectively not produced any of them. But, Seligman adds, "it is not the labor theory, but the social utility theory, which is the real defense of private property."[13]

However, Seligman neither defines "social utility," nor does he derive this principle by deductive argument. So because there is no natural entitlement to ownership, but only one justified by social utility, Seligman maintained that where government provides an individual with a particular benefit or service it may credibly assess him for that service, but where what it provides is a collective benefit and so cannot be easily individuated "the principle of contribution is no longer that of benefits or of give and take, but of ability, faculty, capacity. Every man must support the government to the full extent, if need be, of his ability to pay."[14]

◆

Why is that? Because, at bottom, what stands behind Seligman's arguments is a sweeping redefinition of the relationship between the individual and the government:

> It is now generally agreed that we pay taxes not because the state protects us, or because we get any benefits from the state, but simply because the state is a part of us. The duty of supporting and protecting it is born with us. In civilized society the state is as necessary to the individual as the air he breathes; unless he reverts to stateless savagery and anarchy he cannot live beyond its confines. His every action is conditioned by the fact of its existence. He does not choose the state, but is born into it; it is interwoven with the very fibres of his being; nay, in the last resort, he gives to it his very life. To say that he supports the state only because it benefits him, is a narrow and selfish doctrine. We pay taxes not because we get benefits from the state, but because it is as much our duty to support the state as to support ourselves or our family; because, in short, the state is an integral part of us.[15]

And so, without any logical demonstration, Seligman asserts the organic nature of the state and the individual's cellular relationship to it, following the Germanic nationalism of his Hegelian mentors.

Should we accept Seligman's position and agree that the principle justifying taxation is ability to pay, what type of taxation most accurately would measure that capacity? Obviously, it must be net worth, not income, since the latter by definition is only a portion of the former and in some cases is a negative portion where an individual's indebtedness exceeds both his income and assets combined. We would expect, therefore, that Seligman's preference for "ability to pay" would lead him to endorse net worth as the most preferable type of taxation. Nevertheless, he rejected net worth.

◆

Its deficiencies, Seligman argued, are practical and insuperable. Its principal defect was the experience with the general property tax by states and localities in the 19th century.[16] One problem involved intangible assets, whose value appreciated dramatically, especially after the Civil War, but were bringing in successively less revenues than taxes on tangible property, since they could be more easily hidden and the taxes on them evaded than their tangible counterparts. Thus, while revenues from the general property tax grew throughout the century, the increasing disparity between revenues from real as opposed to personal property was justifiably resented by the public. Another problem: real estate had to be assessed, and the methods of doing so varied widely and controversially. Third, the tax varied in its treatment of debt from state to state, so that even had all assets been accounted for the tax would not necessarily have been assessed on net worth. In short, it was an extremely difficult tax to assess accurately and in practice did not necessarily accord with taxpayers' financial capacities.

Therefore, instead of supplementing federal revenues with a federal net worth tax, Seligman recommended an income tax because it had two attributes missing from any general property tax. First, income, whatever its source, was stated in monetary terms and, therefore, did not require assessment (unlike, for example, assessing the value of real estate or a privately owned business). Second, the payer of the income could be required to report it and withhold the tax on it. In other words, the singular practical virtue of a tax on income, in Seligman's view, was its collectibility, i.e., its relative invulnerability to fraud, misrepresentation, and/or evasion.

However, the income tax was accompanied by its own set of problems, both philosophical and practical, that escaped Seligman's attention. Philosophically, he had maintained that income, like wealth, most accurately reflected an individual's capacity

◆

to pay tax when compared with his fellow citizens. Of course, nothing could be further from the truth.

A contemporary example demonstrates the problem. Warren Buffett said that he had $11,563,931 in adjusted gross income in 2015, on which he paid $1,845,557 in federal tax; *Forbes* magazine recently pegged Buffett's net worth that year at $72.7 billion.[17] Had he been assessed the wealth tax that Elizabeth Warren initially proposed in 2019 (2% on $50 million–$1 billion and 6% above $1 billion) Buffett would have paid about $4.3 billion instead of $1.8 million (roughly 2,400 times what he actually paid). The former amount is obviously more precisely correlated with Mr. Buffett's ability to pay than the latter.

The same calculation could be made for any one of the growing numbers of millionaires in Seligman's day. Whatever its practical advantages as an instrument of government finance, the income tax's *moral* superiority to a wealth tax as calibrated by the ability-to-pay standard is delusional. Seligman seemed oblivious to this ethical non sequitur.

Despite the lack of correlation between income and financial capacity, Seligman amplified the discord further by suggesting that the ability-to-pay principle required that the income tax not be levied proportionately, but progressively. His argument was that, as the government's duties are to enhance social utility rather than to protect property, the appropriate instrument to maximize that utility is to reduce the distance between those with lesser and those with greater financial capacity.

Seligman had three reasons. First, the income required for the necessities in life should not be subject to taxation at all. Second, more financial capacity amplifies an individual's potential future accretions to wealth geometrically and so must be taxed in successively greater proportions with respect to additional pecuniary increments in order that it accords with his financial capacity. Such progressive assessments will decrease the collective utility of the few while increasing the collective utility of the many. Finally, lesser financial capacity means that each additional pecuniary increment will yield greater marginal utility than that same increment when added to the assets of a higher-income individual. A progressive income tax will address both difficulties by reducing the future potential amplification of wealthy individuals' reinvested assets and by reducing the marginal utility of the final increment of their income while increasing that of the majority to whom that income's utility is transferred.[18]

In practice, the income tax, as Seligman correctly anticipated, has been the most collectible and, hence, an abundant source of government revenue. However, as a mechanism of the type of redistributionist reform sought by Seligman—reducing the distance between the final utilities of the rich and the poor—it has been a failure of monumental proportions. In fact, "progressivity," particularly in Europe, has increased the distance between the middle class and the ultrarich, as the high marginal rates on income in these countries hit middle-income earners. And when combined with typical European payroll taxes (usually at least double those in the United States) and value-added sales taxes, they have served principally as a means of making the middle class dependent upon state provision while reducing their capacity to save and purchase medical care and other necessities from private providers.

For an illustration, consider the 2022 tax rates on personal income in Germany, the grandfather of today's welfare states (see table 3.1). A middle-income taxpayer in Germany would have paid a 42% tax rate once he reaches $59,769. In the U.S., by contrast, a single taxpayer with an equivalent income would be in the 22% tax bracket. The top tax rate in Germany is 45%, which hit a single taxpayer whose income reaches $282,383; in the U.S.,

Table 3.1. Income and Payroll Taxes in Germany: 2022 (1€ = $1.02)

SINGLE TAXPAYER		MARRIED TAXPAYERS		RATES
Euros	Equivalent U.S. Dollars	Euros	Equivalent U.S. Dollars	
€0–9,984	$0–$10,184	€0–€19,968	$0–$20,367	0%
€9.985–€58,595	$10,185–$59,786	€19,969–€119,220	$20,368–$121,604	14%–42% (rates rise geometrically as income increases)
€58,597–€277,825	$59,769–$282,382	€119,221–€555,569	$121,614–$565,722	42%
€277,826 and higher	$282,383 and higher	€555,570 and higher	$565,723 and higher	$45%
Payroll Taxes				Single Rate
Pension Insurance				9.3% paid by employee 9.3% paid by employer
Unemployment Insurance				1.2% paid by employee 1.2% paid by employer
Health Insurance				7.3% paid by employee 7.3% paid by employer
Long-Term Care Insurance				1.525% paid by employee 1.525% paid by employer
Total Additional Taxes on Wages				19.325% paid by employee 19.325% paid by employer
VAT				19% (some goods and services taxed at 7%)

The income brackets for Germany varied in the sources consulted, as did the exchange rates used to compare euros to dollars. In this table, 1 euro = $1.02. The income ceiling (as of January 2022) for pension insurance and unemployment insurance taxes was €84,600 [$86,202], the income ceiling for health insurance and long-term care insurance was €58,050 [$59,211]. In 2022, the income ceiling for Social Security taxes in the U.S. was $147,000; there was (and is) no income ceiling for Medicare taxes.

the top tax rate is 37%, and it applied to a single taxpayer whose income reaches $539,901.

The tax withheld from a German employee's income for *pension insurance* is 9.3%, compared with 6.2% for *Social Security* in the U.S. In Germany, 7.3% is withheld from an employee's income for the *government-run health care system*, and an additional 1.525% withheld for *long-term care*. (In the U.S. by contrast, 1.45% is withheld from an employee's income for Medicare, which bumps up to 2.35% for a single taxpayer once his income exceeds $200,000, or $250,000 for married taxpayers). In Germany, regressive payroll taxes, in short, add up to 19.325% of the taxpayer's income. Finally, there is a sales tax, called the VAT (value-added tax), which is 19% generally for goods and services, with a 7% rate for a smaller percentage of goods and services.

The irony is that when the 19th-century tariffs and excises, which American progressives deplored as regressive, were added in Germany in the form of a value-added sales tax to the "progressive" income tax and the "regressive" payroll tax on income, its effect was to diminish the distance between the middle class and the poor, but not between the wealthy and the rest.

Ultimately, the progressive income tax is not justified by the benefits principle, the ability-to-pay principle, or even a redistribution-of-wealth principle. The sole justification is that it is an accessible and easily allocated collectible source of government revenue. But to repeat: its effect is to diminish the ability of those who depend upon income, not wealth, to support themselves. That is, it increases their dependence upon the state's redistribution of their own confiscated income.

In the second edition of his treatise *The Income Tax: A Study of the History, Theory, and Practice of Income Taxation at Home and Abroad* (1914), published after the Sixteenth Amendment was passed and a federal income tax was assessed, Seligman restates its practical virtues and then concludes, stunningly, that "so far as national taxation is concerned, it will scarcely be doubted that the income tax is not needed."[19] Practically, he wrote, it is only needed to fight wars.[20] Otherwise, he noted, tariffs and excise

◆

taxes were perfectly adequate sources of federal revenues. And he added that the maligned general property tax was similarly adequate in providing needed revenues for states and localities.

As a piece of political or economic reasoning, Seligman's justification for the social utility theory is, absent a deductive argument, nothing but a series of moral assertions with an occasional appeal to the ethical views of his fellow progressive academics ("It is now generally agreed") followed by the non sequitur claim that the ability to pay implies a progressive tax on a percentage of your income.

Seligman's current successors among progressives—including Thomas Piketty, professor at the Paris School of Economics—are well aware that income taxes, no matter how progressive, have scant relation to a taxpayer's capacity or ability to pay.[21] "The explosive dynamic of wealth inequality," Piketty writes, "especially when larger fortunes are able to garner larger returns," ensures that outcome, "and only a direct tax on capital can correctly gauge the contributive capacity of the wealthy."[22]

Instead, Piketty and other progressives now endorse wealth redistribution as a third justification for taxation (as distinguished from the benefits and ability-to-pay justifications)—although they have carefully rephrased the public formulation of their general egalitarian prescriptions as the reduction of *income* inequality. Moreover, 19th-century impediments to collecting accurate information on personal intangible property are irrelevant. The federal government could easily compel citizens to file forms listing their assets and liabilities and use the information to calculate their net worth. This information, Piketty noted, can be demanded as well from "banks, insurance companies, and other financial intermediaries."[23] To reach assets invested abroad, Piketty recommended something like the 2010 Foreign Account Tax Compliance Act, under which foreign financial institutions

◆

must report the financial assets they hold for American taxpayers to the U.S. Treasury.[24]

None of the three possible justifications for taxation—Wayland's benefits principle, Seligman's ability-to-pay principle, or Piketty's redistributive-wealth principle—support an income tax. All three justifications, in fact, suggest that wealth should be taxed, proportionately for Wayland and progressively for Piketty. As for Seligman's ability-to-pay principle, it is entirely unclear what formula it may imply for wealth taxation. Does it imply a proportional wealth tax, a progressive one, or some other formula? Seligman would have had to, first, recognize that the ability-to-pay principle does not support income taxation and, second, define it with greater specificity to see what sort of wealth tax this principle implies.

Later in this book, we will propose that both income and wealth taxes can be replaced entirely by a tiny sales tax upon all purchases of goods and services with no reduction in government revenues as a result (see chapter 11). In any case, progressive intellectuals who followed Seligman in the New Deal period did not recommend an annual wealth tax. Its principal advocate, Louisiana governor (and U.S. senator) Huey Long, was treated as a pariah by most progressives. Rather it was not the wealth of the rich that they wanted to reach. It was the income of the middle class that could be taxed and its payers gradually reduced to government dependency or servility. So, instead of higher marginal rates on extraordinary levels of income, progressives during the 1930s repeatedly advocated increased rates for the middle classes.

Wisconsin's progressive senator Robert La Follette Jr. spoke for most of them. "The important [income tax] brackets that must be made to carry their fair share of the tax burden," he said in 1935, "are those below $50,000 annual taxable income."[25] The late historian Mark Leff noted that "even before Roosevelt took

◆

office, a position paper approved by 101 economists counseled him to slash income—and estate—tax exemptions and to elevate rates on 'moderate-sized incomes' of $5,000–$30,000." He added that "when the *New Republic* sponsored a forum of liberal economists in 1938, a majority favored cuts in income tax exemptions and higher middle-bracket rates." The People's Lobby, led by the elite stratum of progressive intellectuals—such as John Dewey, Reinhold Niebuhr, Paul Douglas, and Stuart Chase—produced a petition with 900 signatures arguing for broad-based progressive taxation that would include lower- and middle-income earners. "The gold is in the foothills, not in the mountains," alleged one economist from the Twentieth Century Foundation.[26]

University of Chicago economist Henry Simons was blunt. Current taxes, he wrote in 1938, were "absurdly low in the case of what conventional discussion strangely refers to as the lower and middle-sized incomes." Looking ahead, "the main question is whether our taxes shall fall mainly on people with incomes ranging from $3,000 to $20,000 or largely on people below the $2,000 level. What happens to the rates beyond $20,000 is not of major importance."[27]

All of them had to await the attack on Pearl Harbor to have their hopes realized when the class tax was converted to a mass tax to finance World War II.

EVOLUTION RUNS BACK

John Burgess was incredulous when the Sixteenth Amendment, enabling the federal taxation of income, was ratified in 1913. "It simply made waste paper of the Constitution in respect to the relation of Government to the constitutional rights of the Individual to his property," he wrote in 1915.[28] "Constitutional law is a body of limitations on governmental power and you dare not call any document a Constitution, no matter from what source it may come, which is not such," adding:

> Now, the sovereign, through the Sixteenth Amendment to the Constitution, has done just this in regard to the rights of the Individual to his property. It has made over to the Government the whole power of the sovereign, unlimited and unqualified, to take what it will and in any way it will from the Individual, to take from one Individual and not from another, as it will, and to take in different proportion from different Individuals, as it will. This is not a power of constitutional taxation. It is the power of confiscation.[29]

Burgess returned to the subject a few years later, heaping blame for the amendment on Theodore Roosevelt—one of his former law students—for a resolution proposing an amendment to the Constitution that was passed by Congress on July 12, 1909, when he was no longer president. "The first highly important product of the Rooseveltian radicalism and the triumph of the so-called Democracy of 1912," Burgess wrote, was an amendment that meant that there was nothing in the Constitution to prevent the government from "exercising completely arbitrary, despotic and discriminating powers over the property of the individual through the levy and collection of this unlimited tax upon incomes."[30]

But this criticism, bereft as it was of a natural-rights justification, was too little and, written in 1915 after the fact, it was too late. Seligman, building on Burgess's rejection of natural rights (including the right to one's property), had been publishing in favor of progressive income taxation relentlessly since 1894. Burgess had remained silent; and in the three books written by Burgess after its passage, Seligman's name appears only in his

◆

1931 memoirs, and there he is portrayed flatteringly, with no mention of his views.

As for his protégé, what we can conclude is that as a competent tax economist, he had discovered that the revenue from an income tax was not required by the federal government to cover its expenses. His recommendations for a progressive income tax he invalidly derived from a moral principle from which it does not logically follow. And that principle is itself derived from an argument about ownership that does not follow from his premise that no one is entitled to anything that is comprised of natural resources. Like his progressive contemporaries, Seligman's conclusions are not empirically derived but normatively asserted—and thus any pretense that they had equal status with the empirical natural sciences is fraudulent and undeserved.

TRASHING THE CONSTITUTIONAL SEPARATION OF POWERS

The damage that Burgess caused by training and hiring Seligman, thereby giving him a platform for views Burgess would condemn as disastrous for America, was equaled if not exceeded by his appointment of Frank Johnson Goodnow to the faculty. Goodnow, like Seligman, was both an undergraduate and graduate student of Burgess. Older by two years than Seligman, his undergraduate degree was earned at Amherst while Burgess taught there; he then obtained his law degree at Columbia under Burgess, who, in addition to his professorial position in political science, held a professorship at Columbia's Law School. Also, like Seligman, Goodnow was trained in Germany (at the University of Berlin) and in Paris at the École Libre des Sciences Politique (the model Burgess had used for his School of Political Science at Columbia that its trustees authorized him to establish in 1880).

◆

Goodnow's views were so appallingly reactionary that one is tempted to quote his manuscripts in their entirety rather than summarize them, lest the reader think they are being exaggerated. In *The American Conception of Liberty and Government* (1916), Goodnow, who was then the president of Johns Hopkins, not only rejected the view that people own themselves, their liberty, their labor and its fruits but failed utterly to grasp the salient features of these rights. First, he seemed oblivious to the fact that in the history of human civilization, these rights were first discerned and explicated by John Locke in 1690, at least 5,000 years after the first governed countries were founded. He continually referred to rights as inconsistent with the developments of modern life and insisted on the return to the autocratic forms of governance from which they extricated us. Second, when commenting upon the advances in industry, commerce, and medicine, he failed to grasp that these were the direct result of the protection of these rights. That freedom of ownership and exchange depends upon the protection of these rights escaped him entirely. Instead, the rapid economic growth in the late 19th century that made America the envy of the world— and resulted from the protection of rights—he attributed only to social and economic circumstances that happened to exist but are not based on permanent principles or conditions.

Goodnow did not deny that America's unique economic prosperity derived from the protection of natural rights, but he claimed it was a mistake to believe that they were either "eternal or immutable." They were, as the other progressives announced, "influenced in large measure by the social and economic conditions of the time when the recognition was made." That was then; but now, he wrote in 1916, those conditions had changed radically:

> The accumulation of capital, the concentration of industry with the accompanying increase in the size of the industrial unit and

the loss of personal relations between employer and employed, have all brought about a constitution of society very different from that which was to be found a century and a quarter ago. Changed conditions, it has been thought, must bring in their train different conceptions of private rights if society is to be advantageously carried on. In other words, while insistence on individual rights may have been of great advantage at a time when the social organization was not highly developed, it may become a menace when social rather than individual efficiency is the necessary prerequisite of progress. For social efficiency probably owes more to the common realization of social duties than to the general insistence on privilege based on individual private rights. As our conditions have changed, as the importance of the social group has been realized, as it has been perceived that social efficiency must be secured if we are to attain and retain our place in the field of national competition which is practically coterminous with the world, the attitude of our courts on the one hand towards private rights and on the other hand towards social duties has gradually been changing.[31]

"It has been thought," "it has been perceived." By whom? These vague references are the basis, according to Goodnow (the first president of the American Political Science Association), of the fact that

whatever may have been formerly the advantages attaching to a private rights political philosophy—and that they were many I should be the last person to deny—this question of private rights has been reëxamined with the idea of ascertaining whether, under the conditions of modern life, our traditional political philosophy should be retained.

The political philosophy of the eighteenth century was formu- lated before the announcement and acceptance of the theory of

◆

evolutionary development. The natural rights doctrine presupposed almost that society was static or stationary rather than dynamic or progressive in character.[32]

Here, the obvious empirical fact that every living thing has its own body and that human beings uniquely are capable of grasping this fact abstractly and, therefore, can make rules among themselves prohibiting murder, kidnapping, assault, rape, slavery, theft, and fraud in the protection of what is, in fact, essentially their own, seems to have escaped Goodnow. His thesis that evolution is a progressive force in human affairs was about to be falsified one year after his book's publication by Lenin's coup d'état in Russia, a few years later by Mussolini's dictatorship in Italy, several years later by Hitler's Germany, and many years after that by Mao's China. So much for evolutionary advancement. No matter—and no worry about this country either. Goodnow told his readers in whom they should trust the education of their children to guide them through the gates of evolution and past the erroneous doctrine of Locke and America's Founders:

> We teachers are in a measure responsible for the thoughts of the coming generation. This being the case, if under the conditions of modern life it is the social group rather than the individual which is increasing in importance, if it is true that greater emphasis should be laid on social duties and less on individual rights, it is the duty of the University to call the attention of the student to this fact and it is the duty of the student when he goes out into the world to do what in him lies to bring this truth home to his fellows.[33]

As was the case in Germany, Goodnow had in mind a place in government for students enlightened by their progressive teachers: government bureaucracies. Specifically, this meant a fourth branch of government staffed by appointees endowed with leg-

◆

islative powers (and some judicial ones as well) without having to go through the rigors of congressional elections. The vehicle the new class of academic mandarins would ride was Article I, Section 8, Clause 3 of the U.S. Constitution, which accorded to Congress the power "to regulate commerce with foreign nations, and among the several states, and with the Indian tribes." "The content of the subject to be regulated," Goodnow explained, "is not determined, the methods of regulation are not stated, nor are the words 'among the several states' defined." In short, it was a perfect opening for "a body or bodies representing the nation as a whole" to fill in the details of laws Congress might pass, and in so doing, vastly expand "the power of the federal government. It is the one clause in the constitution which lends itself most readily as a means for the reconstitution of our political system in accordance with changing economic needs."[34]

That meant abandoning "the strict application of the principle of the separation of powers whenever the demand for administrative efficiency would seem to make such action desirable, and it may be expected that this tendency will continue and even increase in force if it is apprehended that even conservative social reform is impossible under the former conception of the proper relations of governmental authorities."[35] This proposal, or prediction, essentially meant delegating legislative power—the power to make laws—to unelected administrators serving in the executive branch—a goal that Goodnow shared with Woodrow Wilson in his academic years.[36]

In Germany, universities specialized in the training of such administrators, empowering them with legislative authority that in America was reserved for elected legislators. That training function progressive academics here looked forward to assuming. Philip Hamburger, a law professor at Columbia University, recently traced the genesis. "German scholars," he wrote, "were perfectly comfortable in distinguishing between constitutional and administrative matters." Thus, "when Treitschke rejected the separation of powers, he instead divided power into 'the constitutional and administrative categories'—the one being the state's 'unified will,' and the other being the detailed expression and application of this will."[37]

Hamburger also points to the dangerous consequences of this separation of constitutional and statutory matters on the one hand and administrative matters on the other:

> Agencies increasingly make law simply by declaring their views about what the public should do. Agencies, for example, offer "guidance," propose "best practices," declare "policy," give "advice," take positions in briefs, or make naked demands—all of which is done with the unmistakable hint that it is advisable to comply. These statements officially are not binding on the public, and they usually evade even the notice and comment required for lawmaking interpretation. Nonetheless, the Supreme Court has not rejected these statements, but rather has said that they deserved "respect" as interpretations of statutes.... As a practical matter, it is not always predictable whether guidance, etc. will get judicial "respect." Agencies therefore often enforce such demands with "arm-twisting"—something that... often amounts to extortion.[38]

◆ ◆ ◆

In his 1915 book *The Reconciliation of Government with Liberty*, the outrage Burgess expressed over the enactment of the Sixteenth Amendment singled out for scorn a "School of Sociologists and Political Economists" that "impatient of the voluntary methods of religion, charity, and philanthropy, have sought to accomplish what they call social justice, the social uplift, by governmental

◆

force. There is no question that they have exercised a strong influence in directing the thought of the present."[39] Burgess went on to say that the "programme of Caesaristic paternalism" to which this school would lead the country was spreading:

> All parties are now declaring themselves to be Progressives, and all mean in substance the same thing by this claim, viz.: the increase of governmental power over the constitutional Immunities of the Individual, the solution by force of the problems of the social relations heretofore regulated by influence, by religion, conscience, charity, and human feeling, the substitution of the club of the policeman for the crosier of the priest, the supersession of education, morals, and philanthropy by administrative ordinance.[40]

It was a remarkable, and remarkably prescient, statement—yet nowhere does Burgess reveal the identity of any leader of this "School." The names Seligman and Goodnow are nowhere to be found; nor were the names of any of the other colleagues he appointed to the faculty of Columbia University. Unlike in the epic World War II film *The Bridge on the River Kwai*, there would be no "Colonel Nicholson" moment for Burgess—no recognition of his own role in building a bridge to a political future he despised, no horrified "What have I done?" moment.[41]

◆

CHAPTER 4

JOHNS HOPKINS UNIVERSITY

In August 1883, Cornell University professor Herbert Tuttle, an eminent historian of Germany, took to the pages of the *Atlantic Monthly* to discuss an emerging trend—that American "higher education is rapidly becoming Germanized." While a diploma from a German university, he noted, does not guarantee "employment in American colleges...it is a powerful recommendation." As such, the "number of Americans studying in Germany is accordingly now reckoned by hundreds, or even thousands, where it used to be reckoned by dozens." That this turn of events, he added, "is fraught with vast possible consequences for the intellectual future of America is a proposition which seems hardly open to dispute; and the only question is about the nature, whether good or bad, of those consequences."[1]

Tuttle had spent much of the 1870s in Paris and Berlin; his two-volume *History of Prussia* became a classic, praised by the noted jurist Rudolph von Gneist, who taught at the University of Berlin.[2] Intimately familiar with Germany's intellectual currents, the answer to the question Tuttle posed in the *Atlantic* about the consequences of the ongoing "scholastic pilgrimage" was that "as a people, we have cause not for exultation, but for grave anxiety, over the class of students whom the German universities are annually sending back to America."[3]

The reason, he explained, was that Germany's professoriate in the humanities and social sciences was filled with so-called

◆

55

Kathedersozialisten, men who taught socialism from their academic chairs. Their theory of government was the opposite of America's founding ideals; it "assumes as postulates the ignorance of the individual and the omniscience of the government," a government, moreover, "removed as far as possible from" the influence of elected legislatures and public opinion. In short, Tuttle concluded, if America's academic "pilgrims are faithful disciples of their masters," they will return as "advocates of a political system, which, if adopted and literally carried out, would wholly change the spirit of our institutions, and destroy all that is oldest and noblest in our national life."[4]

Tuttle's prescient warning applied to intellectual currents already visible at Columbia University. It applied as well to a university established less than a decade earlier.

THE FOUNTAINHEAD OF ANTI-NATURAL-RIGHTS PROGRESSIVISM

Johns Hopkins University, founded in 1876, was a distinctive addition to the country's institutions. Remarkably, the overwhelming majority of the faculty was in the natural sciences. It also produced a flood of influential economists, political scientists, historians, and political philosophers. They included America's most famous progressive philosopher, John Dewey; a leading progressive economist at the University of Michigan, Henry Carter Adams; and the founder of Hopkins's political science department, political theorist Westel Woodbury Willoughby, as well as his twin brother, William F. Willoughby, professor of jurisprudence and politics at Princeton and the first director of the Brookings Institution. Not least among the PhDs minted at Hopkins was Woodrow Wilson.

Even more impressive: the institution's extraordinary output of humanities faculty and social scientists was primarily accomplished

◆

by a mere three faculty members, only one of whom (historian Herbert Baxter Adams) became a full professor, the other being a junior faculty member (economist Richard T. Ely), and the last (philosophy professor George Sylvester Morris) a part-time faculty member. When one thinks of the combined size of the initial Johns Hopkins and Columbia social science and philosophy faculty and the dramatic change that they wrought in America's academic political culture in one generation, one cannot help but be astounded.

The institution stood out for another reason. Unlike Columbia, Yale, Harvard, Princeton, the University of Pennsylvania, the University of Wisconsin, the University of Michigan, and other older institutions, Hopkins did not grow from an existing college. It emerged *de novo* in emulation of the University of Berlin, with graduate education, not undergraduate education, as its principal function. Under its first president, Daniel Coit Gilman, the new university was to be nonsectarian. This was unlike most colleges in America, which were typically associated with a particular sect of Christianity and had a minister as both their president and, frequently, their principal instructor in moral philosophy, political economy, and history. Most (though not all) of the faculty in these colleges were comprised of other ministers, who taught a variety of subjects from classical languages to mathematics. Gilman, by contrast, sought faculty with doctorates in specific disciplines, with demonstrated research abilities, and without a ministerial background. He had sought to make the university a purely graduate institution, but local pressures in Baltimore induced him to abandon that objective.

Gilman focused on employing natural scientists of proven stature or obvious potential and sought to avoid appointing faculty based on their political preferences. In a letter to a trustee, Gilman was unambiguous:

♦

The Institution we are about to organize [he wrote] would not be worthy [of] the name of a University, if it were to be devoted to any other purpose than the discovery and promulgation of the truth; and it would be ignoble in the extreme if the resources which have been given by the Founder without restrictions should be limited to the maintenance of ecclesiastical differences or perverted to the promotion of political strife.

As the spirit of the University should be that of intellectual freedom in the pursuit of truth and of the broadest charity toward those from whom we differ in opinion it is certain that sectarian and partisan preferences should have no control in the selection of teachers, and should not be apparent in their official work.[5]

Gilman's initial faculty appointments included Harry A. Rowland, a brilliant young physics instructor at the Rensselaer Polytechnic Institute, and James Joseph Sylvester, an established older mathematician trained at Cambridge who had taught at the Royal Military Academy. These were followed by other highly qualified mathematicians, physicists, chemists, physiologists, and morphologists educated here and in Europe.[6]

Sylvester returned to England in 1883 to teach geometry at Oxford.[7] His replacement was Simon Newcomb, head of the Naval Observatory in Washington, editor of the *Nautical Almanac*, and associate editor of the *American Journal of Mathematics*. In his history of Johns Hopkins University, Hugh Hawkins described Newcomb as "the most famous living American mathematician in 1884,"[8] and Gilman appointed him as a professor of mathematics and astronomy. Over the course of his long career, Newcomb published 318 works in astronomy and 35 in mathematics—but he also contributed 42 publications in economics, many of which were methodologically pathbreaking.

Harvard economist Joseph Schumpeter regarded Newcomb's *Principles of Political Economy* (1885) as the best book of its kind

◆

produced between the publications of John Stuart Mill and Alfred Marshall, and Keynes "gave acclaim to Newcomb as an original thinker."[9] Columbia University economist Joseph Dorfman would also write that "it was unfortunate for economics that Newcomb's primary interest was in astronomy. His talents were such that he might easily have been the outstanding contributor to economics in his time."[10] Newcomb was part of the cutting-edge marginalist school that began with the British economist William Stanley Jevons and culminated in the work of Jevons's countryman, Alfred Marshall, as well as the later work of American John Bates Clark and Austrian economist Carl Menger. Marginal utility theory is the essential basis of microeconomic theory—which attempts to account for relationships between the supply of a product, the demand for it, and its price. The theories in that school began with certain assumptions and its conclusions were deduced from these, frequently mathematically.

Philosophically, Newcomb was a firm believer in natural rights and the liberties that flowed from them. As an economist, Newcomb prescribed what he called "the Let Alone Principle" as most conducive to the interests of all people most of the time:

> In the first case, the principle declares that society has no right to prevent any individual who is capable of taking care of himself from seeking his own good in the way he deems best, so long as he does not infringe on the rights of his fellow-men. In the second case, the principle forms the basis of a certain theory of governmental policy, according to which that political system is most conducive to the public good in which the rightful liberty of the individual is least abridged.[11]

Newcomb was a professor of mathematics and astronomy at Hopkins; his economic writings were, in a sense, an avocation—and they would lead to a momentous confrontation touched off by

◆

Richard T. Ely, to whom Gilman had given a faculty appoint-ment in economics. Ely, who earned his PhD at the University of Heidelberg, was one of those "pilgrims" that Tuttle warned the country about.

At Heidelberg, Ely studied under the historian and political scientist Johann Bluntschli and the economist Karl Kneis, under whose supervision he obtained his doctorate. Subsequently, Ely attended the lectures of the prominent economist Adolph Wagner at the University of Berlin.[12] Knies and Wagner were members of the "historical school of economics." This school rejected theoretical (deductive) economic reasoning; instead, it held that the proper study of economics should be based on an empirical and historical (i.e., evolutionary) analysis of human society and institutions. All of them, as Tuttle told readers of the *Atlantic*, rejected natural rights; most professed one form or another of state socialism.[13]

Bluntschli, for his part, dismissed the view that "the State, according to the whole philosophy of natural rights, is essentially based upon contract and association."[14] The historical school, on the other hand, had "the merit of having restored the conscious-ness of the organic theory of the state."[15] According to Bluntschli, individuals are mere cellular components of the state who live and die, while the state's existence persists. The state, therefore, is sovereign over all people who have whatever rights and duties the state chooses to assign to them.

From Knies, a founder of the historical school, Ely absorbed the view that economics cannot be merely a science that deduces market relationships from a set of axioms about human prefer-ences but must be a study of what economic institutions ought to be promoted by discovering the evolutionary trajectory of eco-nomic history. The economist, in other words, should be engaged in moral improvement and reform. In history, Ely argued, the ideal exists, but not universally. "The ethical aim of reformers is to render in general that excellence which at the time is isolated," he wrote. "Past, present, and future are organically connected. The germs of a better future always exist in the present, but they require careful nursing. They do not develop spontaneously."[16]

Yet the Americans trained and influenced by German professors found themselves in a quandary. On the one hand, they could not refrain from political advocacy; on the other, they needed to portray themselves as disinterested empirical scientists, as devoted to objectivity in their conclusions as any natural scientist.[17] But if the role of the social scientist is to become an expert in discovering which historical trends are of greatest benefit to society—and then educate and proselytize for them—which social scientists possessed those powers of discernment, according to Ely? Certainly not ones like Simon Newcomb.

IS ECONOMICS A SCIENCE?

In *The Past and the Present of Political Economy* (1884), Ely dismissed what was and are now the central insights of what we call microeconomics, i.e., the benefits of the freedom of production and exchange. The laws of supply and demand are used to analyze transactions that presuppose property rights in what individuals produce, a right dismissed by Ely (and his ilk) as an impediment to the autocratic powers sought by them in the name of "progress" or "reform." But these were the same autocratic powers that, taken to the limit, would be sought by Lenin in the name of the "workers," by Hitler in the name of the "Aryans," the New Left in the name of "the people," and by contemporary progressives in the name of income redistribution, the climate, race, or gender. Each of these justifications is a pretext by its proponents for autocratic privileges for themselves.

◆

"The nation in its economic life is an organism," Ely wrote, dutifully repeating the notions of his teachers, "of which individuals, families, groups and even towns, cities, provinces, etc., in their economic life form parts. This is strictly and literally true, as is shown conclusively by comparing the facts of economic life with the ideas embraced in the conception, organism." The claim that society is "literally" an organism rests on an observation that

> the people does not consist simply of a sum of individuals, nor does the national economic life—which it is the province of political economy to investigate—mean a sum of individual economies. This notion, the fictitious assumption of the classical individualistic political economy, holds only of men living in an isolated barbarous condition, which is a low, mean state of independence. But the first and foremost factor of modern economic life is dependence.[18]

What Ely called "dependence" is nothing more than the division of labor—a mundane fact from which it is absurd to leap to the conclusion that society is "literally" an organism. Nevertheless, in support of his thesis, Ely relies upon the "discoveries" of his teacher, Adolph Wagner, which can be summarized by saying that it is within the state's province to determine how much or little freedom the individual should be permitted to have.[19] After the unification of Germany, historian Daniel T. Rodgers noted, Wagner urged "the extension of state enterprise into railroads, canals, banking, insurance, utilities, mining, and housing."[20] He also wanted the government to own all the land in cities, put limits on private profits, and redistribute income through taxation. Wagner called his proposals "state socialism." Its "goal, without the 'craziness' and 'criminality' of revolutionary socialism, was to lead the economy 'more and more out of private into public organizational forms.'"[21]

◆

"In Germany," Ely told his American readers in 1884, the members of the historical school "have carried the day."[22] In 1931, Ely called Adolph Wagner "one of the great economists of his age."[23] Four years later, one of Hitler's followers paid tribute to Wagner "as one of the fathers of Nazism."[24]

Ely's graduate sojourn in Germany provided him with a glimpse of a world very different from that of the typical American academic. "The leading German professors served in the upper houses of the state diets, where the universities had special representation," historian Rodgers explains. "Their seminars, way stations to higher government service, were heavily salted with lawyers and state officials. They managed their own (often contentious) journals, pursued research, wrangled publicly over public issues, grasped hard for political influence, and stocked the government bureaus with loyal students."[25] The example was congenial. "I am," as Ely said of himself, "an aristocrat rather than a democrat; but when I use the term 'aristocrat,' I have in mind not a legal aristocracy, but a natural aristocracy...an aristocracy which lives for the fulfillment of special service."[26] He was determined to replicate the political philosophy and high professional stature of his mentors in Germany. In pursuit of his goal, he had plenty of help from other Americans who had trained in Germany—men such as Edmund J. James and Simon Patton at the University of Pennsylvania's Wharton School of Finance; Henry Carter Adams at Cornell and the University of Michigan; Columbia's E. R. A. Seligman and Frank Goodnow.

But Ely and the others faced a problem that Adolph Wagner had not. Two of America's greatest economists—Hopkins's own Simon Newcomb and Yale University's William Graham Sumner—held views that were the antithesis of the German economic professoriate. In the view of Ely and his academic allies, these two men, along with others who defended natural rights and free competition, would have to be professionally marginalized.[27]

PROGRESSIVES MOUNT A PURGE

In pursuit of this end, as historian Mary O. Furner explains, Ely in 1884 "ridiculed Newcomb before campus gatherings and got his former students to repeat the charges in their journals"; and "friends who had access to journals kept up a steady flow of criticism against the laissez-faire economists, calling them either hopelessly outdated as scholars or clients of the unscrupulous rich."[28]

The first to do this was Edmund J. James at the University of Pennsylvania's Wharton School of Finance (who had obtained his doctorate at the University of Halle under Johannes Conrad, one of the Kathedersozialisten). James published a sneering attack on Newcomb's 1885 *Principles of Economics* (which would remain a classic in the development of both micro- and macroeconomics). He called Newcomb "a great and successful astronomer and physicist wandering over into the economic field" who had undertaken "to write a treatise on a science of whose present status he knows next to nothing." The attack was political; Newcomb was chastised for his "extreme individualism," his reliance on and repetition of "exploded theories and almost universally rejected laws," that is, rejected by Ely and those of like mind.[29]

Newcomb dismissed the attempt by James to discredit him and defended the application of mathematical deductive theories to social science:

> The objections to the deductive features in this school can arise only from a misapprehension. Its deductions being only hypothetically true, are not to be applied in practice unless the actual case is shown to apply to the hypothesis. But it does not follow that

◆

the method is useless because it needs modification when applied to particular cases, because this is true of all science.

Deduction is an essential process in every rational explanation of human affairs. To say that we are not to apply it to any subject is equivalent to saying that we can have no rational conception of the relation of cause and effect. A subject of which this is true would be quite unworthy of the study of men.[30]

The problem, Newcomb correctly observed, was that his critics, with all their emphasis on the gathering of statistics and various historical investigations, had discovered no new system or laws at all, nor could they. Harvard economist James Laurence Laughlin agreed, writing to Newcomb that "I don't see where the 'new method' men have a peg to hang a new system on."[31]

Ely wanted to establish a professional organization of economists that would not include Newcomb and other "men of the Sumner type," and ultimately drive them out of academic economics.[32] The name of his proposed organization was the American Economic Association (AEA), and it was modeled on a professional association of anti-free-market economists in Germany, the Verein fur Sozialpolitik.[33] "We regard the state as an educational and ethical agency," Ely's 1886 platform for the new organization began, "whose positive aid is an indispensable condition of human progress. While we recognize the necessity of individual initiative in industrial life, we hold that the doctrine of laissez-faire is unsafe in politics and unsound in morals; and that it suggests an inadequate explanation of the relations between the state and the citizens." Ely went on to claim that America was suffering from "a vast number of social problems whose solution is impossible without the united efforts of Church, state and science."[34]

Newcomb would wryly note that Ely's manifesto amounted to "a sort of church, requiring for admission to its full communion a renunciation of ancient errors, and an adhesion to the supposed new creed."[35] And in fact, the belligerent nature of the platform put off many academic economists. No one from Harvard or Yale joined, stigmatizing the professionally disinterested pretensions of the organizers.[36]

Ely's plan exposed the dilemma that a discipline faced whose practitioners insisted that it be treated as an empirical science but injected moral prescriptions into its theories. Pre–Civil War American colleges made no secret of their denominational moral perspectives. Their presidents were ministers, and the insertion of Christian moral values was part of the mission of their institutions. Ely and other economists trained in Germany claimed the mantle of "science" while actively seeking to professionally excommunicate opponents who had different moral views.

As the members of the "new school" strove to extricate themselves from the obvious disparity between their disciplines and the natural sciences, E. R. A. Seligman, in the case of economics, argued that they viewed economic history as evolving toward greater and greater progress. The role of the economist, then, is to identify the beneficial trajectory of economic history before it becomes apparent and thereby accelerate its realization. This, he claimed, supplied the discipline with the objectivity associated with the natural sciences:

> The paramount question of political economy to-day is the question of distribution and in it the social problem (the question of labor, of the laborer),—how, consistently with a healthy development on the lines of moderate progress, social reform may be accomplished; how and in what degree the chasm between the "haves" and the "have-nots" may be bridged over; how and in what degree private initiative and governmental action may strive, separately or conjointly, to lessen the tension of industrial

◆

existence, to render the life of the largest social class indeed worth living. This and other complex problems of the present day cannot be solved by a simple adherence to the principles of a bygone generation. The tenets of a bald individualism have been placed in the scales of experience, and have been found wanting.[37]

Seligman's "solution," in fact, was simply to assert moral principles, claim they were revealed by historical developments, and then use them to propose policies—a similar ploy to his tortured philosophical, not economic, argument to abandon the benefit principle and substitute the ability to pay.

America's new universities in the late 19th century included disciplines that *were* strictly empirical and mathematical, along with those combining observation, deduction, and moral prescription. The latter disciplines claimed equal status with the former—but the effect of doing so was to encourage moral conformity to the *values* of the majority.

Worse, after the founding of the first generation of doctoral programs, academic appointments devolved from the presidents and trustees to the faculty. This was a reasonable transition for the natural sciences. In the empirical-cum-normative disciplines, however, ambitious graduate students would, over time, tend to conform to the moral preferences of their mentors if they wanted to get jobs and rise in the profession. By the 1960s, the conformity in the political views of philosophers, political scientists, economists, historians, and sociologists had reached an extreme, resembling that of faculty in schools of theology rather than that of schools of natural science, engineering, finance, and agriculture (see chapter 6 for more detail).

As for the American Economic Association, the sense of some of those involved that they were indeed being perceived as moral advocates rather than objective scientists caused them

◆

in 1887 to drop from its platform any "overt ideological tests of fitness for the profession."[38] Ely, too, was pressed to leave his position as one of its officers, which he reluctantly did. Unhappy at Johns Hopkins and longing for a position at an institution of similar potential prestige at which he could exercise decisive control over faculty appointments, Ely was appointed director of a new School of Economics, Political Science, and History at the University of Wisconsin in 1892, with a salary of $3,500, the highest salary among professors or deans.[39] It was a dream come true: he was able to hire only faculty who agreed with him and to produce (as he had at Johns Hopkins) principally a coterie of fellows who would fill positions in other universities and colleges.[40]

At Wisconsin, two famous progressives—both militant racists—became his most auspicious faculty appointments. John R. Commons had helped Ely at Hopkins with his *Introduction to Political Economy*.[41] He opposed giving the vote to African Americans, writing that "this race, after many thousand years of savagery and two centuries of slavery, was suddenly let loose into the liberty of citizenship, and electoral suffrage."[42] Edward Alsworth Ross had been fired at Stanford because of his opposition to immigrants from the Orient, whom he dismissed as inferior to Caucasians. Of blacks, he had this to say: "'One man, one vote' does not make Sambo equal to Socrates in the state, for the balloting but registers a public opinion. In the forming of this opinion the sage has a million times the weight of the field hand."[43]

This troika set about turning Wisconsin into a laboratory of progressive "reform." As historian Thomas C. Leonard writes, "Governor Robert LaFollette, the Republican Progressive, empowered the University of Wisconsin faculty and released them on the state. By 1908 all the economists and one sixth of the Uni-

♦

versity's entire faculty held appointments on Wisconsin govern-ment commissions, including Charles Van Hise, the University President."[44] Frederic C. Howe, one of Ely's former students at Hopkins, touted the result:

> Wisconsin is doing for America what Germany is doing for the world. It is an experiment station in politics, in social and industrial legislation, in the democratization of science and higher educa-tion. It is a state-wide laboratory in which popular government is being tested in its reaction on people, on the distribution of wealth, on social wellbeing.[45]
>
> The university is the state research laboratory. Graduate students investigate pending questions, while the seminars in economics, politics, and sociology are utilized for the exhaustive study of state problems. There is scarcely a big legislative measure that was not first thoroughly studied at the university end of Madison before it was placed on the statute books at the other. Wisconsin adopted a state income tax in 1911.[46]

Today, some economists continue to present themselves as scien-tists although they are indistinguishable from moral and political philosophers. In their book *The Triumph of Injustice: How the Rich Dodge Taxes and How to Make Them Pay*, Emmanuel Saez and Gabriel Zucman at the University of California, Berkeley, for example, ground their approach to taxes on the late philosopher John Rawls, whose views on social justice, they explain, enjoy "broad support among social scientists." Thus:

> It is acceptable, according to Rawls, to have social and economic inequalities if these inequalities increase the living standards of the most vulnerable members of society. When applied to tax policy, this perspective suggests we should not concern ourselves

◆

with the monetary interests of the rich. We should care only about how taxing them affects the rest of the population.[47]

The foundation of the two economists' prescription, in short, is a moral assertion that they expect the reader to accept. Since the foundations of what Rawls called the "difference principle" have been philosophically exploded (see chapter 5), the combined support of it by "most social scientists" is irrelevant. Ironically, the Rawlsian philosophical edifice rests on the same claim that defenders of slavery such as George Fitzhugh adopted—that human beings have no right to self-ownership. While economics as a discipline may not suffer as much as history or political science from undue dependence on normative rather than scientific investigation, it nevertheless is afflicted with the malady that all the quasi-empirical, quasi-normative social science disciplines share. They are not natural sciences and do not deserve to be treated as if they were.

GERMANY LOSES ITS LUSTER

Johns Hopkins did produce a serious political philosopher, Westel Woodbury Willoughby, who attempted a reasoned refutation of the natural-rights principle rather than a simple assertion of its lack of authority with the new class of Germany-trained progressives. Willoughby was the founder of, and the first professor at, Hopkins's political science department.

But his treatise, *An Examination of the Nature of the State* (1896), fell short. The basis of Willoughby's refutation was the equation of having a right to oneself with its protection. Nature provides individuals only with powers, he claimed, not rights. Rights exist only in society, as defined by law, by authority. Since the protection of rights, Willoughby asserted, is impos-

◆

sible without a state—and if its protection and its existence are one and the same—then rights are therefore only what the state grants and protects.[48] However, there is no basis for this equation in the philosophy of John Locke or by this nation's Founders. Rights are in their view the intrinsic entitlement that one has to one's person. How such rights are to be secured—the means by which they are to be protected—is simply a separate question. But Willoughby did not agree and thus moved on from Locke to Rousseau, who said that when individuals consent to form a state they implicitly agree to obey the collective or General Will, which is different from the combined separate wills of its individual citizens:

> It therefore appears that the origin of the State must be conceived as an act of a People rather than of individuals. The existence of a common or "General Will" must be predicated, and the creation of the State held to be due to its volition.... Hence, by adding together a sum of private interests, we can never get a public interest, nor from a sum of private rights obtain a public right. The General Will, as distinguished from the sum of individual wills, is rather a volitional unit that is obtained by extracting from each of the individual wills certain sentiments and inclinations that concern general interests, and from a combination, equating, and balancing of them obtaining a single result that is based upon elements that exist in the individual wills, but is thus distinct from their sum. But even this is a more mechanical description of the General will than its essentially unitary character properly permits.[49]

This means, Willoughby concluded, that no individual can be "considered apart from the whole, of which he is an integral and inseparable part.... He is coerced by the law, not as a free autonomous person, but as a constituent element of the authority that coerces him. He is an integral and inseparable part of the political body, and his will cannot be separated from its will."[50]

Willoughby inferred from this that the United States was not created by the Constitution but preexisted as a "national feeling that unites its People."[51] Drawing on the ideas of Bluntschli, he maintained that "the State is a person because it has a will of its own, that is recognized in the national consciousness in a manner very similar to that by which the feelings of an individual organism are recognized by the animal consciousness."[52]

As rights are nothing but the creation of the state, they do not impede state powers. As to whether his theory points "necessarily to ultimate socialism," Willoughby wrote that "a categorical answer cannot be given. They do point, undoubtedly, to an inevitable extension of the State's activities far beyond those at present exercised."[53] These activities might include "the ownership and operation by the State of railroads, of canals or of telegraph lines; the ownership by the city of gas, water and electric light works, and the provision of model tenement houses for the poor by the public authorities."[54] All that matters, Willoughby added in his next book on political philosophy, *Social Justice*, is whether, "as a matter of fact, political control will be followed by beneficent results."[55] He also agreed with John William Burgess—the superior nations of the modern world are those that are racially Teutonic, and the obligation of such nations is to organize the rest of the world politically.[56]

Willoughby's next contribution to political philosophy, *Prussian Political Philosophy: Its Principles and Implications*, appeared in 1918. Humiliated by Germany's autocratic, imperialistic venture in World War I, he performed an about-face. "The Declaration of

◆

Independence," he now wrote, "declares that all men are endowed by their creator with inalienable rights to life, liberty and the pursuit of happiness, and that to secure them, governments are instituted among men."[57] In America "the legal powers of the government should not be permitted to extend to all matters of public control, but that from their operation should be excepted certain private rights of the individual with reference to his life, liberty and use of his property."[58]

Better late than never, one might suppose. Nevertheless, he also admitted that, in his view, citizens can strike such rights by amendment from the Constitution, a conclusion that Locke or Jefferson would reject. After all, in his first two books on political philosophy, Willoughby distinguished the state from its citizens and asserted that it had a personality of its own, and that its will is the General Will of the people, which is not to be identified with the sum of their wills. And if "the State...has a will of its own,"[59] he previously argued that the sovereignty of the state is unalienable.

Willoughby's effort, then, to distinguish himself from his Germanic philosophy required that he attempt, without contradicting himself, to defend positions that he had unequivocally rejected. First, he rejected the racial superiority of the Teutonic people, which he had previously affirmed. Then he said, disparagingly, that the Germans see the state as having an existence apart from its citizens, the precise view that he had formerly accepted by stressing that the state has a personality and will of its own, distinct from that of the citizens whom it governs. He even rejected the Hegelian philosophy of the state, which he had previously embraced.[60]

In point of fact, progressives like Willoughby, who had proudly advertised the Germanic roots of their political philosophy, may have suffered embarrassment at World War I but did not abandon

◆

their statist opposition to the principles of the American Founding. And not content with merely rejecting the Founding's natural-rights origins, progressives would next ascribe base motives to the Founders holding them.

◆

CHAPTER 5

THE PROGRESSIVES' SEARCH FOR A USABLE AMERICAN PAST

If—as John W. Burgess, E.R.A. Seligman, Frank Goodnow, and Westel Willoughby argued—the natural rights announced in the Declaration of Independence were false, how can one account for the adoption of a Constitution that protected them? The Fifth Amendment, for example, states that "no person shall...be deprived of life, liberty, or property without due process of law"; the Ninth Amendment declares that "the enumeration in the Constitution, of certain rights, shall not be construed to deny or disparage others retained by the people." Charles A. Beard, a historian trained at Columbia University, would provide a famously influential answer.

TRASHING THE U.S. CONSTITUTION'S FOUNDING FATHERS

Beard grew up in Indiana, and after graduating from DePauw University, spent four years (1898–1902) at Oxford University at his wealthy father's expense. Before he arrived in England, Beard had already consumed *Unto This Last* (1860), a diatribe against capitalism and the modern world written by John Ruskin, a celebrated English art critic and philosopher. Ruskin, along with Thomas Carlyle, Robert Southey, Samuel T. Coleridge, and Benjamin Disraeli "offered a conservative critique of industrialism that rejected the mechanistic market economy in favor of

◆

an organic, hierarchical world associated with the preindustrial past." Ruskin and Carlyle, in particular, idolized the medieval world, especially its "feudal hierarchy."[1] Ruskin also argued that political equality is impossible, so workers should look to their political superiors—like Ruskin—to help them improve their standard of living:

> My continual aim has been to show the eternal superiority of some men to others, sometimes even of one man to all others; and to show also the advisability of appointing such persons or person to guide, to lead, or on occasion even to compel and subdue, their inferiors, according to their own better knowledge and wiser will.[2]

Ruskin's influence on Beard was profound. In a biography of her late husband, Mary Ritter Beard wrote that he "regarded Ruskin's philosophy as set forth in his small book, *Unto This Last*, as an acme of wisdom and usually had it in his hand or pocket as a bracer."[3] In his years at Oxford, Beard borrowed Ruskin's paternalism, appending it to his own racial convictions in a pair of essays recommending a new world order.

"Under the auspices of an 'international bureau,'" as historian Ellen Nore explained his proposal, "arid plains would be irrigated, swamps would be reclaimed for agriculture, and new canals and railroads would be built to bind the nations. The physical labor would be done by 'mongol and negro' workers, 'always under white foremen.'"[4]

Now equipped with the conviction that a Ruskin-like superior class ought to formulate policies that would ameliorate the human condition, Beard returned to America where he received a doctorate at Columbia University under Burgess, Seligman, Goodnow, and a more recent addition to the political science faculty, James Harvey Robinson (PhD, University of Freiburg).[5] At

◆

Burgess's School of Political Science, Beard would not encounter objections to his autocratic inclinations from defenders of natural rights; there were none.

Among his instructors, Seligman, in particular, provided an analytical framework for Beard's most famous scholarly endeavor. In his 1902 book *The Economic Interpretation of History*, Seligman concluded that

> civilization indeed consists in the attempt to minimize the evils, while conserving the benefits, of this inevitable conflict between material resources and human desires. As long as this conflict exists, the primary explanation of human life must be the economic explanation—the explanation of the adjustment of material resources to human desires.[6]

Eleven years later, Beard published his own take on this thesis: *An Economic Interpretation of the Constitution of the United States*. In it, he attempted to answer the following question: If the Constitution was not genuinely intended to protect the alleged natural rights of human beings, what caused it to be written? What motivated its authors to craft it as they did?

Like other progressive social scientists of his generation, Beard posed as a disinterested empirical investigator. That is, he implied that he would take his inquiry wherever the historical facts led him. And since he assumed, with Seligman, that the most important causal facts determining historical outcomes are economic ones, he asked which of these determined the content of the Constitution. To be sure, Seligman did not deny the causal importance of moral, political, religious, aesthetic, and other human motives—but he did argue that all of these require economic means, making the latter the most important determinant of historical outcomes. Beard agreed. If there was

◆

unassailable evidence of specific economic causes for important events in human history, then empirical objectivity required the scholar to acknowledge them.

For Beard, then, the question to be resolved was not whether the Constitution was an instrument designed to protect the universal rights of every member of the human species, but rather *whose economic appetites* it was designed to satisfy. And he intended what he wrote to destroy the last vestige of the Founders' philosophical commitments as the grounds for their Constitution. In a letter to a student after his *Economic Interpretation* was published, Beard wrote that "the thing to do is to lay a mine, store it with nitro, and then let it off in such a fashion that it rips the bowels out of something important, making it impossible for the fools to travel that way any more."[7]

His principal thesis was simple. "Instead of being a document drawn up by patriotic men for the protection of life, liberty, and the pursuit of happiness," as Beard's leading critic, historian Robert Brown, would summarize it, "the Constitution was the work of consolidated economic groups—personal property interests including money, public securities, manufacturers, and trade and shipping—groups that were personally interested in the outcome of their labors."[8] Specifically, what Beard claimed to demonstrate was that the U.S. Constitution was not designed to protect property as the fruits of anyone's labor, but to protect only specific types of property known as "personalty." Personalty included all movable instruments of credit and securities, as opposed to real estate and personal and business indebtedness. Beard emphasized particularly the dominance of holders of government debt that was sold to raise funds to fight the Revolutionary War. He attempted to show that the Constitutional Convention was dominated by holders of such instruments and, hence, produced a constitution designed principally to protect them.

Brown went through Beard's evidence for his thesis, meticulously and thoroughly discrediting its research: in fact, more of the members of the convention owned realty than owed personalty. The Founders were not interested in protecting only the rights to one type of property, Brown concluded, but to all types:

> Since most of the people were middle-class and had private property, practically everybody was interested in the protection of property. A constitution which did not protect property would have been rejected without any question, for the American people had fought the Revolution for the protection of life, liberty, and property. Many people believed that the Constitution did not go far enough to protect property, and they wrote these views into the amendments to the Constitution.[9]

The problem was that Brown's convincing refutation was published more than forty years after Beard's book. By that time, Beard had long since achieved his mission—which was to "rip the bowels out" of anyone who claimed that the protection of natural rights was central to the considerations that led to the Constitution. Most progressives had already formed an opposition to natural rights as unyielding as that of slavery's antebellum defenders. To this, Beard added a deeply cynical view of the motives that inspired the Constitution's drafters. Decades of academic historians and their students would be schooled in the notion that their country was the setting for a contest between intrinsically antagonistic classes—capitalists versus farmers and laborers.

Beard had professed moral neutrality when researching and writing *An Economic Interpretation of the Constitution of the United States.* Later, he admitted the impossibility of such neutrality. Responding to a charge of bias in the 1930s, he called neutrality a "Noble Dream" that was impossible for a historian to achieve. Indeed, Beard encouraged "the task of exploring

◆

the assumptions upon which the selection and organization of historical facts proceed."[10]

By the end of World War I, the decades-long assault on Lockean-based natural rights seemed impregnable in the higher reaches of the American academy. And yet, in 1922, this consensus was challenged by Carl Becker—an intellectual historian at Cornell who had been educated at the University of Wisconsin, a progressive bastion. In his book *The Declaration of Independence*, Becker stood apart. He took seriously the *thinking* that explained and motivated the Revolutionary generation:

> Whenever men become sufficiently dissatisfied with what is, with the existing regime of positive law and custom, they will be found reaching out beyond it for the rational basis of what they conceive ought to be. This is what the Americans did in their controversy with Great Britain; and this rational basis they found in that underlying preconception which shaped the thought of their age—the idea of natural law and natural rights.[11]

These ideas, he argued, were absorbed by the revolutionaries from Locke. Moreover, Becker understood that Locke was part of a Newtonian tradition that had deified nature, so in deducing God's intentions from human nature (that each person is a distinct individual) he concluded that God could not have intended that one person should own another, but that each should own himself. "The channels through which the philosophy of Nature and Natural Law made its way in the colonies in the eighteenth century were many," he explained:

> A good number of Americans were educated at British universities, where the doctrines of Newton and Locke were commonplaces; while those who were educated at Princeton, Yale, or Harvard

◆

could read, if they would, these authors in the original, or become familiar with their ideas through books of exposition.... The revolutionary leaders do not often refer to the scientific or philosophical writings of either Newton or Locke, although an occasional reference to Locke's *Essay* is to be found; but the political writings of Locke, Sidney, and Milton are frequently mentioned with respect and reverence.[12]

Becker traced the effect of these ideas on the growing inclination in the colonies to sever their relationship with the British monarchy. One of the earliest manifestations appeared in a 1768 letter written by Samuel Adams which declared that "it is an essential natural right that a man shall quietly enjoy and have the sole dispersal of his property," and therefore, it followed that "Americans must enjoy this right equally with Englishmen."[13] And citing a pamphlet probably composed in 1770, Becker quotes James Wilson on the dispute about the authority of the British Parliament: "All men are, by nature, equal and free: no one has a right to any authority over another without his consent: all lawful government is founded in the consent of those who are subject to it."[14] As Becker noted, "This reminds us of the Declaration of Independence, and sounds as if Wilson were making a summary of Locke."[15]

Also in 1774, the Declaration and Resolves of the First Continental Congress that was sent to the British government stated that the "inhabitants of the English colonies in North America, by the immutable laws of nature...are entitled to life, liberty and property."[16] It followed, Becker noted, that "the foundation of the United States is indissolubly associated with a theory of politics, a philosophy of human rights which is valid, if at all, not for Americans only, but for all men."[17]

Beard's denigration of the Constitution's alleged origins ultimately faded away, given its shoddy evidence. But opposi-

◆

tion to the natural-rights tradition that Becker traced in his study of the Declaration of Independence remained—and remains—dominant in the academy and among intellectuals generally.

LIBERALISM: THE STRANGE CAREER OF AN IDEA

That opposition became more complicated among America's academic progressives during World War I, touched off by Germany's aggression. After the war, the rise of fascism and communism in the 1920s was an additional source of unease. Progressives seeking to obscure the Prussian autocratic roots of their ideas came to substitute the term "liberal" for "progressive" as a label for their outlook.

The word itself apparently had been introduced as a substitute in the July 1916 *New Republic*.[18] But there was a problem: "liberal" was also used by pro-natural-rights types like Columbia's then-president Nicholas Murray Butler.[19] In 1923, for example, Butler complained that enemies of individual rights of liberty were attempting to appropriate the term liberal to describe illiberal ideas. E. Martin Hopkins, president of Dartmouth College, agreed with Butler's analysis that autocrats, professionally organized, were attempting to appropriate the term liberal with the intention of meaning its antithesis.[20] In 1924, the *New York Times* also bemoaned changes "in names and labels. One such notable change," since the end of the war, "has been the expropriation of the time-honored word 'Liberal.'" The weeklies using the word "are not Liberal at all in the established sense, but...represent a blend of pre-war Radical and Red." The *Times* writer wondered if at some point "the Radical-Red school of thought might be compelled to hand back the word 'Liberal' to its original owners."[21] Six years later, the *New York Times* repeated the complaint, protesting the appropriation of the term "Liberal" by domestic friends of autocracy.[22]

Unpacking the meaning of, and confusion surrounding, the term liberal would have lasting consequences in 20th-century American politics, and, as such, deserves discussion.

In England, the term was first employed by members of the British Whig Party in 1832. "Liberal" became associated with the protection of individual liberty, property rights, and freedom of exchange. However, there was an irreconcilable philosophical disparity between the two branches of British liberalism—natural-rights liberalism and utilitarian liberalism.

Many British liberals based their preferences for liberty not on natural rights but on the utilitarian philosophy of Jeremy Bentham and John Stuart Mill. Political and economic liberty, these utilitarians believed, was the most useful means of attaining the greatest happiness for the greatest number of people. Of course, when socialists began to claim that their institutional "reforms" would produce a superior result, they too could call themselves liberals.

The other wing of British liberalism was led by Herbert Spencer, a proponent of natural rights. Spencer denounced interferences with the right to use and dispose of one's property as what he called, in 1885, "the New Toryism."[23] He accused liberal politicians in Britain of doing whatever succeeded in getting them elected. Previously, Spencer argued, the removal of government coercion made them popular; now they found that government interference led to electoral success. The disparate uses of the same term by political opponents led to the elasticity of its meaning.

In England, the final authoritative definition of liberalism was made by an opponent of both the Benthamite and Spencerian wings, L. T. Hobhouse, a professor of sociology at the University of London. In *Liberalism* (1911),[24] Hobhouse first dismissed the natural-rights liberalism of Locke, Blackstone, and Spencer. He did so not by analyzing the arguments of Locke or Spencer, its two most distinguished proponents, but by criticizing this principle in the French Declaration of the Rights of Man (1789), which was derived from Rousseau—who held that there were no natural rights.

Hobhouse then turned to Bentham and exposed the obvious weaknesses of the utility principle. Some people can suffer a hellish existence as long as the sum of happiness of the greatest number is greater than their suffering. These are hardly firm grounds for a liberty principle, according to Hobhouse. If the majority is made ecstatic by the government's torture of a minority, the utility principle is satisfied.

Turning away from both Lockean natural rights and utilitarianism, Hobhouse proposed that the liberal should distinguish between that portion of wealth due solely to the efforts of the individual and that portion contributed by society taken as a whole. The latter, he suggested, should be taken by taxation to the benefit of those who have enjoyed no inheritance, a portion of which is the contribution of the community. Hobhouse argued that forms of unearned income such as inheritance, gifts, and financial speculation, as well as very large incomes, are suitable objects of taxation. He recommended a progressive surtax on incomes exceeding £5,000 (in 1911). The revenues should go to the poor. And as for business, its revenues should be limited by the state and transferred to its workers.

Each of these suggestions, of course, implied that the state is the ultimate owner of what is produced within its borders, not its citizens. This radical transformation of the idea of "liberalism" served two purposes. It took advantage of the favorable public opinion of its association with the protection of human liberty from potential autocracy, while simultaneously restoring autocratic rule with a new pretext—the improvement of the economically poorest members of society.

This revised conception of liberalism suited many progressives in the early decades of the 20th century, including President Franklin Delano Roosevelt and his advisers and admirers, who appropriated the term. In doing so, however, these self-defined liberals were faced with a dilemma: How can this new version of liberalism be squared with this country's traditions? John Dewey, a philosopher trained at Johns Hopkins who taught at Columbia, would provide the answer.

JOHN DEWEY REBRANDS LIBERALISM

The problem Dewey confronted was how to reconcile liberalism's genesis in Lockean natural rights with the coercive legal and bureaucratic regime that Roosevelt was erecting. He accomplished his improbable task by first recounting liberalism's history. Beginning with Locke, natural rights, and their inclusion in the American Declaration of Independence, Dewey emphasized Locke's conviction that every human being has ownership of himself, his liberty, and his property.[25] He then argued that liberalism became associated with the economic theory of Adam Smith, which emphasized the economic benefits that result when property can be freely produced and exchanged. This gave rise, Dewey said, to the idea that interferences with one's natural liberty should be prevented, and the result was the formulation of laissez-faire liberalism.

The principal advocate of laissez-faire, Dewey claimed, was Jeremy Bentham, who was an opponent of natural rights but based his liberalism on grounds of utility. Bentham opened the way for legal innovations that impeded economic freedom if they could be shown to advance utility. "When he disallowed the doctrine of inalienable natural rights," Dewey wrote, "he removed as far as theory is concerned, the obstacle to positive action by the state whenever it can be shown that the general well-being will be promoted by such action."[26] Moreover, Dewey noted, liberalism

came, if gradually, to be disassociated from the laissez-faire creed and to be associated with the use of government action for those at economic disadvantage and for the alleviation of their conditions. In this country, save for a small band of adherents to earlier liberalism, ideas and policies of this general type have come to define the meaning of liberal faith.[27]

It was a neat trick: progressives would retain the term "liberalism" because of the personal freedom and economic growth that it produced—while discarding the means necessary to achieve these ends. "The notion that organized social control of economic forces lies *outside* the historic path of liberalism," as Dewey would have it, "shows that liberalism is still impeded by remnants of its earlier *laissez faire* phase, with its opposition of society and the individual.... Earlier liberalism regarded the separate and competing economic action of individuals as the means to social well-being as the end. We must reverse the perspective and see that socialized economy is the means of free individual development as the end."[28]

So, in order to capture a term and its historical associations while jettisoning its meaning and replacing it with its antithesis, the libertarian principles and institutions to which it originally referred must be removed. Dewey found in liberalism's original British *opponents*—Carlyle, Ruskin, Coleridge, and other Tory antimarket sympathizers with feudal institutions—allies of his transformed liberalism. The irony is that Dewey's liberalism closely resembled 19th-century *conservatism*.

◆

Dewey's attempt to rebrand liberalism, however, proved problematic. Progressives in the 1930s who wanted to claim the liberal mantle recognized that in the age of totalitarianism, the implied repudiation of Lockean unalienable rights made them vulnerable to the charge that they were skirting close to various species of European totalitarianism. This charge (or, from their perspective, this fear) arose from the experience of the New Deal itself.

Exhibit A was Roosevelt's initial response to the Great Depression: the National Industrial Recovery Act (NIRA), enacted in June 1933. The purpose of this legislation, and its creation of a National Recovery Administration (NRA), was to "stabilize" prices and wages by a massive reorganization of the economy under the federal government's supervision. As historian Burton Folsom explains, "It allowed American industrialists to collaborate," i.e., to collude,

> to set the prices of their products, and even the wages and hours that went into making them. Leaders in all industries, from steel and coal to shoulder pads and dog food, were invited to sit down together and write "codes of fair competition" that would be binding on all producers in their industry. Laborers were often allowed to organize and anti-trust laws were suspended.[29]

John T. Flynn, a well-known journalist and New Deal critic, noted that the transformation of the economy via the NRA "was the one thing that appealed most strongly to Roosevelt's imagination. He imagined he had been the instrument of creating a revolution in American industry. This was his idea of a planned economy."[30] The resemblance of this scheme to fascist Italy was obvious:

> The country was divided into provinces—economic provinces as distinguished from geographical provinces. The geographical

♦

provinces—the states and counties—continued to be run on the democratic plan by popularly elected legislators and executives. The economic provinces—the province of steel, of textiles, of millinery, etc.—were run by legislators and police (compliance officers) elected not by the people in the industries on the democratic principle but by a handful of employers. And if this system had continued in force and our development had progressed along that line, we would have continued to move further and further from the democratic plan and in the direction of the corporate state of Mr[.] Mussolini.[31]

In reality, the price- and wage-fixing cartels established by the NRA did nothing to revive the economy, nor did they survive, at least in the law. In 1935, the Supreme Court unanimously struck down the NIRA because it unconstitutionally delegated legislative power to the executive branch of the government.[32] "The strangest feature of this episode," Flynn would write, "was that this serious blow to our democracy was carried on to the cheers of many of the so-called liberals who flocked to Washington to support the New Deal."[33]

Walter Lippmann was another contemporary critic of the New Deal policies. Lippmann was one of America's most distinguished journalists and, in his youth, a proponent of socialism and progressivism. But his influential 1937 book *The Good Society* rejected gross economic interventionism and economic planning as threats to freedom and prosperity. He labeled these threats "gradual collectivism."[34] The "real nature of" it, he wrote, was revealed by the NRA and what it portended:

No clearer, no more naked, illustration could be offered of what is meant by the statement that gradual collectivism means the conferring of privileges upon selected interests. For the right to

◆

make laws and to enforce them by fines and imprisonment is the basic attribute of sovereignty, and the delegation of sovereignty to selected interests is exactly what the word "privilege" means. In the case of the NRA privilege was conferred upon certain trade organizations and theoretically at least upon industrial employees also.[35]

Small, incremental interventions in the economy, Lippmann believed, could be made without jeopardizing individual liberty and general prosperity. But no central coercive economic plan that interferes with the first can preserve the second.

LOUIS HARTZ REBRANDS LIBERALISM, AGAIN

Given the odor of totalitarian dictatorships, something had to be done to insulate liberals from the accusation that the New Deal they supported bore a greater resemblance to the country's European and Asian adversaries in World War II than to America's founding institutions. Louis Hartz, a professor of government at Harvard, attempted to provide that insulation by redefining liberalism. Rather than discard Locke, he attempted to square the Lockean circle, making it flexible enough to accommodate progressives and yet not exclusionary enough to separate these new liberals from the natural-rights Lockeans.

In his landmark book *The Liberal Tradition in America* (1955), Hartz wrote that he "insists on using" liberal "in the classic Lock[e]ian sense."[36] What is remarkable about this book is the author's recognition of the vulnerability of American progressivism to the charge that its economic policies frequently seemed indistinguishable from those of socialist or fascist regimes.

Hartz reminded readers that two European traditions have made no headway in America, and both are equally alien to its

♦

Lockean roots. The first was the feudal aristocracy of the slave-holders, which was rejected intellectually by the heirs of Locke and Jefferson, and the second was the new European opponents of feudalism—the socialists and fascists. Both are philosophically antithetical to the Lockean principles of self-ownership and the ownership of the fruits of one's labor. If, as Hartz argued, neither the contemporary forms of European autocracy nor its feudal predecessors have ever advanced in undermining America's attachment to Lockean principles, why should progressives identify themselves as opponents of Locke?

In attempting to include the New Deal in the Lockean liberal tradition, Hartz portrayed it as only a series of pragmatic adjustments rather than a substantial impediment to individual liberty by means of a central coercive authority. Lippmann, on the contrary, had presented a far more incisive characterization of the intellectual forces responsible for the outlook and policies of the Roosevelt administration:

> Though the progressives prefer to move gradually and with consideration, by persuading majorities to consent, the only instrument of progress in which they have faith is the coercive agency of government. They can, it would seem, imagine no alternative, nor can they remember how much of what they cherish as progressive has come by emancipation from political dominion, by the limitation of power, by the release of personal energy from authority and collective coercion. For virtually all that now passes for progressivism in countries like England and the United States calls for the increasing ascendancy of the state: always the cry is for more officials with more power over more and more of the activities of men.[37]

Lippmann was not alone. Herbert Hoover, Roosevelt's predecessor, saw in the New Deal a radical departure from liberalism *(The*

Challenge to Liberty, 1934). In 1935, Lewis W. Douglas, a lifelong Democratic congressman from Arizona and FDR's first budget director, published *The Liberal Tradition: A Free People and a Free Economy*—delivered as Harvard's Godkin Lectures—which condemned virtually all of Roosevelt's legislation as illiberal. Several others recognized the illiberal consequences of economic planning: Isabel Paterson, *The God of the Machine* (1943); Rose Wilder-Lane, *The Discovery of Freedom* (1943); F. A. Hayek, *The Road to Serfdom* (1944); Ludwig von Mises, *Liberalism* (1927), *Human Action: A Treatise on Economics* (1949), and *Socialism: An Economic and Sociological Analysis* (1951).

With the exceptions of Hartz, Mises, and Hayek, however, the other authors were not academics; and the term "liberalism" had been seized by New Dealers as a replacement for "progressive," exploiting its continuity with the country's Founding while rejecting its philosophical basis. As a result, those who retained a commitment to the natural-rights basis of the American republic abandoned the term "liberalism," replacing it with terms like "individualism" and "libertarianism." But they mostly were writers outside of the universities where the progressives—or "liberals," as they now called themselves—were well on their way toward cementing control of the social sciences and humanities (see chapter 6).

There was a great irony in the claim by New Dealers and New Deal sympathizers that laissez-faire economic policies brought about the Great Depression, and that Roosevelt's response saved capitalism. The reality is that the Depression was not the result of a government paralyzed by an irrational attachment to laissez-faire in the face of an economic catastrophe. Instead, it was due to the one part of the economy over which the government had quasi-monopolistic controls—the currency, credit, and banking system.

The failure of the Federal Reserve to recognize and rectify a dramatic contraction of the money supply from 1929 to 1933 led to

◆

depression. While the money supply contracted by a third—some say due to the gold-exchange standard, which left the dollar as the convertible currency,[38] others because the Federal Reserve sterilized incoming gold so that it would not enhance the money supply[39]—the Great Depression was the fault of government, not of the unregulated sectors of the market.[40] Simply expanding the money supply would have brought about a prompt recovery, but progressives were unwilling to let a good crisis go to waste. Instead, the Roosevelt administration and an overwhelmingly Democratic Congress enacted a blizzard of ill-conceived measures to restructure the economy. And it was these measures, including (but not limited to) the National Industrial Recovery Act, the Agricultural Adjustment Act, and the Wagner Act (compulsory unionism), that impeded an economic recovery. A damaging tax on undistributed corporate profits, and another contraction of the money supply that the Federal Reserve caused by increasing the required reserves held by banks that could not be expended, resulted in a severe recession in 1937 and 1938.[41]

The Depression had illustrated the following: first, its causes were from the sector of the economy controlled by the government, not its unregulated sectors; second, its government remedies failed to end it; and third, the claim initiated by Hoover, reiterated by Roosevelt, and finally repeated by the British economist John Maynard Keynes and his American follower Alvin Hansen that lack of consumer demand was its source, was utterly mistaken.

Claims that government expenditures during World War II ended the Great Depression—and that their abrupt cessation at the war's conclusion would cause the return of the Depression—were equally erroneous. As economist Robert Higgs documented, the measures usually treated as indicants of an economy's health are completely irrelevant during wartime: "In 1940, before the military mobilization, the unemployment rate (Darby concept) was

◆

9.5%. During the war, the government pulled the equivalent of 22% of the pre-war labor force into the armed forces. Voila—the unemployment rate dropped to a very low level."[42]

Unlike most civilian jobs, however, military service in wartime risked death as well as severe and lasting physical and psychological damage. As Higgs commented, "To treat military jobs as commensurate with civilian jobs during World War II, as economists do in comparing the tradeoffs between them, betrays a monumental obtuseness to their realities."[43] Moreover, while there was no unemployment in the statistical sense during the war, "four-tenths of the total labor force was not being used to produce consumer goods or capital capable of yielding consumer goods in the future."[44]

Put bluntly, selling goods at the counter in a pharmacy is not equivalent to getting shot to death by a German machine gun, although both are counted as employment. Tracking only *personal consumption* more accurately measures prewar, war, and postwar consumer welfare. Using the price deflator produced by Milton Friedman and Anna Jacobson Schwartz, Higgs concluded that "real consumption per capita reached a prewar peak in 1941 that was nearly 9% above the 1939 level; it declined by more than 6% during 1941–43, and rose during 1943–45; still, even in 1945, it had not recovered to the 1941 level. In 1946, however, the index jumped by 18%, and it remained at about the same level for the rest of the decade."[45]

Moreover—because most goods were rationed during World War II—personal consumption took on an entirely different meaning than in peacetime. As Warren Buffett's biographer explained, "money mattered less and less":

> Everyday life was measured in points and coupons: 48 blue points
> a month for canned goods; 64 red points for perishables; coupons

◆

for meat, shoes, butter, sugar, gasoline and stockings. No amount of money would buy meat without coupons; only chicken went unrationed....To take an automobile trip, you pooled the family's gas coupons. Blowing out a tire could mean serious trouble, since automobile tires were among the most strictly rationed commodities.[46]

Ultimately, it was government policies—during the years that Herbert Hoover and Franklin D. Roosevelt were presidents—that failed to prevent a depression and failed to extricate America from it during peace or war. Only the end of the wartime command economy saw an increase in consumer welfare, in contrast to the Keynesians' dire prediction of the effects that ending wartime expenditures would have.

Given the failure of New Deal policies and Lippmann's warnings about the political and social consequences of centralized economic planning, Hartz nevertheless described an America not racked by opposed ideologies, but one united by a common philosophical ancestry—Lockean liberalism. There are references to Locke on forty-three pages of Hartz's book. How is one to reconcile the Lippmann-Hartz embrace of Lockean liberalism with its unqualified rejection by the entire academic progressive tradition that evolved since the Civil War? The answer is that no such reconciliation is possible. Meanwhile, another movement away from the implications of Lockeanism arose in the 1950s, partly as a result of help from an improbable source.

ERASING NATURAL RIGHTS: RUSSELL KIRK, GORDON WOOD, GARRY WILLS

In 19th-century English political history, "conservative" was a term used to describe the anticapitalist views of Tories like John

Ruskin and Thomas Carlyle—hardly suggesting any connection to America's founding principles. Nevertheless, Russell Kirk—an obscure instructor at Michigan State University—advised Americans interested in conserving their traditions to turn away from John Locke. His advice helped progressives consummate their annexation of the term liberal.

In his 1953 book *The Conservative Mind*, Kirk made the preposterous claim that defenders of America's Founding should find its source in Edmund Burke. This claim made no historical sense, as the British parliamentarian's writings did not influence the authors of the Declaration of Independence or the U.S. Constitution. But so there should be no misunderstanding of his intent, Kirk explained that "Burke disavowed a great part of the principles of Locke, the official philosopher of Whiggism."[47] He declared that

> the theories of Locke were inherited by such diverse legatees as Rousseau in Geneva, Price in Old Jewry, Fox in St. Stephens, Bentham in his library, and Jefferson at Monticello; but from among the general ideas of that philosopher, conservatism after Burke retained almost nothing but Locke's contention that government originates out of the necessity for protecting property.[48]

Demonstrating his ignorance, Kirk wrote that "Rousseau deduces natural rights from a mythical primeval condition of freedom and a psychology drawn from Locke."[49] The problem, of course, is that Rousseau rejected the existence of natural rights (as discussed in chapter 2). "It may be asked how individuals," he wrote in *The Social Contract* (1762), "who have no right to dispose of their own lives can transmit to the sovereign this right which they do not possess."[50] Instead of natural rights, Rousseau posited a General Will by which society is to be governed,

◆

understanding by it what is really intended by all human beings no matter what they say they want. That General Will is to be grasped by a Platonic Guardian of superior insight whom Rousseau calls "the Legislator," and whose unique insight into the "real" collective will permits him to govern the citizenry. The "legislator" turned out to be Robespierre, the bloody dictator of the French Revolution.

That Locke and Rousseau are polar opposites on this central issue seems to have escaped Mr. Kirk. What did not escape him were two examples of what he dubbed the "conservative mind" that he recommended for Americans' admiration: John C. Calhoun and John Randolph. "The affection for state rights, the duties of a gentleman, and the traditions of society which Randolph and Calhoun extolled found their finest realization in General Lee," Kirk wrote. He added that "the political representative of those principles was a man of parts less exemplary than Lee's, but still a man of high courage and dignity, Mr. Jefferson Davis."[51]

Effusive and laudatory reviews of *The Conservative Mind* appeared in the *New York Times* and *Time* magazine.[52] And why not? A conservatism that wrote off John Locke was no problem for postwar liberals (née progressives); a conservatism that held up for admiration two die-hard defenders of slavery—and two traitors—was even less of a problem. Among the first to recognize the use that could be made of Kirk's conservatism was Clinton Rossiter, a Cornell historian and political scientist who provided an effusive cover blurb for Kirk's book, calling it "splendid."

Progressives had for generations attacked Lockean natural rights as false because it impeded their political project: a boundless role for the state. All that was left was to delete Locke as an influence on America's political tradition—which Kirk was happy to help them do. Contemporary liberals could continue to propose laws and regulations to erode rights, all the while professing

◆

their loyalty to them. And given Kirk's obfuscatory account of something he called "conservatism," liberals were free to describe falsely the ideological alternative that their progressive forebears in the late 19th century had unambiguously defined. Building upon Kirk's vacuities, Rossiter thus created a fictitious history of American political theory:

> The Liberal ideal, even among progressives of the twentieth cen-
> tury, has been one of government that exists primarily to protect
> the individual's rights and clear the way for his energies. The
> conservative reality, in America as in all countries, has been one
> of government that intervenes repeatedly to guide and reduce the
> free play of the individual's interests, always in behalf of a larger
> interest described as "the community" or "the public."[53]

The task of eliminating the natural-rights tradition from American history was a project left to others. In 1969, for example, Brown University historian Gordon Wood published *The Creation of the American Republic*, which claimed that what inspired American revolutionaries was less the protection of individual rights than it was the desire to establish a republic where "each man must somehow be persuaded to submerge his wants into the greater good of the whole. The willingness of the individual to sacrifice his private interests for the good of the community—such patriotism or love of country—the eighteenth century termed 'public virtue.'"[54] In elaborating his conception of a republic as an organism requiring the sacrifice of the interests of its constituent parts (individual human beings), Wood has been characterized by critics, especially political scientist Michael Zuckert, as having transformed the Lockean concept of liberty into "the corporate involvement of the people in ruling, and not the individual security of natural rights."[55]

◆

Several years later, in his aptly named *Inventing America*, Garry Wills (then at Johns Hopkins), conjured an America that he would have created, not the one fashioned by the Declaration of Independence or the Constitution of 1787.[56] Wills downplayed Locke's connection to Jefferson's thought while giving priority to Francis Hutcheson, an 18th-century philosopher at Scotland's Glasgow University. While Hutcheson's writings (as the writings of other Scottish Enlightenment figures) were well-known to Jefferson and other Founders, his vaguely defined rights are capacious and ambiguous enough to accommodate Wills's view of the Founding as a loosening of the boundaries on government discretionary authority— precisely the antithesis of Locke's confinement of government power to the protection of rights.

A colleague in the history department at Johns Hopkins University—Kenneth S. Lynn—published a sharply critical essay of the book. Wills's thesis "that the Declaration is not grounded in Lockean individualism," Lynn wrote, but "a communitarian manifesto" would, if true, be "a stunning accomplishment." But it wasn't:

> Far from being a careful work of scholarship, *Inventing America* is the tendentious report of a highly political writer whose unannounced but nonetheless obvious aim is to supply the history of the Republic with as pink a dawn as possible. That his book has been prominently reviewed and lavishly praised—by academic authorities no less than by newspapermen—is a telling indication of the intellectual temper of the times. In an age of ideology, the inventions of ideologues have come to seem plausible, even though they are fantastic.[57]

Historians in the postwar decades who attempted to submerge natural rights were ultimately following the program initiated by the first generation of academic progressives, who were themselves following the programs of their Prussian mentors. But it was an American philosopher who sought to administer the coup de grâce: John Rawls. In his book *A Theory of Justice* (1971), the Harvard professor instructed his readers that human beings collectively should

> regard the distribution of natural talents as a common asset and...share in the benefits of this distribution whatever it turns out to be. Those who have been favored by nature, whoever they are, may gain from their good fortune only on terms that improve the situation of those who have lost out.[58]

Rawls would have us envisage a storehouse where a fund of natural human attributes is housed and somehow arbitrarily distributed to empty human selves, who then become undeservedly benefited or deprived by their good or bad fortune. Harvard political theorist Michael Sandel clarified the implications of Rawls's conception of what constitutes a person: "Regarding the distribution of natural talents as a common asset does not violate the difference between persons nor regard some as means to others' welfare, because not *persons* but only 'their' *attributes* are being used as means to others' well-being."[59]

That distinction will likely appear peculiar: how can you separate the individual self—his identity—from the attributes he was born with? Rawls's answer, Sandel explained, was that

> To say that *I* am somehow violated or abused when 'my' intelligence or even effort is used for the common benefit is to confuse the self with its contingently-given and wholly inessential attributes (inessential, that is, to me being the particular self I am). Only on a theory of the person that held these endowments to be essential

constituents rather than alienable *attributes* of the self could the sharing of assets be viewed as using *me* as a means to others' ends. But on Rawls' account all endowments are contingent and in principle detachable from the self.[60]

Given that your attributes, physical or mental, are not yours, according to Rawls, they belong to everyone. Of course, neither Rawls nor Sandel answers the obvious question raised by this bizarre conception of human identity. If you do not own your attributes because they do not intrinsically constitute you, but are only accidentally a part of you, why does society collectively own them? Since society collectively considered is not intrinsically constituted by these attributes either, they hence are created by no one, constitute no one, and are owned by no one, and therefore no one—whether severally or collectively considered—is entitled to use them.

That is the absurd conclusion implied by Rawls's conception of human identity. And it most certainly follows that any principle of how the products of individual human endeavor should be divided among people must be rejected, since that principle assumes that its author is entitled to distribute objects that were produced by attributes not owned by him or her.

And there we have it: liberalism as interpreted by its illiberal proponents, explained and justified. Individuals have no right of self-ownership because what we think of as persons don't really exist. What exists are innumerable empty containers arbitrarily filled with attributes that do not belong to them but to society. But if the attributes belong to no one, how does it follow that they belong to everyone? It will come as no surprise that the liberal Rawls was also a socialist. But what, according to this theory of ownership, requires us to obey any of his normative rules?

◆

Rawlsian liberalism is the antithesis of Lockean liberalism; they are not the same things but opposites employing the same name. Rawls had rules of production and distribution of goods and services that he deduced for the rest of us to obey. He called these rules liberal; they are in fact the arbitrary autocratic dictum of the philosophical emperor who somehow is entitled to compel the distribution of that which he does not own. Rawlsian antiliberal "liberalism" also represents, in a sense, the dead end of the road taken a century earlier by the American students who imbibed their theory of society at the feet of state-socialist professors in Germany.

Fittingly, President Bill Clinton presented a National Humanities Medal to Rawls in 1999, whom he called "perhaps the greatest philosopher of the 20th century. In 1971, when Hillary and I were in law school, we were among the millions moved by a remarkable book he wrote, 'A Theory of Justice,' that placed our rights to liberty and justice upon a strong and brilliant new foundation of reason."[61]

CHAPTER 6

THE POLITICAL CONVICTIONS
OF ACADEMICS

By the end of World War II, the transformation of higher education begun by American college students trained in Germany in the 1870s and 1880s was complete, profoundly altering the political and cultural outlook of faculties in colleges and universities, especially in the social sciences and humanities. This change was not a matter of common knowledge or widespread discussion among the general public. That would begin to change with the publication of a controversial book in 1951.

The book was *God and Man at Yale*, and the author was William F. Buckley, a recent graduate. Buckley's book contained a remarkable account of the economics department at one of the country's oldest and most prestigious universities. All the department's faculty, he contended, displayed an anti-individualist, anti-free-market perspective. Professors not only engaged in moral proselytizing but did so from the same ethical vantage point without any contrary faculty opinion.[1]

Yet the economics department was not a part of the university's divinity school or philosophy department. Economics, most Americans would have assumed, was an empirical, scientific discipline, not morally prescriptive.

The immediate response to Buckley's book was a wave of denunciations from inside the university, as well as a review

◆

in the *Atlantic Monthly* by McGeorge Bundy, a prominent Yale graduate. Bundy characterized Buckley as "dishonest," as well as "a twisted and ignorant young man."[2] In reality, Buckley's characterization of the Yale economics department was as much an indicant of the social sciences at American universities generally as it was of his alma mater.

Several years after the uproar over Buckley's book another striking example of campus political leanings occurred at the University of Virginia.[3] In the spring of 1960, UVA's free-market-oriented Thomas Jefferson Center for Studies in Political Economy applied to the Ford Foundation for financial support. The application was turned down on the grounds that its economists were politically biased—holding, in the view of foundation officials, to "a single 'point of view,'" unlike supposed bastions of intellectual diversity such as Yale or Harvard.[4] Ronald Coase, one of the center's economists, wrote privately of a meeting he had with a Ford Foundation official, noting that this person had "pointed to the statement in the brochure of the Thomas Jefferson Center, in which it said that the Center encouraged scholars who believed in individual liberty, as being particularly objectionable." Coase, an Englishman, wrote that he was "bowled over" by the comment.[5]

The Ford Foundation episode was only the beginning. A few years later, G. Warren Nutter, chairman of UVA's economics department, accidentally received a secret report prepared by the dean of the faculty that showed that the *university administration* had planned to push leading center scholars out of the university altogether. Citing "considerable adverse criticism" for the center's "close association with a particular viewpoint"—i.e., that of the University of Chicago's economics department, which housed Milton Friedman and George Stigler, and was "regarded by the vast majority of economists as of a distinctly unfavorable character"[6]—UVA refused to match a job offer by the University of

◆

Chicago to Ronald Coase. Coase left UVA in 1964. In 1967, another center economist, James M. Buchanan, resigned when, among other things, the university thrice turned down the economics department's recommendation to promote Gordon Tullock. Tullock also left the center.

Despite the "adverse criticism" cited in the UVA report, Coase won the Nobel Prize in Economics in 1991. Buchanan won the Nobel Prize in Economics in 1986. Tullock enjoyed a distinguished career in the economics profession for decades. And despite the "distinctly unfavorable character" of the University of Chicago's economic viewpoint cited in the UVA report, Friedman (in 1976) and Stigler (1982) also won Nobel Prizes in Economics.

As far as individual liberty goes, the Ford Foundation's 1958–1959 Research Fellow—MIT economist and Nobel Prize winner Paul Samuelson—had this to say the very year the USSR, along with its command economy, collapsed:

> The Soviet economy is proof that, contrary to what many skeptics had earlier believed, a socialist command economy can function and even thrive. That is, a society in which the major economic decisions are made administratively, without profits as a central motive force for production, can grow rapidly over long periods of time.[7]

LIFTING THE VEIL

Yale's public attack on William F. Buckley and the University of Virginia administration's quiet evisceration of the Thomas Jefferson Center might be shrugged off, but the political mindset in the academy would become clear as surveys and reports gauging the left-leaning convictions of American academics piled up. One set of surveys measured self-descriptions of political leanings and presidential votes, sometimes comparing faculty responses

◆

to those of the general public. Other surveys or data included reports on the ratio of Democrats to Republicans among the faculty by self-description or by party registrations at the national, university, or department level, or among members of academic associations, including editors of academic journals. Numbers and ratios differed depending on how large the survey was, how many faculty members responded, or how the questions and choices of an answer were worded. There are too many of these surveys and reports to examine, and in any case, the results have been consistent, if anything revealing disparities that have increased over time. This chapter will present results from a few of the most comprehensive or illustrative.

The first major study of faculty political opinion, by Paul F. Lazarsfeld and Wagner Thielens Jr., was based on personal interviews conducted in 1955 and published in 1958. It showed that liberals outnumbered conservatives, but their book, *The Academic Mind*, reported on only a few hundred academics in a limited number of disciplines.[8] *The Academic Mind* was superseded in 1975 by *The Divided Academy: Professors and Politics*, a book written by Everett Carll Ladd Jr. and Seymour Martin Lipset.[9] They analyzed a comprehensive survey of faculty opinion in 1969 sponsored by the Carnegie Commission on Higher Education and the American Council of Education (Ladd and Lipset's working sample exceeded 60,000), and a smaller follow-up survey—several hundred respondents—that the authors conducted themselves in 1972.

Ladd and Lipset's interest in faculty political opinion was based on the increasing role that higher education had come to play in American culture. They noted that the number of faculty members in colleges and universities, fewer than 50,000 in 1920, exceeded 600,000 in 1972; meanwhile the number of students, "2.5 million in 1950," grew "by 4 million" in the 1960s. And crucially, "persons not armed with a bachelor's degree need not bother to

◆

apply for executive positions in private industry or government." Ultimately, "the greatest source of influence of academics may stem from their control of the process of certification as to competence for virtually the entire range of elite occupations, and in particular their position as key reference group for the larger community who live by the manipulation of ideas."[10]

In the 1969 Carnegie survey, Ladd and Lipset reported, the *overall* political profile of faculty differed significantly from the American public—46% of academics described themselves as "Left" or "Liberal," compared with 28% who described themselves as "moderately or strongly conservative." By contrast, 20% of the general public described their political leanings as Left and Liberal, and 42% described themselves as moderately or strongly conservative.[11]

Breaking down the 1969 survey by academic disciplines showed a greater imbalance: 64% of faculty in the social sciences described themselves as "Very Liberal" or "Liberal" while only 20% described themselves as "Conservative" or "Very Conservative." In the humanities, 54% of the faculty identified themselves as Very Liberal or Liberal while 29% characterized themselves as Conservative or Very Conservative. Among the law school faculty, 52% were Very Liberal or Liberal and 28% Conservative or Very Conservative.[12]

Twenty years later, in 1989, the Carnegie Foundation for the Advancement of Teaching published another major survey of faculty attitudes. Overall, the faculty at four-year colleges or universities self-identified as 62% "Liberal" or "Moderately Liberal" and 23% as "Moderately Conservative" or "Conservative." However, within the humanities and social sciences overall, 70% were Liberal or Moderately Liberal. In the humanities, 18% were Moderately Conservative or Conservative, and in the social sciences, 15% were Moderately Conservative or Conservative.[13]

◆

POLITICAL PARTY REGISTRATION

A different series of reports began to emerge in the latter half of the 1980s, not involving self-descriptions of faculty political leanings, but rather their party affiliation. In 1987, for example, the *Colorado Review*, a student publication, reported on the party registrations of all faculty and administrators at the University of Colorado.[14] Out of 56 administrators, only 3 were Republicans; out of 602 faculty members, only 45 were Republicans.

The results by *academic department* were more significant. In economics, 9 faculty members were Democrats, 16 were unaffiliated, and 2 were Republicans. Of the 57 professors in the English department, 43 were Democrats, 14 were unaffiliated, and none were Republicans. In history, of 28 professors, 21 were Democrats, 6 were unaffiliated, and 1 was a Republican. In philosophy, of 25 professors, 22 were Democrats, 3 were unaffiliated, and none were Republicans. In political science, there were 25 faculty members, of whom 18 were Democrats, 3 were unaffiliated, and 4 were Republicans. In sociology, 14 of the 20 members of the department were Democrats, 5 were unaffiliated, and 1 was a Republican. In the school of law, there were 30 faculty members, of whom 27 were Democrats, 1 was unaffiliated, and 2 were Republicans.

The student report caused a major uproar in the state, though there were no consequences or changes made by the university in response. Similar voter-registration studies by students at some other institutions were done in the next decade, all of which showed similar results.[15]

In 2002, *The American Enterprise* magazine reported faculty political party registration by department that it collected from local records, dividing the results into "professors registered in a party of the Left [Democratic, Green, Working Family], or in a party of the Right [Republican, Libertarian]."[16] Among the institutions and departments in the article, the data revealed a remarkable imbalance (see table 6.1).

Table 6.1. Faculty Political Affiliations at Select Universities (2002)

COLLEGE	DEPARTMENT	LEFT	RIGHT	COLLEGE	DEPARTMENT	LEFT	RIGHT
Brown				UCLA			
	Economics	5	1		English	29	2
	Engineering	7	2		History	53	3
	English	10	0		Journalism	12	1
	History	17	0		Political Science	16	1
	Political Science	7	0		Women's Studies	31	2
	Sociology	8	0	Total		141	9
Total		54	3				
				University of Colorado, Boulder	English	37	0
Harvard					History	28	1
	Economics	15	1		Journalism	14	0
	Political Science	20	1		Political Science	17	2
	Sociology	15	0		Sociology	14	1
Total		50	2		Women's Studies	6	1
				Total		116	5
Penn. State				University of Maryland	Economics	8	4
	Economics	8	4		Political Science	17	3
	Political Science	17	3		Sociology	34	3
	Sociology	34	3	Total		59	10
Total		59	10				
				University of Houston			
Syracuse	Economics	15	1		English	12	5
	Political Science	20	1		History	10	3
	Sociology	15	0		Journalism	3	1
Total		50	2		Political Science	12	3
					Sociology	8	3
				Total		45	14

Source: Data are drawn from Karl Zinsmeister, "The Shame of America's One-Party Campuses," *The American Enterprise*, September 2002, 18–25.

◆

A few years later, the National Association of Scholars published two significant studies under the rubric "Documenting the One-Party Campus" in their journal *Academic Questions.* The first study, "Political Diversity in Six Disciplines," surveyed the U.S. members of six national *social science and humanities associations* (American Anthropological Association, American Economics Association, American Historical Association, American Society for Political and Legal Philosophy, American Political Science Association, American Sociological Association). The survey received 1,678 responses to the question, "To which political party have the candidates you've voted for in the past ten years mostly belonged?"[17] The *overall* results are shown in table 6.2.

Table 6.2. Membership Voting Preferences in Social Science and Humanities Associations (2004–5)

Democratic Party	80.47%
Republican Party	7.87%
Green Party	1.55%
Libertarian Party	1.17%
Other	.39%

The study also reported on the ratio of Democratic to Republican voters *by academic discipline* (see table 6.3).

Table 6.3. Ratio of Democratic to Republican Voters in Six Academic Disciplines (2004–5)

Anthropology	30.2 to 1
Economics	3.0 to 1
Political and Legal Philosophy	13.5 to 1
History	9.5 to 1
Political Science	6.7 to 1
Sociology	28.0 to 1
Average Ratio over Six Disciplines	15.1 to 1

Source: Data are drawn from Daniel B. Klein and Charlotta Stern, "Political Diversity in Six Disciplines," *Academic Questions* 18, no. 1 (Winter 2004–5), 40–52.

The second study reported the political party registration in several social science disciplines at the University of California, Berkeley, and Stanford University (see table 6.4).[18] This study was far more comprehensive than similar such studies in the past because the authors included six surrounding counties for each institution, not just the county in which the university was physically located. The gulf between registered Democrats and Republicans in the social sciences and humanities faculties was overwhelming:[19]

Table 6.4. Party Registration in Several Disciplines at UC Berkeley and Stanford (2004–5)

UNIVERSITY OF CALIFORNIA AT BERKELEY		
	Registered Democrats	Registered Republicans
Anthropology	12	0
Economics	22	2
Political Science	28	2
Sociology	17	0
English	29	1
History	31	1
Philosophy	9	1
STANFORD UNIVERSITY		
Anthropology	6	0
Economics	14	6
Political Science	18	2
Sociology	10	0
English	22	1
History	22	0
Philosophy	10	1

Source: Data are drawn from Daniel B. Klein and Andrew Western, "Voter Registration of Berkeley and Stanford Faculty," *Academic Questions* 18, no. 1 (Winter 2004–5), 60.

The authors of the "Six Disciplines" study illustrated the incentives to conform politically and disincentives to dissent by quoting Robert P. George, a conservative political scientist at Princeton University, about the advice he would give to an "outstanding" conservative undergraduate who wanted to get a doctoral degree

◆

and teach at an American university. George replied that if a student sought entrance to a top graduate school, he would probably be turned down; if he was accepted, he would "face pressure to conform," and if he resisted, he would be discriminated against.

> But say he gets through. He's going to run into intense discrimination trying to find a job. But say he lands a tenure-track job. He'll run into even more intense discrimination because the establishment gets more concerned the closer you get to the golden ring. By the time you come up for tenure, you're in your mid-30s with a spouse and a couple of kids. It's the worst time to be uncertain about your career. Can I really take the responsibility of advising a kid to take these kinds of risks?[20]

Professor George's frank comments brought up a key factor behind the campus monoculture: tenure.

While academic tenure is now all but universal in American higher education, college and university presidents traditionally appointed and dismissed faculty throughout the 19th century and into the 20th century. But the question of employment security arose in the 1880s and 1890s after several professors were dismissed for public statements on political or social issues that riled up the college president, trustees, or donors of the institution.[21]

Tenure was sold as a guarantee of free inquiry. In the natural sciences, free inquiry was rarely if ever a problem. Faculty members in disciplines that included moral prescriptions, as well as empirical facts, were quite another matter. But in these disciplines, the regnant paradigm had already taken shape as the social scientists with German doctorates ceaselessly—and speciously—claimed, as historians Richard Hofstadter and Walter P. Metzger put it, that "the prescriptions of social science were presumably based on facts and social laws. The distinguishing

◆

badge of competence that natural scientists wore was claimed by social science by right of direct descent."[22]

Beginning in the early years of the 20th century, a series of protracted negotiations took place between the American Association of University Professors (AAUP) and an association of college presidents, the Association of American Colleges (AAC); both organizations were established in 1915. Tenure in its modern form took hold with the AAUP's "1940 Statement of Principles on Academic Freedom and Tenure." It represented, of course, a shift in the terms of employment, but there was more at stake. During the early years of negotiations, the AAC's Academic Freedom Commission agreed that "all appointments and termination of contracts should be made in conference with the departments concerned, and 'might well' be approved by a faculty committee or the faculty itself."[23]

Over time, "should be made in conference with" and "'might well' be approved" evolved. Today, in practice, faculty appointments are made by faculty. The actual role of the president and trustees, regardless of any formal institutional language, was and still is, with rare exceptions, to rubber-stamp a department's decision to make an offer of employment or promotion that includes tenure.

While this state of affairs has, for the most part, meant employment security inside the academy—at least for tenured faculty—it is not, and was never meant to be, a means for protecting moral, intellectual, or philosophical *diversity*. And as Robert George's statement indicated, such diversity in the social sciences and humanities is the exception, not the rule. This has vastly increased the incentives for more political conformity on the part of aspiring faculty with little incentive for moral dissent. Indeed, in recent years, even tenured faculty members have been at risk for even slight acts of political nonconformity.[24]

◆

THE ACADEMIC CASTE SYSTEM

"Faculty Voter Registration in Economics, History, Journalism, Law, and Psychology,"[25] a 2016 study in *Econ Journal Watch*, investigated the voter registration of 7,243 faculty members at forty leading American universities as determined by *U.S. News & World Report*. Overall, 3,623 were registered Democrats and 314 were Republicans, with the ratios shown in table 6.5.[26]

Table 6.5. Faculty Voter Registration in Five Disciplines at Forty American Universities (2016)

Economics	4.5 to 1
History	33.5 to 1
Journalism/Communications	20 to 1
Law	8.6 to 1
Psychology	17.4 to 1

Source: Data are drawn from Mitchell Langbert, Anthony J. Quain, and Daniel B. Klein, "Faculty Voter Registration in Economics, History, Journalism, Law, and Psychology," *Econ Journal Watch* 13, no. 2 (September 2016): 425.

The study's three authors—Mitchell Langbert, Anthony J. Quain, and Daniel B. Klein—offered a hypothesis about the causes of the political one-sidedness:

> Academia is an array of disciplinary pyramids, settlements of which are financed and sustained as departments at a university. In History, for example, the pyramid's apex consists of the top History departments, which produce most of the Ph.D.s and place them best, producing what Val Burris (2004) called in Sociology the "academic caste system," but it is the same everywhere.[27]

In practice, these *disciplinary pyramids* maintain and intensify the observable disparity in political outlook across the university:

> Once the apex of the disciplinary pyramid becomes predominately left-leaning, it will sweep left-leaners into positions throughout

◆

the pyramid (or, at least, it will exclude vibrant dissenters). At the micro level of a particular university department—no matter where in the pyramid—once it has a majority of left-leaners, it will, in serving, enjoying, protecting, advancing, and purifying sacred values, tend to hire more left leaners (or at least not vibrant dissenters).

Over time, the authors noted, those not on the left will "naturally tend to select themselves out of academia."[28]

Professional associations represent yet another means for maintaining the caste system. A 2020 study in *Econ Journal Watch* by Mitchell Langbert documented the partisan leanings of the American Economic Association's membership.[29] Predictably, the membership was heavily Democratic. But within the association itself, the profile was even more skewed:

> For contributors to PACs and candidates, the D:R ratio is 67:0, with 139 not making political contributions. There are no Republican, neutral, or minor party donors among the AEA's current and recently past officers and editors. With respect to voter registration, the D:R ratio for the officers and editors is more than double the ratio for the membership (8.1:1 versus 3.8:1).[30]

In a commentary[31] on Langbert's study, John Cochrane, an economist at Stanford University's Hoover Institution, singled out the role of *journal editors*, who "decide what gets published and what does not get published in the association's [eight] journals." This is no small matter, as publication is a crucial metric for career advancement or even survival. "The AEA plainly has almost no political diversity in its operational roles," Cochrane commented, and the "AEA's official statement on racial diversity states that a divergence in percentages between the AEA membership and general population is proof of a 'hostile' 'climate.'" He declined to conclude whether "the AEA should draw the same conclusion regarding political diversity." Nevertheless, Cochrane had to wonder if "research that advocates new or expanded [economic or social] programs sells better than research that documents unintended consequences of existing programs."

Columbia University law professor Philip Hamburger recently provided another perspective about how the academic caste system operates against law professors and students who don't conform to regnant ideological currents. "On account of mere dissent," he explained, "deans investigate faculty for their views, give them meager salary increases, bar them from teaching some subjects, and even threaten to fire them.... It's not only deans. Faculties or their appointment committees regularly refuse to hire people with the wrong views."[32] Hamburger described a top-to-bottom machine, noting that "student law-review editors exclude dissenting students from their boards and even threaten to fire editors whom they discover to have the wrong views, whether on pronouns or matters of law." Some journals block articles that offer views or perspectives they disfavor; as a result, "Many students and faculty therefore shy away from exploring such viewpoints. Quietly in the background, members of faculty oversight boards encourage or permit this narrow-mindedness."

Langbert, one of the authors of the 2016 *Econ Journal Watch* report, published a follow-up study in 2018.[33] He reported, for example, the ratio of Democratic-to-Republican-registered faculty at 65 colleges in the *U.S. News & World Report* rankings (for 2017). The figures for some of the top colleges are shown in table 6.6.[34]

THE DEFENSE OF THE STATUS QUO

Repeated confirmations of the overwhelming dominance of progressive faculty in crucial disciplines that were purportedly

♦

Table 6.6. Number of Faculty and Their Political Party Registrations in Fifteen Liberal Arts Colleges (2018)

College	Sample Size	Not Registered	Registered but No Party	Democrat	Republican	D:R Ratio
Williams	254	71	50	132	1	132:1
Amherst	184	42	37	102	3	34:1
Wellesley	240	53	48	136	1	136:1
Swarthmore	182	51	6	120	1	120:1
Bowdoin	166	24	26	107	2	53.5:1
Pomona	195	41	29	119	3	39.7:1
Claremont-McKenna	161	28	37	74	20	3.7:1
Davidson	161	20	45	87	9	9.7:1
Colby	184	36	28	109	9	12.1:1
Colgate	246	54	27	153	8	19.1:1
Hamilton	149	23	22	99	4	24.8:1
Haverford	109	33	9	62	4	15.5:1
Annapolis	337	72	67	136	59	2.3:1
Smith	233	39	57	131	4	32.8:1
Vassar	221	52	20	140	4	35:1

Source: Mitchell Langbert, "Homogeneous: The Political Affiliations of Elite Liberal Arts Colleges," *Academic Questions* 31, no. 2 (Summer 2018). The colleges here are drawn from a list of sixty-five.

empirical—but in reality are shot through with moral perspectives, such as economics, sociology, political science, history, and anthropology (as well as strictly moral sciences such as political philosophy)—are properly controversial. Nevertheless, there have been attempts to explain away the obvious.

While admitting the virtual nonexistence of conservatives or Republicans in the social sciences and humanities, there have been arguments to brush this aside, primarily by making one or more of three claims. First, the conclusion that the academy is dominated by the left is denied. Second, the one-sided character of instruction involving political policy and philosophy is claimed to have little influence on the subsequent political convictions of students. Lastly, the one-party campus is supposedly not the result of discrimination or hostility to conservative, classical liberal, or libertarian views, but stems rather from the fact that

◆

students with such views are typically not inclined to be interested in academic careers for reasons having to do with their intrinsic vocational inclinations.

In 2005, John Tierney, then a columnist for the *New York Times*, brought up the claim of some academics "that their political ideologies don't affect the way they teach." This argument, Tierney commented, "is proof of how detached they've become from reality in their monocultures. This claim is especially dubious," he added, "if you're training lawyers and journalists to deal with controversial public policies."[35]

Tierney's statement touched off a chorus of denials from the academy. Tierney discussed the responses he received in a subsequent column—responses he found risible. Liberal scholars, he wrote, "sent me treatises explaining that the shortage of conservatives on faculties is not a result of bias." Instead, they offered him other reasons, including that conservatives don't "value knowledge for its own sake," "do not care about the social good," are "too greedy to work for professors' wages," and "are too dumb to get tenure." "I've studied these theories as best I could (for a conservative)," Tierney wrote, "but somehow I can't shake the notion that there just might be some bias on campus."[36]

Tierney also commented that conservatives' alleged lack of interest in careers focusing on ideas was peculiar given the success of conservative politicians, as well as the growth of right-leaning student groups and publications on campus. "Plenty of smart conservatives have passed up Wall Street to work for right-wing think tanks that often don't pay more than universities do, and don't offer lifetime tenure and summers off." Ultimately, Tierney perceived a simple reason why the professoriate leaned so heavily to the left: "Once liberals dominate a department, they can increase their majority by voting to award tenure to like-minded scholars. As liberals dominate a field, conservatives' work comes to be seen as fringe scholarship."

◆

Two years later, sociologists Neil Gross and Solon Simmons defended the status quo based on a claim that the dramatic political imbalance on campus was vastly exaggerated, indeed an illusion.[37] They conducted surveys that added two political categories, "Slightly Liberal" and "Slightly Conservative," and then added those so classified to those describing themselves as "Middle of the Road." The result was a category that exceeded those classifying themselves as "Extremely Liberal" or "Liberal." Therefore, the authors claimed that the university, while still virtually bereft of conservatism, is not as left-leaning as others have reported. But the political disparity across all disciplines was not the central concern among critics of the academy—instead, it was the absence of significant conservative opinion in the social sciences and humanities.

Lawrence Summers, a liberal economist at Harvard (and the university's former president), was not at all comforted by the conclusions reached by Gross and Simmons. "The data in this paper surprised me in the opposite direction that it surprised the authors," he said at a symposium. "It made me think that there is even less ideological diversity in the American university than I had imagined." Summers noted the "overwhelming tilt toward the progressive side," especially in the humanities and social sciences at elite universities that offered doctoral degrees. He also disputed the notion that the instruction students receive has little influence on their political convictions. "Given that faculties control what perspectives people are exposed to at the most formative moment of their intellectual life, it is hard to believe that the nature of their beliefs and the availability of alternative beliefs is a matter of irrelevance."[38]

In a subsequent book, Gross discussed the paucity of conservatives in the social sciences and the humanities (strangely omitting philosophy, which, of course, includes political philosophy).[39] His first inclination was to examine the history of

◆

American higher education for an answer to the question of why there is a disparity between the left and right on its faculties. Unfortunately, his investigation was woefully inadequate, as the pivotal role of Germany in training the first doctoral faculty in humanities and social science between 1870 and 1890 went unrecognized. The organic view of society and state sovereignty these Americans learned from the German historicists and state socialists—combined with their rejection of the natural-rights philosophy of Locke and the Declaration of Independence—was replaced with their self-conception, like their German mentors, as an elite guardian class. The dominant status that this cohort attained in the academy made others—whose views grew out of the philosophy of America's Revolutionary generation—unwelcome from the outset.

Ultimately, Gross retreated to the self-selection defense—students with classical liberal, conservative, or libertarian views are typically not inclined to be interested in or attracted to academic careers for reasons having to do with their intrinsic vocational inclinations. But self-selecting out of an academic career is based less on a lack of interest than it is on the recognition that with their political views, they are less likely to be accepted into departments at the top graduate schools, less likely to get strong job recommendations from their professors, and less likely to get tenure-track job offers (or achieve tenure) from top universities.

The reality that dissenting views from the academic consensus very much play a role in discouraging a student's pursuit of an academic career was made plain by Princeton's Robert George in 2003. The atmosphere two decades later was made even plainer when Jordan Peterson—a clinical psychologist, widely read popular commentator, and tenured professor—resigned in frustration from the University of Toronto in January 2022. For years, Peterson had come under intense pressure

◆

to conform to the wave of politically correct opinion sweeping through Canada as well as America. He was also disgusted that "the accrediting boards for graduate clinical psychology training programs" in his country "are now planning to refuse to accredit university clinical programs unless they have a 'social justice' orientation." The last straw was his realization that even his best "heterosexual white male graduate students" faced "a negligible chance of being offered university research positions, despite stellar scientific dossiers."[40]

As for the political convictions of academics, recall the fierce criticism and denials that greeted William F. Buckley's 1951 book about Yale University's one-party campus. Today his book would barely raise an eyebrow there, or anywhere else. In 2022, for example, a survey by the *Harvard Crimson*, the student newspaper, reported that 80% of Harvard's Faculty of Arts and Sciences "characterized their political leanings as 'liberal' or 'very liberal,'" while "only 1 percent of respondents stated they are 'conservative,' and no respondents identified as 'very conservative.'"[41]

More recently, the board of trustees at the University of North Carolina, Chapel Hill, announced that it would attempt to rectify the problem of ideological uniformity at their institution. Voter data from the North Carolina Board of Elections showed that Democrats outnumber Republicans 16 to 1 in humanities and STEM departments. In response, the trustees announced that they would establish a School of Civic Life and Leadership, staffing it with 20 faculty members from across the political spectrum.[42]

Is this likely to change UNC? Suppose there were Schools of Religious Studies across the country, and all of them were dominated by theologians of one particular faith or sect. If only one of these institutions were to add a single department whose faculty had a diversity of views, would it be likely to change the rest of that institution, or any others?

◆

UCLA's Higher Education Research Institute (HERI) has confirmed the extent of the problem that the UNC trustees are attempting to address and why their particular solution will fall far short of its goal. "In the 1989–90 HERI survey," as Phillip W. Magness and David Wauth noted recently, "only 21% of faculty indicated that their institutions placed a high priority on 'help[ing] students learn how to bring about change in American society.'" That changed dramatically over the years. "By 2017–18, this number increased to 80.6% of all faculty. Together, these data indicate that the leftward ideological shift among the professoriate has been accompanied by a clear rise in instructional approaches that prioritize political activism in the classroom."[43]

POSTSCRIPT

Based on the sheer numbers presented in this chapter, the classical liberal tradition might appear dead in the academy. Yet, there are (and have been) scholars who would be characterized as classical liberals, libertarians, or conservatives.

Over the years, a long and distinguished group of political scientists have pushed back against the entire "progressivist" reinterpretation of the Declaration and the Constitution. They have included, among many others, Harry Jaffa, Martin Diamond, James Ceaser, Daniel J. Mahoney, Thomas Pangle, Arthur M. Melzer, David Lewis Schaefer, William B. Allen, Ken I. Kersch, Peter C. Myers, Ronald J. Pestritto, Hadley Arkes, Robert George, Jean Yarbrough, Edward Erler, Thomas G. West, James R. Stoner, Bradley C. S. Watson, Charles Kessler, Tiffany Miller, Michael Zuckert, John Tomasi, Keith Whittington, Aaron Wildavsky, and Gottfried Dietze.

In history, they have been joined by Forrest McDonald, Arthur Ekirch, Ronald Hamowy, Paul Moreno, Gary Dean Best, Robert

♦

Hessen, Herman Belz, Burton W. Folsom Jr., David Beito, Donald T. Critchlow, Larry Schweikart, Wilfred M. McClay, Allen C. Guelzo, C. Bradley Thompson, Paul Rahe, and many others. In law, they include James W. Ely Jr., Richard Epstein, Randy Barnett, Ilya Somin, David E. Bernstein, Philip Hamburger, Stephen Gilles, Jonathan H. Adler, Gary Lawson, Michael McConnell, John Hasnas, Scott Gerber, and again, many others.

In philosophy, virtually the only professor to discuss political theory in the 1930s was John Dewey, a Johns Hopkins PhD (1884) who taught in the philosophy departments at the University of Michigan, the University of Chicago, and Columbia University. He was a defender of democratic socialism in the 1930s, calling for "'the socialization of all natural resources and natural monopolies, of ground rent and of basic industries.'"[44] But within the academy, he was a lonely figure—because philosophy departments generally were concerned with portraying themselves as similar to mathematics departments and, therefore, discouraged the appointment of moral and political philosophers. Philosophy departments tended to confine themselves to logic, the theory of knowledge (epistemology), the philosophy of science, and the analysis of language. This situation began to change slowly in the 1950s, more rapidly in the 1960s, and explosively in the 1970s and 1980s. One would think that in this one discipline, there might have been a chance that natural rights would not be marginalized.

Initially, like the rest of the academy, the first major political philosophers were progressives. Harvard's John Rawls was the most influential figure in political philosophy after Dewey's passing. But three years after his book *A Theory of Justice* appeared in 1971, Rawls was challenged by Robert Nozick, a fellow professor in Harvard's philosophy department. Nozick's book *Anarchy, State, and Utopia*[45] won the National Book Award. It devastated Rawls's argument while defending a Lockean view of individual

◆

rights. I have already explained Rawls's bizarre, implausible view that a human being's attributes were somehow separate from his identity—from his existence as a human being. That view exposed the Rawlsian edifice to the indictment of the unfounded normative claims that he derives from it. However, Thomas Nagel, then a professor of philosophy at Princeton, criticized Nozick's foundational claims as similarly indefensible. Nozick announced in the preface of his book that he was converted to libertarianism by the decisive force of the arguments of classical liberals. As Nagel put it in an essay, "Libertarianism without Foundations,"

> Nozick starts from the unargued premise that individuals have certain inviolable rights which may not be intentionally transgressed by other individuals or the state for any purpose. They are the rights not to be killed or assaulted if one is doing no harm, not to be coerced or imprisoned, not to have one's property taken or destroyed, and not to be limited in the use of one's property so long as one does not violate the rights of others. He concludes that the only morally permissible state would be the minimal nightwatchman state, a state limited to protecting people against murder, assault, theft, fraud, and breach of contract. The argument is not one which derives a surprising conclusion from plausible premises. No one (except perhaps an anarchist) who did not already accept the conclusion would accept the premise, and the implausibility of each can only serve to reinforce a conviction of the implausibility of the other.[46]

Nagel's criticism was correct. Nozick did fail to provide a foundational argument for the rights that he attributed to individuals and, therefore, for the limited state function (the protection of those rights) that he believed he justified.

◆

But the foundations are obvious because they are merely two factual truths: that every living thing possesses its body, not that of another, and that only human beings have the mental capacity to recognize and claim what they possess. The right is a "claim," but it is a claim to what I already have as a matter of existential and empirical fact. To those who claim that to have a body does not imply that one owns it, it follows that either no one owns their body, or some other person or persons owns it.

When Nagel goes to the doctor, Nagel goes, not someone else. When Nagel is examined by the doctor it is his, not someone else's, body that is examined. When he is correctly diagnosed with a disease, it is he who has it with its particular attributes at the moment of its diagnosis, not someone else. When he is told about it he understands what it is, unlike a pet cat he might have who is given a similar diagnosis. When he is told that the disease he has is terminal, he understands what his cat could not understand under similar circumstances.

When Nagel wrote "Libertarianism without Foundations," *he* composed it, not someone else, no matter what their claim. If I say that I composed any of his books, then I am lying. If Nagel produces something that no one else produced and claims ownership in virtue of its existence deriving from him, not anyone else, what argument can I use to claim it and the revenue from its sales? That I need it? Suppose my heart is failing and Nagel's is perfectly fine. Am I entitled to Nagel's heart? On what grounds, if it factually is part of Nagel? That is the foundational argument that Nozick failed to supply.

Nozick was not the only contemporary philosopher to have defended natural rights and/or limited government. He was accompanied by, among others, Loren Lomasky, Fred D. Miller Jr., Horacio Spector, David Gauthier, John Tomasi, Juliana Pilon, Scott Arnold, John Thrasher, Tara Smith, James R. Otteson, John

◆

Kekes, Geoffrey Sampson, George Mavrodes, Norman Barry, Michael Huemer, Matt Zwolinski, Jan Narveson, Douglas B. Rasmussen, Douglas J. Den Uyl, Ellen Frankel Paul, Kevin Vallier, Lorenzo Infantino, Guido Pincione, Eric Mack, Antony Flew, George H. Smith, Stephen R. C. Hicks, Ed Feser, Steven Wall, David Schmidtz, Jason Brennan, and preceded by Ayn Rand (the novelist), John Hospers, and Murray Rothbard (economist and historian). And this is not a complete list.

Tragically, the revival of classical liberalism, broadly speaking, has been far too little and too late. The dominant status established by progressives at the outset of American doctoral education has, as surveys confirm, completely transformed the political culture of American higher education. The control exerted by the academic caste system that has evolved over training and appointments is irreversible.

CHAPTER 7

THE MEDIA

In their book *The Divided Academy*, Everett Carll Ladd and Seymour Martin Lipsett stressed the role of college in credentialing men and women for employment in the upper reaches of private businesses or government.[1] They pointed out that "the people who write for major newspapers, magazines, and news services, and who direct network broadcasting have values and political orientations similar to academics," and cited a report that noted "'almost one third of the nation's most influential journalists'" were graduates of the Ivy League and that the "'suggestion that many national journalists now function as a kind of "lesser" clergy for the academic elite is not far from correct.'"[2] Given the political coloration of their teachers, journalists and others in the mass media inevitably skewed their reportage and opinion writing in the decades following the Second World War. Over the past few decades, the liberal—or more accurately, illiberal—bias became profound. Today, the press, and the mass media generally, operate functionally as a propaganda arm of the Democratic Party.

Before considering the evidence, it is helpful to begin with an example of how the right type of overt bias is rewarded in today's media.

During the 1992 presidential campaign, the Clinton election team allowed a recording of its activities, which was released a year later as a movie, *The War Room*. At one point in the film,

George Stephanopoulos, Clinton's campaign communications director, takes a phone call from a reporter inquiring about the candidate's sexual affairs and suggesting that he will have to report on what he has found. Stephanopoulos responded with a threat. "I guarantee you that if you do this," he said, "you'll never work in Democratic politics again," adding that by not publishing the story, "You'll know that you did the right thing, and didn't dishonor yourself."[3]

After leaving the White House in 1996, Stephanopoulos became a political analyst for ABC News and a correspondent for the network's *This Week*, *World News Tonight*, and *Good Morning America*. His rise continued, and in 2015 he was named chief Washington correspondent for ABC News, after comoderating the Democratic Party presidential debate between Barack Obama and Hillary Clinton. Subsequently, Stephanopoulos replaced Diane Sawyer on *Good Morning America* and, after a brief departure, returned as the host of *This Week* in December 2019. At that time, he signed a contract to stay on at the network until 2021 for $105 million. He is one of three hosts of *Good Morning America* and is also the host of *This Week with George Stephanopoulos* on ABC News.

One might ask: Could someone who managed a Republican campaign and threatened a reporter in the way Stephanopoulos did have been hired by any major network? The question answers itself.

"THE ELEPHANT IN THE LIVING ROOM"

S. Robert Lichter, Stanley Rothman, and Linda S. Lichter commissioned a detailed survey in the late 1970s of the political opinions held by 238 (randomly chosen) journalists at several elite media institutions: the *New York Times*, *Washington Post*, *Wall Street Journal*, *Time*, *Newsweek*, *U.S. News & World Report*, ABC, NBC,

CBS, and public television. They published the results in *The Media Elite: America's New Power Brokers* (1986).[4] The political leanings of the reporters, columnists, bureau chiefs, film editors, and the like were apparent from the choices they made in four prior presidential elections: 94% voted for Lyndon Baines Johnson in 1964; 87% chose Hubert Humphrey in 1968; 81% chose George McGovern in 1972; and 81% chose Jimmy Carter in 1976.[5]

The authors reviewed several other surveys conducted between 1971 and 1985—all of which found far more liberal than conservative reporters (as well as newspaper managing editors and news directors of television and radio stations). One of them, a September 1976 *Washington Post*–Harvard University poll of accredited reporters in the nation's capital, "found that 59% called themselves liberal and 18% conservative," which the authors noted was "strikingly close to the 54 to 17 margin we found among the media elite four years later."[6] Another, by the Brookings Institution's Stephen Hess (*The Washington Reporters*, 1978), also found a liberal-leaning press corps in the nation's capital.[7] A major survey by the *Los Angeles Times* in the mid-1980s reported "a gap of 25 percent between the attitudes of journalists and their audience."[8]

Younger journalists in the *Media Elite* survey were far more liberal than their predecessors. In trying to account for this, the authors conducted another survey, this time a random sample of 1982 degree candidates at Columbia University's Graduate School of Journalism, the country's most prestigious such institution. Of the one-sixth of that class randomly sampled, 85% were politically liberal and 11% were conservative. For the implications of this survey, the authors of *The Media Elite* turned to a statement made a decade earlier by Daniel Patrick Moynihan (a member of the Kennedy and Nixon administrations, Harvard University professor, and Democratic U.S. senator from New York), who noted that the political consequence of the rising social status of journalism is that the press grows more and more influenced by attitudes genuinely hostile to American society and American government. This trend seems bound to continue into the future. On the record of what they have been writing while in college, the young people now leaving the Harvard *Crimson* and the Columbia *Spectator* for journalistic jobs in Washington will resort to the [Lincoln] Steffens [muckraking] style at ever-escalating levels of moral implication.[9]

The trend identified in *The Media Elite* continued. In 1996, a survey of 139 Washington bureau chiefs and congressional correspondents by the Freedom Forum's Media Studies Center and the Roper Center found that 89% of the journalists voted for Bill Clinton in 1992, compared with 44% of nonjournalist voters; 7% of the journalists voted for George H. W. Bush, compared with 37% of nonjournalist voters.[10]

Once the survey was released, Howard Kurtz (then the *Washington Post* media writer) said on *Fox News Sunday*, "Clearly anybody looking at those numbers, if they're even close to accurate, would conclude that there is a diversity problem in the news business, and it's not just the kind of diversity we usually talk about, which is not getting enough minorities in the news business, but political diversity, as well. Anybody who doesn't see that is just in denial."[11] Tom Rosenstiel, at the time the director of the Project for Excellence in Journalism affiliated with Columbia University's Graduate School of Journalism, echoed Kurtz: "Bias is the elephant in the living room. We're in denial about it and don't want to admit it's there. We think it's less of a problem than the public does, and we just don't want to get into it."[12]

By the time Donald Trump was elected president in 2016, the political bias and hostility exhibited by the prestige media reached unprecedented heights. "News Coverage of Donald Trump's First 100 Days," a study released by Harvard University's Kennedy School in May 2017, announced that "Trump has received unsparing coverage for most weeks of his presidency, without a single major topic where Trump's coverage, on balance, was more positive than negative, setting a new standard for unfavorable press coverage of a president."[13] The study looked at CBS, CNN, NBC, Fox, the *New York Times, Washington Post,* and *Wall Street Journal,* concluding that CNN and NBC's coverage was the most unrelenting; negative stories about Trump outpaced positive ones 13-to-1 on the two networks. Trump's negative coverage on CBS was more than 90%. His negative coverage exceeded the 80% level in the *New York Times* (87%) and the *Washington Post* (83%). Coverage in the *Wall Street Journal* was 70% negative, a difference largely attributable to the *Journal*'s more frequent and more favorable economic coverage. The Harvard report also noted that the coverage "was not merely negative in overall terms. It was unfavorable on every dimension. There was not a single major topic where Trump's coverage was more positive than negative."[14]

For a long time in American history, newspapers were the only vehicle for news reporting and editorial commentary. Radio began broadcasting in the 1920s, with television following in the 1940s. During print's dominant period, newspapers were privately held corporations that frequently reflected the political views of their owners, who tended to be (but were not uniformly) conservative and Republican in party affiliation. Radio and television networks, however, were publicly held companies whose ability to broadcast was licensed by—and subject to the regulation of—the Federal Communications Commission.

For decades, the political journalism that the three broadcast networks (CBS, NBC, and ABC) daily fed the public increasingly reflected the views of reporters, most of whom were college-educated. Moreover, the managers and executives of these networks were also college-educated and held views that reflected those of their university mentors. What this meant was a growing divide

◆

between the political views of what was broadcast and those of viewers. It also meant scrutiny of what was being fed to the public.

One of the earliest to do so was Edith Efron, a staff writer for *TV Guide* (and a graduate of Columbia University's Graduate School of Journalism). Efron surveyed the news broadcasts of the three networks, meticulously documenting the biases of their political coverage of the 1968 presidential election. She published the results in *The News Twisters* (1971),[15] after which CBS orchestrated a full-on PR campaign to trash her careful findings. Efron dismantled their critique in a follow-up work, *How CBS Tried to Kill a Book* (1972).[16]

The network ran a sequel two decades later when Bernard Goldberg—who won several Emmy Awards during more than two decades as an employee of CBS News—published an account of the consistent bias of the television journalists with whom he had worked. His anecdotal book, *Bias: A CBS Insider Exposes How the Media Distort the News* (2002), shocked no one except his fellow journalists. And like Efron's *News Twisters*, Goldberg's book was attacked by CBS and its claims dismissed.

Eight years after Goldberg's critique of the CBS television network, the political coverage of the *New York Times* was examined by William McGowan in his book *Gray Lady Down: What the Decline and Fall of the* New York Times *Means for America*.[17] McGowan argued that the separation of news reporting and editorial opinion had broken down at the *Times*, frequently transforming reportage into political proselytizing.

SILENCING CONSERVATIVES: THE ROLE OF THE FEDERAL GOVERNMENT

Given the lock that CBS, NBC, and ABC established in commercial television broadcasting by the mid-1950s, it would be easy to assume that the mass media version of the news favoring the Democratic Party generally and Democratic presidents specifically was a done deal. It wasn't. In the late 1950s and early 1960s, the major *networks* began turning their attention from radio to television, leaving myriad independently owned (and licensed) radio *stations* to scramble for revenue-producing programming that had been transferred to the new medium. These stations found what they needed in a growing number of conservative broadcasters that attracted enormous audiences.

Consider: while William Buckley's conservative magazine *National Review* had nearly 73,000 subscribers by 1964, a single conservative radio program, Carl McIntire's *Twentieth-Century Reformation Hour,* had an estimated 20 million listeners.[18] McIntire's program was the largest conservative radio broadcaster, but there were several others including H. L. Hunt's *Life Line,* Billy James Hargis's *Christian Crusade,* and Clarence Manion's *Manion Forum.* These programs were broadcast across the country on hundreds of independent radio stations to audiences in the millions.[19] The conservative radio broadcasters were relentlessly anticommunist and relentlessly critical of John F. Kennedy during the 1960 presidential campaign.

Kennedy won a narrow victory, and members of his administration began gearing up for the 1964 election soon after the inauguration. They viewed conservative radio broadcasters as a political threat, and—as the broadcasters were also critical of organized labor—enlisted the help of Walter Reuther, president of the United Auto Workers, and his brother Victor, a UAW official. As historian Paul Matzko explains, JFK's brother, Attorney General Robert Kennedy, met with the Reuther brothers "multiple times in 1961 to discuss campaign strategy" for the 1962 midterms as well as the 1964 presidential election. In December, Victor Reuther had a document titled "The Radical Right in America Today"—

colloquially known as the "Reuther Memorandum"—sent to the attorney general.[20]

The Reuther Memorandum outlined a strategy to silence conservative radio that included the IRS:

> The growing power of radical right propagandists and groups is directly related to their expanding ability to secure large sums of money. As funds are a source of power to the radical right, action to dam up these funds may be the quickest way to turn the tide now running in their favor.... Prompt revocation [of the federal tax exemption] in a few cases might scare off a substantial part of the big money now flowing into these tax exempt organizations.[21]

"Ironically," as Matzko noted, "these were the same tactics used during the 1950s to squash radical left-wing groups."[22]

The Reuther Memorandum also suggested that "the Federal Communications Commission might consider examining the extent of the practice of giving free time to the radical right and could take measures to encourage stations to assign comparable time for an opposing point of view on a free basis."[23] This tactic was based on the FCC's 1949 Fairness Doctrine. These recommendations were music to the Kennedy administration's ears, as Matzko explains:

> Walter Reuther shared some of his ideas about the Radio Right with Robert Kennedy at a meeting during the second week of November 1961. A few days later on November 16, John Seigenthaler, who was Robert Kennedy's administrative assistant, contacted Mitchell Rogovin, the IRS commissioner's assistant and legal adviser, to inquire about the tax-exempt status of "four or five organizations generally considered to be right-wing" and to ask whether they had been audited recently.[24]

◆

The IRS went after Hargis's *Christian Crusade* early the next year. The local agent in Tulsa, Oklahoma, concluded that there was no basis to rescind the organization's tax exemption, as there was no violation of the tax code. IRS headquarters in Washington, however, told him to take another look; when that didn't work, Washington asked the office to look again. That third look also failed, as did a fourth and a fifth—so Washington took over the investigation, revoked the organization's tax exemption, demanded $100,000 in back taxes, and ruled that the contributors to the *Christian Crusade* "could no longer claim the money they had donated as a tax deduction."[25] Hargis sued (as would another organization that lost its tax exemption, H. L. Hunt's *Life Line*). His lawsuit dragged on through the courts for years. Hargis ultimately won, but only at great cost. Meanwhile, other conservative radio broadcasters and contributors also lost their tax exemptions.

The IRS campaign, known internally as the "Ideological Organizations Project," cost the conservative broadcasters considerably in legal fees and fewer contributions but did not drive them off the airwaves. The Reuther Memorandum's suggestion about using the Fairness Doctrine, however, helped the Kennedy administration deliver a body blow. In 1963, the FCC demanded that radio stations broadcasting paid attacks on an individual, organization, or political position offer a comparable opportunity to respond—for free.[26] By the late 1960s, thanks to Fairness Doctrine complaints, as well as a thinly veiled threat of a Senate investigation, "hundreds of radio station owners decided to drop right-wing programming altogether," and by the early 1970s, it was a spent force.[27]

The FCC repealed the Fairness Doctrine in 1987 during the Reagan administration. But the Clinton administration dusted off JFK's IRS playbook to audit free-market think tanks; so too did the

Obama administration, in an even more dramatic fashion. Early in 2010—after the *Citizens United* Supreme Court decision—the IRS began targeting organizations seeking tax-exempt status as 501(c)(4)s that would publicly oppose various administration policies. Lois Lerner, director of the Exempt Organizations Division, put out a "Be on the lookout" for applicant groups whose names included "Tea Party" or "Patriots" or "9/12," and/or whose applications mentioned government spending, debt, or taxes—in other words, that were politically conservative. The organizations were asked for reams of irrelevant information, and their applications were put on indefinite hold. The Exempt Organizations Division also demanded that many of these organizations provide lists of donors, many of whom had their taxes audited. Judicial Watch, a nonprofit organization that employs FOIA (Freedom of Information Act) requests and lawsuits to investigate government corruption and fraud, concluded that:

> Over the course of twenty-seven months leading up to the 2012 election, not a single Tea Party–type organization received tax-exempt status. Many were unable to operate; others disbanded because donors refused to fund them without the IRS seal of approval; some organizations and their donors were audited without justification; and many incurred legal fees and costs fighting the unlawful conduct by Lerner and other IRS employees.[28]

Ultimately, the Tea Party was snuffed out, Barack Obama got a second term, and no one involved in the misuse of IRS power was held accountable.

CONFIRMATION OF THE MEDIA'S TRAJECTORY BY ONE OF ITS OWN

The decades of liberal-leaning journalism reached an apogee with the 2016 presidential election and administration of Donald

♦

Trump. According to Jeff Gerth, a longtime investigative journalist for the *New York Times*, the result has been a collapse in the public's trust in the news media.

Gerth's conclusion appears in "The Press versus the Presidents," published by the prestigious *Columbia Journalism Review* (*CJR*) on January 30, 2023. The exhaustive report—accompanied by an introduction by *CJR*'s editor-in-chief and publisher, Kyle Pope—is an analytical history and critique of the national media's biased and misleading coverage of "Russiagate"—the phony scandal launched by a made-up "dossier" financed by the Hillary Clinton presidential campaign and relentlessly pushed by the *New York Times*, *Washington Post*, and most of the national broadcast and digital media.

Of course, the nearly two-year investigation led by Special Counsel Robert Mueller utterly failed to substantiate any collusion between Trump and Russia. With its conclusion, the scandal crumbled and along with it, the media's reputation. "Before the 2016 election," Gerth noted, "most Americans trusted the traditional media and the trend was positive according to the Edelman Trust Barometer.... Today, the U.S. media has the lowest credibility—26 percent—among forty-six nations, according to a 2022 study by the Reuters Institute for the Study of Journalism."[29] He added that 86% of Americans think that the media is biased.[30]

Gerth also reported what he called a "lack of transparency by media organizations in responding to my questions." He contacted more than 60 journalists, but only somewhat more than a dozen agreed to be interviewed; and "not a single major news organization made available a newsroom leader to talk about their coverage."[31] *CJR*'s editor and publisher praised Gerth's report as "important" and "worthy of deep reflection."[32]

◆

CHAPTER 8

A CENTURY OF DICTATORSHIPS

Collective Ownership or Control of the Means of Production

This nation was based on the explicit understanding in the Declaration of Independence that individual human beings have an unalienable right to self-ownership and the fruits of their labor, whether or not these rights are protected by law. These rights were natural, that is, "prelegal." This is in sharp contrast to governments before and after that have conferred various *privileges* in various degrees on some inhabitants while withholding them from others.

For centuries, the privilege-granting power was most often exercised by a sovereign who justified his or her rule on theistic grounds. That is, the sovereign was either *chosen by a deity* or *was a deity*—which implied his or her ultimate ownership of the people and the lands he or she governed. The sovereign might assign to some subjects the privileges of limited self-ownership as well as the privilege of land ownership. Others might be consigned to slavery or involuntary servitude.

The theistic pretexts for sovereign power began to be replaced in the 17th, 18th, and 19th centuries with nontheistic ones. Sometimes majority rule was deemed to confer sovereign power, a notion that had antecedents in the Roman Republic and ancient Athens. In other cases, it was conferred on or seized by those

◆

with purported special insight into the aggregate welfare of the governed. Or it was assumed by those who claimed to represent the interests of a previously exploited group of people entitled to what had been taken from them. Or it was assumed by those who claimed to speak for a race of people whose legitimate entitlement to participate in the elections of the government had been unfulfilled. Or it sprung from a fanciful notion that society was an organism, in which the subjects were like cells or bodily organs and the rulers were endowed with the intellectual powers of the brain and, therefore, the privilege of sovereignty over others. Over the centuries, the pretexts for the exercise of dictatorial power are legion—Divine Right, one religion's superiority over all others, one race's superiority over all others, one class's unjust exploitation by another, the need for an equal distribution of income and/or wealth, "equity," or the declaration of an environmental or climate emergency. The latest pretext is "gender" discrimination. The list of pretexts is probably inexhaustible.

These various pretexts do not nullify what, in fact, belongs to every human being—ownership of his or her person, liberty, labor, and its fruits. Still, human history has been almost entirely filled with regimes in which self-ownership has been unrecognized and routinely violated.

The crucial question is what sorts of threats to individual rights have been or are currently being posed, by whom, and on what grounds. This chapter considers the three structural forms that dictatorships have principally taken over the past century; the two chapters that follow take the story down to the present.

COLLECTIVE OWNERSHIP OF THE MEANS OF PRODUCTION: SOCIALISM AND COMMUNISM

Socialism and communism posed the foremost 20th-century challenges to America's capitalist order, although the threats have

◆

been foreign, not domestic. These two "isms" have a variety of meanings, but the principal definition specifies that the means of production, distribution, and exchange of goods and services should be owned by the community as a whole. There were many socialist theories in the 19th century (not only the version proposed by Karl Marx); indeed, voluntary and isolated social-ist communities were launched in the United States and Britain during the early decades of the 19th century. The first major transformation of an entire country by socialists began in Russia after its czar, Emperor Nicholas II, abdicated in March 1917. He was succeeded by an elected parliamentary government, which was overthrown by the Bolsheviks—a Marxist faction that had been part of the Russian Social Democratic Party—in an October 1917 coup. The new government ended Russia's participation in the First World War in March 1918.

Led by Vladimir Lenin, the Bolsheviks imposed com-munism upon the territories they had taken, "inspired," as historian Richard Pipes explained, "by an ideological belief in the need to deprive the citizens of ownership of disposable assets because they were a source of political independence."[1] As Pipes summarized them, the policies of the new dictator-ship would include:

1. The nationalization of (a) the means of production, with the important (albeit temporary) exception of agriculture, (b) transport, and (c) all but the smallest enterprises.
2. The liquidation of private commerce through the national-ization of the retail and wholesale trade, and its replacement by a government-controlled distribution system.
3. The elimination of money as a unit of exchange and account-ing in favor of a system of state-regulated barter.
4. The imposition on the entire national economy of a single plan.

◆

5. The introduction of compulsory labor for all able-bodied male adults, but on occasion also for women, children, and elders.[2]

The results were disastrous. These included "peasant revolts," "unrest among the workers," and a famine that ultimately cost five million lives.[3] Unemployment among industrial workers doubled between 1918 and 1921—and inflation reached stratospheric heights. By 1923, prices rose by 648,230,000% over 1913.[4] In addition, "the foodstuffs consumed in Russian cities in the winter of 1919–1920 (cereals, vegetables, and fruits) as measured by their caloric value, the free market furnished from 66 to 80 percent," virtually all of which was obtained by illicit street trade.[5]

Ultimately, the capitalist "enemy" had to be allowed to provide charitable relief. From October 1, 1921, to June 1, 1923, the American Relief Administration (ARA), headed by Herbert Hoover, "fed approximately 10 million people" at the "height of its activity."[6]

As far as the working class was concerned, Lenin's fellow communist Leon Trotsky argued that socialism—the abolition of the market in everything—requires compulsory labor because "man is basically indolent and driven to work only by the fear of starvation: once the state assumed responsibility for feeding its citizens, this motive disappeared and it became necessary to resort to compulsion."[7] Compulsory labor meant that there could be no independent labor unions (that is, unions not controlled by the Communist Party),[8] nor any right to strike in a government enterprise.[9] And finally, like their Jacobin predecessors in revolutionary 18th-century France, the Bolsheviks resorted to terror on a massive scale to enforce their will.

Lenin's commissar of justice, Israel Steinberg, commented in 1920 that after the civil war was over, rule by terror remained an integral component of social control:

◆

Terror is not an individual act, not an isolated, fortuitous—even if recurrent—expression of the government's fury. Terror is a *system*...a legalized plan of the regime for the purpose of mass intimidation, mass compulsion, mass extermination. Terror is a calculated register of punishments, reprisals, and threats by means of which the government intimidates, entices, and compels the fulfillment of its imperative will.[10]

In Steinberg's view—written from the safety of Germany—the "atmosphere of terror," its ever-present threat, poisoned Soviet life even more than the executions.[11]

After three years of economic implosion, Lenin decided to restore private ownership of capital in some sections of the economy, which he euphemistically referred to as the New Economic Policy (NEP) in an internal government report republished in October 2021.[12] The policy itself was announced in January 1922 in a document titled "The Role and Functions of the Trade Unions under the New Economic Policy."[13] On the one hand, the NEP included "a free market and capitalism, both subject to state control," and "on the other hand, the socialized state enterprises are being put on what is called a profit basis, i.e., they are being reorganized on commercial lines." Lenin called this new economic arrangement "State Capitalism," which he claimed, by way of justification, would "permit freedom to trade and the development of capitalism only within certain bounds, and only on the condition that the state regulates (supervises, controls, determines the forms and methods of, etc.) private trade and private capitalism."[14]

To paper over the regime's previous—and calamitous—economic policies, Lenin's officials invented the term "War Communism" for them.[15] True, the Bolsheviks were fighting against the South Russian White Army led by former czarist commanders, the Japanese in Vladivostok, British, French, and U.S. troops, as well as the Czechoslovakian army—but these forces occupied

◆

only the periphery of the Bolshevik-controlled territory and did not constitute a cohesive force. The regime's economic policies were not dictated by the circumstances of the war, nor were these policies even called War Communism until the regime decided to abandon them and, as Pipes noted, "blame the disasters of the immediate past on circumstances beyond their control."[16]

The economic and human calamities produced by collectivizing the means of production—placing them in the hands of a few or even a single person—replicated on a national scale the obscene criminality and suffering that so appealed to the first American, George Fitzhugh, to understand the indistinguishability of slavery and socialism while asserting their equal moral virtue. Lenin's successor, Joseph Stalin, eventually canceled the NEP, renationalized industry, and introduced central economic planning—though he kept money as the means of exchange as well as rule by terror. In the decades that followed, Stalinist communism posed a military threat to America, but its appeal as a system domestically has been marginal. The suffering that a communist system necessarily produces makes it unlikely to appeal to a significant number of citizens. Today, only Cuba and North Korea remain exclusively in its orbit.

◆ ◆ ◆

Histories of fascism typically begin with the dictatorship established in Italy after World War I. Yet this common understanding is flawed: it overlooks Lenin's New Economic Policy (NEP), which introduced to the Western world what can properly be called the first experiment in fascism *before* Benito Mussolini came to power in October 1922. This conclusion follows ineluctably from the NEP itself. While still describing himself and his regime as communist, Lenin abandoned the state ownership of all capital and opted instead for a mixture of state and private ownership

◆

of businesses that he called "State Capitalism"—that is, allowing private *ownership of the means of production under the control of a one-party government.*

From the inception of the NEP until Stalin canceled it several years later, Russia was a one-party, semicapitalist dictatorship. Aside from sheer survival, part of the NEP strategy was to lure private capital from abroad into investing in Russia by awarding it various concessions, including access to Russian minerals. Lenin assumed that U.S., British, and German capitalists would vie with one another for the concessions, and to get better terms they would pressure their respective governments to lift restrictions against trading with the Soviet Union. (Lenin had even discussed the idea of turning over the port of Vladivostok and the Soviet Far Eastern provinces to American capitalists so as to turn the U.S. government against Japan.) He had little problem persuading his colleagues that the capitalists' presumed greed could be used to Soviet advantage. When one of them asked him where the Soviet state would obtain the rope with which to hang the capitalist nations—since rope, like every other commodity, was in short supply—he reportedly answered, "They'll supply us with it."[17]

The first concession—for asbestos mines—that Lenin awarded was to Armand Hammer, whose father Julius was one of the founders of the American Communist Party.[18] Indeed, as a result of several hundreds of concessions to European and American companies, Soviet industrial development in the 1920s was profoundly dependent on technology transfers from the West.[19]

COLLECTIVE CONTROL OF THE MEANS OF PRODUCTION: FASCISM IN ITALY, GERMANY, AND CHINA

On October 28, 1922, Benito Mussolini—a lifelong socialist and former editor of the Italian Socialist Party newspaper *Avanti!*—was

◆

appointed prime minister of Italy by King Victor Emmanuel III. Several years earlier, animated by hatred of Austria, Mussolini had abandoned his previous pacifist inclinations and supported Italy's participation in World War I. As a result, he was expelled from the Socialist Party. Mussolini went on to create an organization (Fasci Italiani di Combattimento) in 1919. At first it had few members, but their numbers began to swell as former soldiers, home at last from the war, filled the organization's ranks. Mussolini still remained a socialist in his sympathies, but the anti-trade-union wing of his organization forced him to abandon his socialist ties. In 1921, he created the National Fascist Party. Meanwhile, Italy itself was beset by internal strife, including street fights between communists and fascists as well as violent strikes and factory occupations.

Mussolini's control of Italy was not at first all-encompassing, but freedom of the press was abolished in late 1924, and by 1926, as historian F. L. Carsten noted, Italy was a one-party state and all organized opposition was suppressed.[20] Mussolini's regime also initiated a reorganization of the economy. Each industry or trade had syndicates of laborers and business owners that exercised power over their members, and all syndicates were subject to top-down control by the one-party state. The task of these syndicates "was to mediate between the interests of the employers and of the employees according to the needs of production which were declared to be dominant." These syndicates established agreements that "were then binding on all employed in that branch. Disputes were to be decided by labour courts. Membership dues were deducted from wages, as well as those of non-members. The government was to control the appointment of all higher officials of the syndicates."[21] The similarity of this "corporative" state structure to the government control of industry and labor cartels established by President Franklin

◆

Delano Roosevelt's National Industrial Recovery Act in the 1930s has long been noted and was discussed above in chapter 5.

Germany too would reorganize its economy on fascist lines in the 1930s—that is, with the Nazi Party exercising ultimate control over privately owned businesses—although the historical lineage of this transformation goes back much further than Hitler. From the mid-19th century on, the term "socialism" had, for much of Germany's population, positive connotations. It also had a variety of meanings.

The German Social Democratic Party (SDP), founded in 1863, would become principally, for a long period until World War I, a vehicle for Marxist ideology, emphasizing the fundamental opposition between workers and capitalists. And as the interests of these "classes" were supposedly transnational, national governments, including that of Germany, had to be eliminated.

The SDP's doctrinal commitments were opposed by German state socialists, whose adherents were principally university professors. These academics (the so-called socialists of the chair or Kathedersozialisten) emphasized a nation-based—not class-based—socialism under which the country's monarch would remain, but whose government would nationalize some (not all) industries and institute state-financed pensions and medical care for workers. The proponents of German state socialism trained the first generation of America's doctoral faculty, and it was Otto von Bismarck, Germany's first chancellor after the country's 1871 unification, who instituted welfare and social insurance programs for workers in the 1880s, while at the same time restricting the speech of Social Democrats. The principal division among German socialists, then, became the adversarial relations between state socialists and international or Marxist socialists. At the outbreak of World War I, the SPD split into a prowar wing and an antiwar wing (which became the Communist Party of Germany).

◆

In the chaotic aftermath of World War I, the SDP won the 1919 federal elections, and its leader became the first president of the Weimar Republic. But the country in the early 1920s was politically and economically unstable—ravaged by hyperinflation, violent strikes, and violent strife between paramilitary groups.

Adolf Hitler was an army veteran with both strong socialist and nationalist convictions, rendering him hostile to international socialism. In an army course for veterans, he attended lectures by Gottfried Feder (a civil engineer and would-be economist) who distinguished between the collectivization of banking, the stock exchanges, and the abolition of interest—which he approved—and the nationalization of industry—where independence was crucial for national prosperity—which he opposed.[22] Feder then drew a connection between international finance and the Jews, who he felt had monopolized it. Feder's combination of socialism, nationalism, and antisemitism clearly struck a chord with Hitler. He joined the antisemitic, socialistic German Workers' Party (DAP), which subsequently changed its name to the National Socialist German Workers' Party (NSDAP). Its principles, historian Robert Gellately explained, favored

> a strong interventionist state, opposition to finance capitalism and the Jews, as well as Pan-Germanic nationalism. There would be censorship, even laws against certain trends in art and literature, a crackdown on crime "injurious to the common good," confiscation of war profits, opposition to further immigration, and complete denial of citizenship to Jews.[23]

The party platform also featured a collectivist slogan, "Gemeinnutz geht vor Eigennutz," translated variously as "public interest before self-interest" or "the common good before individual

♦

good," and included "certain expropriations of land for communal purposes, without paying compensation," and increased social welfare programs, as well as "profit-sharing in large enterprises."[24]

Hitler said in 1941 of the NSDAP in the 1920s that "90% of it was made up of left-wing people."[25] However, like Feder, he was pragmatic when it came to economic strength and, therefore, was never enthusiastic about the wholesale collectivization of industry. Yet his party included among its leaders Joseph Goebbels, Otto Strasser, and his brother Gregor, who were passionate socialists. The Strasser brothers favored some kind of "state feudalism" that would collectivize heavy industry, give large estates to those who worked on them, and seize all property, which would then be leased to its owners.[26] Otto Strasser would eventually leave the Nazi Party; as historian Gellately explains, while "Otto wanted the Party to oppose capitalism with the same vehemence that it attacked Marxism, Hitler would not hear of such a thing, because that would ruin the economy."[27]

Before the Great Depression, Hitler, despite considerable effort, had attracted only one major supporter from Germany's industrial elite—Emil Kirdorf, an eighty-year-old coal magnate from the Ruhr. Kirdorf joined the Nazi Party and had a pamphlet published, written by Hitler, for his fellow industrialists. But his efforts were largely fruitless, given the identification of Nazism with socialism in popular parlance. Even Kirdorf eventually resigned from the Party because of its socialist inclinations; he only rejoined after the Nazis came to power.[28]

However, the Reichstag elections of July 1932—in which the Nazis had achieved 37.4% of the vote—sent businesses scrambling to meet with its leadership.[29] Hitler asked Wilhelm Keppler, "one of the lesser businessmen attracted to Nazism in the late 1920s and a loyal 'party comrade' ever since," to become his personal economic adviser in 1931. Keppler accepted, and after some effort recruited Hjalmer Schacht, the former Reichsbank president, to join him.[30]

Hitler, however, was a genuine anticapitalist, as was Lenin. He merely grasped that he had to leave German capitalism's major institutions relatively untouched—though subject to government control—in order to prepare for war. What he would have done to them had he won the war one can only conjecture, given his hostility to many of its institutions. In any event, there is little evidence of either major capitalist enthusiasm for (or financial contributions to) Nazism before it assumed power. Yale historian Henry Ashby Turner Jr.'s convincing demonstration of these two points in *German Big Business and the Rise of Hitler* (1985) is decisive.

China is the last of the 20th-century experiments with fascism instituted by a socialist.

In 1949, Mao Zedong became that country's Marxist-Leninist dictator. His regime abolished property rights and individual rights generally—resulting in the deaths through starvation or murder of tens of millions during his reign, which ended in 1976 with his death. Mao's handpicked successor was quickly replaced by Deng Xiaoping, who had opposed the most virulent of Mao's policies, such as the Cultural Revolution. Deng, like Lenin, grasped that communism is thoroughly unproductive, and so began to slowly institute capitalist reforms while retaining one-party rule. Like the NEP under Lenin, this led to a dramatic economic recovery, especially after Deng encouraged greater foreign investment in the creation of business enterprises.

In defending his policies, Deng repeatedly claimed that capitalism and socialism are not incompatible. He slowly reintroduced private property—not as a right, of course, but as a privilege permitted by the Communist Party. Private capital investment was also permitted, and from 1980, foreign companies were attracted

◆

to a series of special investment zones. Armand Hammer, who had collaborated with Lenin in getting the NEP off the ground, planned a $345 million investment in China in 1981, remarking on the similarities between the two communist experiments with capitalism. "I feel now about China as I felt when I first went to Russia in the time of Lenin," he wrote in 1986.[31] Deng, also like Lenin, was not about to give up his one-party autocracy: a protest at Tiananmen Square in 1989 over the death of a reformer in the Party was forcibly put down. Deng passed away in 1997, yet the reforms continued.

However, Xi Jinping, president of China since 2013, abolished term limits in 2018, allowing him to rule indefinitely. The fascist character of his regime has become unambiguous thanks to his unwillingness to give up one-party rule and government control of the economy and society. Xi has explicitly rejected the following Western values: constitutional democracy, universal values, civil society, pro-market neoliberalism, and criticism of past Party errors and its style of socialism.

Meanwhile, China has instituted universal internet censorship and an Orwellian "social credit system" that scores individuals on their obeisance to government rules and priorities, granting or revoking privileges at will—as there is no such thing as "rights" as Americans understand them. As one scholar noted, a "low social credit score will exclude you from well-paid jobs, make it impossible for you to get a house or a car loan or even book a hotel room. The government will slow down your internet connection, ban your children from attending private schools and even post your profile on a public blacklist for all to see."[32]

If four socialists created fascist regimes over the past century, is it possible that a similar transformation could occur in a constitutional democracy such as the United States? And if so, how?

◆

CHAPTER 9

COLLECTIVE OWNERSHIP OF THE MEANS OF CONSUMPTION

If the United States succumbs to a one-party autocracy, it will not be by state expropriation of capital or the abolition of private enterprise. Instead, it would be the result of extracting so much income from people's earnings that they become utterly dependent upon government provision, as well as by controlling businesses so strictly that their freedom to act depends on rules made up by federal agencies.

A regime with these characteristics is best described by its distinctive characteristic: "collective ownership of the means of consumption." This term distinguishes it from the two other principal autocracies of the past century: socialism/communism, which is one-party ownership of the means of production, and fascism, which is one-party control of the means of production.

The groundwork for this autocracy has been laid by two crucial departures from this country's original constitutional order. The first was the Sixteenth Amendment, which enabled the federal government to levy, without limit, taxes on income "from whatever source derived." The second has been to put private businesses under the arbitrary control of bureaucrats who run the federal regulatory agencies—a profound violation of the Constitution's separation of powers. Over time, both changes tend to lead toward a synthesis: a servile class of citizen-serfs and private enterprise

◆

tolerated as a state-authorized and regulated privilege, not as a right. To complete the transformation of this country's original natural-rights republic to a fascistic autocracy, all that is left is the elimination of opposition political parties.

How might this last step take place? Consider, first, that collective ownership of the means of consumption gradually deprives citizens, through higher income taxes, of the ability to care for their own needs. Businesses will depend more and more on government edicts, which means that the system is tailor-made to financially reward politicians and other officials, as well as lobbyists and lawyers after they leave government employment. But this system is also tailor-made to punish enterprises that resist extortion and handsomely reward those that do not. Politicians, political parties, or individual citizens that represent an impediment to such corruption, on the other hand, may suffer permanent marginalization by any means possible. Such means include the acquiescence of journalists confronted by Stephanopoulos-type threats to their futures and CNN/MSNBC-type rewards for ideological conformity. It could also mean freezing out dissenting ideas and voices from dominant social media, including at the behest of various arms of the federal government.

Meanwhile, to protect themselves from hostile, adversarial investigations by progressives, billionaires like Jeff Bezos can also pay the salaries of employees of the *Washington Post*, a company he owns. Bloomberg News was not permitted to report on its billionaire owner's campaign for the Democratic Party presidential nomination in 2020. Progressives, the supposed allies of the "working class" at the turn of the 20th century, have become their adversaries—the 2016 Democratic Party presidential candidate denigrated them as "deplorables." Billionaires who believe in individual rights are targets; those who are, so to speak, "with

◆

the program" are not—so Charles Koch is subject to abuse while George Soros is ignored or celebrated.

"Muckraking" journalists who presented themselves as adversaries of business oligarchies a century ago evolve into the security guards of today's business oligarchies. Members of the media themselves have become wealthy alongside their capitalist political allies. But the wealth, status, and political influence of these media attack dogs are acquired by virtue of their complicity with the oligarchs whom they effectively serve.

Ultimately, what today's progressives seek is what their academic progenitors sought for themselves in the late 19th century—Prussian-like aristocratic power over capitalists and their employees.

THE REDISTRIBUTION CON GAME

It is crucial, in this regard, to understand that the funding for today's democratic socialist regimes and welfare states around the developed world is collected principally from taxes levied on income. In the United States, of course, this was made possible on the federal level by the Sixteenth Amendment. And as explained earlier in this book, the moral pretext for an income tax put forth by E. R. A. Seligman, its most influential theorist, was false. His foundational justification—that people should be taxed on their financial capacity to pay, not on the benefits they receive from the government—logically implies a tax on wealth, not income. Seligman himself noted, after the Sixteenth Amendment was ratified in 1913, that the income tax was unnecessary to fund the federal government's then-budgeted expenses.[1]

In any event, income taxes, no matter how progressive the rates, are not capable of redistributing *wealth*.[2] Thus Thomas Piketty, a contemporary progressive economist, writes that "the

◆

explosive dynamic of wealth inequality, especially when larger fortunes are able to garner larger returns" ensures that outcome, "and only a direct tax on capital can correctly gauge the contributive capacity of the wealthy."[3]

"Raising the top marginal income tax rate," add Piketty acolytes Emmanuel Saez and Gabriel Zucman, is irrelevant for redistribution in the present. Billionaires such as Jeff Bezos and Warren Buffett don't have "much taxable income." Nor is the estate tax going to affect the distribution of wealth today. Bezos, for example, is sixty; and Mark Zuckerberg is not yet forty. As far as redistribution is concerned, the "way to address this issue is by taxing wealth itself, today and not at some distant future date."[4]

Piketty nevertheless has pressed for greater progressivity in income taxation. He claims that it reduces the ability to become rich through income remuneration as opposed to unrealized capital gains on assets. However, the explosion in incomes earned by entertainers and professional sports figures has led to their becoming ultrawealthy with assets in the hundreds of millions and even billions of dollars, e.g., Michael Jordan, LeBron James, Ice Cube, and Taylor Swift. In his latest book,[5] Piketty urges high inheritance taxes because progressive income taxes have not reduced personal wealth significantly. Still, he recognizes that only *global* limitations on wealth will reduce wealth inequality, and the mobility of wealth renders this nearly impossible.

As far as estate and inheritance taxes are concerned, the egalitarian arguments put forth by defenders are deeply misleading. In the first place, they are irrelevant. Out of a total of $4.9 trillion in federal revenues collected by the United States in 2022, only $33 billion—0.7% of the total—was derived from the estate and gift tax.[6]

The same pattern is true elsewhere: on average in OECD countries, gift, inheritance, and estate taxes made up under 2% of

GDP in 2019, while total tax revenue in OECD countries accounted for close to 34% of GDP.[7] In these countries, the inheritance tax brings in a tiny trickle of revenue from ultrawealthy individuals, although it does affect upper-middle and moderately affluent families. This is why "social democracies" like Sweden, Norway, Canada, Australia, Austria, and New Zealand have abolished their inheritance taxes.

Moreover, the estate tax in the United States is easily reduced for the very wealthy through such devices as charitable lead trusts, grantor retained annuity trusts, intentionally defective grantor trusts, discounts for lack of marketability and/or control, irrevocable life insurance trusts, dynasty trusts, and others too numerous to mention. One of these, the "charitable lead trust," as multibillionaire George Soros told a biographer, "is a very interesting tax gimmick." He explained: "You commit your assets to a trust and you put a certain amount of money into charity every year. And then after you have given the money for however many years, the principal that remains can be left [to one's heir] without estate or gift tax. So this was the way I set up the trust for my children."[8]

Soros's biography appeared in 2003, well after he signed a petition in February 2001—along with some Rockefeller heirs, the founder of Ben & Jerry's, and scores of wealthy others— strongly defending the estate tax and denouncing any attempt to phase it out. Their pretext was that ending the estate tax would "enrich the heirs of America's millionaires and billionaires while hurting families who struggle to make ends meet."[9] Ironically, the left-wing news outlet ProPublica released a report several months later, based on IRS records, that "More than Half of America's 100 Richest People Exploit Special Trusts to Avoid Estate Taxes."[10]

This is where the redistribution con game begins. The aforementioned devices make estate taxes irrelevant to the super-rich.

◆

Multibillionaires who publicly defend the estate tax, in short, privately laugh all the way to the bank.

A similar con may be discerned for multibillionaires who profess egalitarian ideals by supporting higher progressive income tax rates.[11] Such rates will leave them practically unaffected, as income is a tiny proportion of their wealth. This point was illustrated in chapter 3. According to his 2015 federal tax return, Warren Buffett had $11.6 million in adjusted gross income on which he paid $1.8 million in federal tax. *Forbes* pegged his net worth that year as $72.7 billion. Had Buffett been assessed Elizabeth Warren's 2019 wealth tax (2% between $50 million and $1 billion, and 6% above $1 billion), he would have owed about $4.3 billion.[12] In 2021, a report compiled by ProPublica noted that the overall wealth of the wealthiest 25 Americans increased by $401 billion from 2014 to 2018, while the federal income taxes they paid came to $13.6 billion, a rate of 3.4%.[13]

In practice—from Sweden to Denmark to Germany to America—the tax policies of the political left from the late 19th century have left capital relatively untouched while dramatically increasing taxes on income as well as on spending (through value-added and other sales taxes) of the middle and working classes. As a result, wealthy egalitarians—or wealthy investors posing as egalitarians—have few impediments to the retention and appreciation of their assets from social democratic or progressive government policies. This may help explain the growing numbers of these individuals in, and their influence on, left-wing political parties and campaigns.

THE "FAIRNESS" HUSTLE

Among the pretexts offered by progressives for progressive income taxes, none have been as influential as the disparities between the "rich" and the "poor." Yet the fixation on the top marginal tax rate—94%, for example, on earnings in excess of $200,000 in 1945—has long served to divert public attention in the United States from the punishing rates on low- and middle-income earners, which were 23% on incomes between $0 and $2,000 in that year. The war was over, but the rates on the lower end of the income scale remained high for decades.

In 1963, for example, the top rate for singles or married persons filing separately was 91% on income in excess of $200,000—but 20% on income between $0 and $2,000 and 38% for earnings between $10,000 and $12,000. President John F. Kennedy's proposed legislation reduced the top rate in 1965 for singles or married persons filing separately to 70% on income exceeding $100,000—but for those earning between $0 and $1,000, the tax rate was 15%. The rates then climbed swiftly for those making between $10,000 and $12,000, for which the marginal rate was at 32%.[14]

Meanwhile, the federal government under President Lyndon Johnson launched a massive program called the War on Poverty. Despite trillions of dollars spent, there is little evidence the war was won. "Though official poverty levels did decrease over the course of the 1960s," author Amity Shlaes wrote, "it is hard to prove that the 1960s decrease did not occur because of private-sector growth rather than government efforts. After the 1960s, official poverty stabilized at 10 to 15 percent."[15] There was, however, a huge downside—the dependency of millions on the government's "new flood of benefits."[16] The poverty in Appalachia explored by socialist Michael Harrington in his 1962 book, *The Other America*, remains, as Ohio senator J. D. Vance noted in his 2016 book *Hillbilly Elegy*.[17] While "Black unemployment," Shlaes noted, "had been the same as whites' in the 1950s," it rose "from the early 1960s" and only continued to rise. Moreover,

◆

welfare programs funded by presidents Johnson and Nixon expanded rolls to an appalling extent—appalling because welfare fostered a new sense of hopelessness and disenfranchisement among those who received it. "Boy, were we wrong about a guaranteed income!" wrote that most honest of policymakers, Moynihan, in 1978, looking back on a pilot program that had prolonged unemployment rather than met its goal, curtailing joblessness.[18]

Since the 1960s, the basic tax rates on personal income have changed several times, including dramatic cuts under Reagan in the 1980s, increases under George H. W. Bush and Bill Clinton, and modest cuts under Trump. Yet none of these changes alter the big picture.

For example, of the $4.49-trillion budget in the United States for 2019—the last year before the COVID-19 pandemic—$3.35 trillion came from tax revenues (the remainder derived from borrowing), of which only $16.2 billion came from wealth, i.e., estate and gift taxes. Breaking this down a bit more, $1.701 trillion (approximately 50% of total tax receipts) in revenue was derived from personal income taxes, $1.409 trillion from payroll taxes—half of which are assessed regressively on employees' income. In addition, $210.5 billion in corporate income taxes were collected. Progressive taxes on personal income, plus regressive payroll taxes (to finance Social Security and Medicare), dominate federal revenues and are the overwhelming source of the financial burden on middle-income and upper-middle-income Americans.[19]

Moreover, contemporary progressives such as law professor and tax historian Ajay K. Mehrotra are frustrated over the absence of a value-added tax (VAT) in the U.S. This he blames on the early progressive argument that such taxes on various consumption goods by tariffs and excises are regressive and should be replaced by a progressive income tax. Mehrotra commented that they "neglected to see how distributional justice could be achieved through the tax *and transfer* process as a whole. They failed to realize how potentially regressive but highly efficient and productive taxes could generate tremendous revenue that could be used, in turn, for progressive social welfare spending that could counter the possibly regressive incidence of consumption taxes."[20] In other words, the early progressives, from Mehrotra's perspective, inadvertently precluded another way to plunder the income of the American people.

Meanwhile, it is hard to identify any American champion of higher progressive tax rates on income who complains about the regressive payroll taxes that burden citizens of more modest means. In Europe, these payroll taxes (often referred to as social security contributions) are significantly higher than in the U.S.

In Belgium, for example, the employee's share of "contributions" to the country's overall social security system (which includes health care and old-age pensions) is 13.07% of total gross compensation, with no cap (unlike the salary cap on Social Security taxes in the U.S.); the employer's share is about double that percentage. Meanwhile, Belgium's standard value-added tax (VAT)—essentially, a retail tax on goods and services—is 21% (6% for some necessities such as food and pharmaceuticals).[21]

In Germany, the tax on employees' income for old-age pensions (called Social Security in the U.S.) is 9.35% (employers pay an additional 9.35%); the tax on employees' income for health insurance is 7.3% (employers pay an additional 7.3%); and there is also a 1.525% tax on employees' income for nursing-care (called long-term care in the U.S.) insurance (employers pay an additional 1.525%). Germany's VAT is 19% (7% on food and books).[22]

These taxes in Germany, Belgium, and other European countries significantly depress the disposable income of middle- and

◆

upper-middle-income earners while making them dependent on government provision of services that they would have purchased themselves.

The progressives' phony redistributionist strategy hit at least a temporary wall after Ronald Reagan's across-the-board reduction in marginal tax rates was welcomed by all classes of wage earners. So far, the tax hikes in subsequent years—such as by George H. W. Bush in 1990 and Bill Clinton in 1993—have remained, by historical standards, relatively modest. Meanwhile, Clinton failed in his attempt to legislate a federal monopoly on health care.

Since then, progressives have sought other pretexts for subordinating individual liberties and assigning autocratic powers to the government. These pretexts include identity politics, i.e., government discrimination by race and sex—in other words, a caste system of favors and quotas. Another power play: establish a political monopoly over the supply of energy in the name of climate protection—which will establish a political bonanza for "green" energy companies, principally in the United States and China, and impoverish individual consumers of electricity and gasoline. When this menu was rejected by the electorate in 2016, progressives in government and the media tried to throw out the winner. Had this succeeded, it would have brought the country perilously close to one-party rule.

Nevertheless, progressives in the public and private sectors have not given up their crusade to deprive individuals of their right to self-defense and the protection of their property (despite the Supreme Court's reaffirmation of the Constitution's Second Amendment in 2022), strangle the country's energy supply, and constrict free speech through government intimidation, including pressure on social media companies to block messages that the current party in power claims are "misinformation," or by labeling protests against public school policies as "terrorism." They

◆

have since Franklin Delano Roosevelt repeatedly used the IRS to intimidate and defeat political opponents. Finally, they have subsidized enemies (e.g., Iran), placing America on the brink of a major war and stimulating the rise of anti-Semitism.

THE TROJAN HORSE: MEDICARE FOR ALL

At present, the most dangerous pretext for depriving Americans of their natural rights is "universal free health care," aka "single-payer," aka "Medicare for All." By whatever name, the goal is to establish a federal monopoly—a single payer—for the provision of medical services. Such a monopoly would lower physicians' incomes while crippling their right to practice privately, deny potential builders of private hospitals the right to build, and deny ordinary citizens their right to purchase the care and health insurance they want and need.

Proposals for a federal monopoly on health care breeze past the nation's experience with a single-payer system: witness the Department of Veterans Affairs, tasked with providing lifelong health care to eligible military veterans. Since World War II, the VA has a long history of scandals involving inferior care.[23] More recently, in 2014, dozens of veterans perished in Arizona while they waited to get an appointment. In the aftermath, the existence of a secret waiting list emerged. "In order not to lose their bonuses," one independent reporter noted, "VA managers at the Phoenix VA facility set up the elaborate scheme to hide the fact that 1,400 to 1,600 veterans had waited many months to see a doctor. However, the wait times shown on documents sent to VA headquarters in Washington did not exceed the mandated 14-day limit."[24]

Five years later, a psychologist at the VA Maryland Health Care Center with two decades of experience was fired for report-

◆

ing another manipulation of a waiting list for veterans in need of treatment for opioids. Her congressional testimony explained that

> in the spring of 2014, following a nationwide Agency [in other words, the VA] scandal concerning lengthy patient wait times, VA management began to convey to me that our waitlist was too long and they were concerned the waitlist would draw scrutiny from VA leadership and Congress. In order to reduce the waitlist, I was instructed to improperly remove veterans from the electronic waitlist by scheduling fake appointments for them in an imaginary clinic. This clinic was not tied to any provider or location, nor did it actually correspond to any real visits and accordingly, the veterans scheduled for these fictitious appointments were not actually receiving VA care.[25]

To this day, serious problems involving the care of military veterans continue to be reported.[26] A government monopoly that continues to be funded whether or not it takes care of its patients responsibly is what "Medicare for All" will produce on a grand scale.

Single-payer plans have been proposed in Congress since the early 2010s; the most recent versions are two "Medicare for All" bills introduced in the Senate and the House of Representatives. A careful analysis by economist Charles Blahous—a former public trustee for Social Security and Medicare—showed that Medicare for All would lead to increased federal spending above $30 trillion over the next decade and require, at the very least, *doubling personal and corporate income taxes*. His estimate was a lower bound, as it assumes that the federal government would reduce payments to physicians and other health care providers to Medicare rates—and such payments are much lower than the reimbursements they get from private health insurance.[27]

◆

In his book *The Case against Single Payer* (2019), health care analyst Chris Jacobs has laid out the inherent problems in the Medicare for All legislation currently in Congress. The first and most obvious is that when the government monopoly defines health care as a "right," it means in practice that the "government has the 'right' to tell you what health care you will and will *not* receive."[28] The Medicare for All plans place restrictions on physicians in the system to practice medicine privately. If payments to physicians are lower than at present, the likely outcome is an expanding doctor shortage; if hospitals must stay within a government budget, that guarantees the denial of care. And of course, "Many single-payer supporters, including President Obama, have spoken favorably about controlling access to costly treatments to save money."[29]

The inevitability of such effects is evident in countries with single-payer health care systems such as those in Canada and Britain. To contain costs, patients in both countries receive substandard care. Using statistics compiled by the Organization for Economic Cooperation and Development (OECD), Jacobs showed that, "expressed as totals per million inhabitants," Canadians, compared with Americans, "have less than one-third as many magnetic resonance imaging (MRI) machines"; "less than half as many computed tomography (CT) scanners"; "one-third the number of mammography machines"; and "one-fourth the number of radiotherapy machines."[30] As a result, according to Canada's Fraser Institute, "Canadians could expect to wait 5.4 weeks for a computed tomography (CT) scan, 10.6 weeks for a magnetic resonance imaging (MRI) scan, and 4.9 weeks for an ultrasound." Overall, the time it takes Canadians to get care has spiraled upward for many years; by the end of 2022, "specialist physicians surveyed report a median waiting time of 27.4 weeks between referral from a general practitioner and receipt of treatment."[31]

◆

The levels of care in Britain's National Health Service (NHS) also reveal a decades-long downward spiral, including fewer "MRI machines, CT scanners, and radiotherapy equipment," hospital bed shortages, drugs restricted that regulators deem are not cost-effective, and long waits to see a doctor or even get operations.[32] Heart-attack and stroke victims "wait more than 1½ hours on average for an ambulance," the *Wall Street Journal* has reported; "a total of 401,537 people in England were waiting more than a year for hospital treatment" at the end of 2022. Horror stories abound. "An 83-year-old woman in Leicester with a suspected stroke waited more than 18 hours in a makeshift tent outside a hospital emergency room. A 90-year-old woman with suspected sepsis waited three days."[33]

As for the United States, the "Medicare for All" bills in Congress stipulate that today's actual Medicare system would be abolished and its trust funds dumped into the overall federal budget pot. The promising Medicare Advantage plans that have proven popular for, and improved the care of, millions of senior citizens would cease to exist.[34]

CHAPTER 10

AMERICA'S EMERGING OLIGARCHY AND ITS FINANCIERS

Thanks to this country's trend toward "collective ownership of the means of consumption," very wealthy egalitarians—or very wealthy investors posing as egalitarians—have come to realize that they have few impediments to protecting their assets, and the appreciation of their assets, from social democratic or progressive government policies. This situation provides the richest of these individuals with an incentive to support higher tax rates on income; the public attention given to demands for such "reforms" will divert attention from these individuals' wealth while burnishing their image in the media as enlightened progressives.

These incentives probably explain a curious phenomenon over the past few decades—the growing numbers of the very wealthiest Americans in, and influencing, left-wing political parties and campaigns. It is a phenomenon that has not gone unnoticed.

David Callahan, a cofounder of Demos, a leftist think tank, is one who has taken note. In *Fortunes of Change: The Rise of the Liberal Rich and the Remaking of America* (2010), he analyzed the paradoxical financing of egalitarian policies in the United States. Callahan noted, for example, that while the base of the Democratic Party came out in droves for Barack Obama in 2008, "a group that *Forbes* dubbed 'Obama's billionaires'" were also staunch supporters:

◆

Among them were some of America's wealthiest hedge fund managers, including Thomas Steyer, Kenneth Griffin, Paul Tudor Jones, James Simons, and—predictably—George Soros, who was the single largest donor to the Democratic push in 2008. These men backed Obama even as the candidate pledged to more than double taxes on hedge fund profits, a move that could cost some of these donors millions of dollars a year.[1]

Warren Buffett was an adviser to the Obama campaign. Wealthy Hollywood types—Stephen Spielberg, David Geffen, Jeffrey Katzenberg—were all in, as was Eric Schmidt, then the CEO of Google. Ultimately, as Callahan pointed out, Obama outraised McCain in most of the country's ten wealthiest zip codes as well as in a variety of financial and technology sectors including investment and commercial banks.[2]

There is another twist to this story—a cohort of what Callahan called wealthy "left-wing heirs of the sixties generation"[3] who have established foundations that have organized and funded left-wing causes. These heirs of large corporate fortunes included Stewart Rawlings Mott (son of Charles Stewart Mott, for many years the largest shareholder of General Motors), George and Sarah Pillsbury (namesake of the company acquired by General Mills), Obie Benz (Daimler-Benz), and Jane Bagley Leman (R. J. Reynolds).[4] Callahan explained that these heirs "built a funding machine that has transformed activism in the United States, nurturing a vast universe of social change groups that might not otherwise exist."[5] And yet, he noted that "in the name of redistributing wealth and power, a tiny group of the most privileged members of U.S. society will help decide which social justice groups—and causes—will thrive in the next half-century and which will wither."[6]

All this led Callahan to wonder if we were headed toward Plato's ideal of a Guardian class of super-citizens who would end

◆

up running the United States—though not by living ascetically as Plato imagined. Instead,

> first, you make a boatload of money or are born to it, and then—keeping your multiple homes and perhaps your private jet—you turn to doing some good in the world.
>
> If oligarchy is government by the rich, for the rich, the contemporary Platonic ideal is about something else: rule by the rich on behalf of the common good, as they define it.[7]

An emerging political order of the kind Callahan described is not "liberal" in the historical sense of a term that had its genesis in Europe—and is still used there—to describe regimes in which the power of the government over persons and their property is limited. Nevertheless, that term has been appropriated by Americans to describe liberalism's antithesis, i.e., an illiberal combination of unconstrained government interference in the individual's self-ownership and liberties, accompanied by property privileges for the very richest not available to those of lesser wealth.

THE SHIP OF FOOLS

There is a deep irony here. Academic progressives in this country and elsewhere in the Anglo-American world have long imagined themselves as the future aristocracy in a radically revised capitalism. It hasn't worked that way. They are not captains of the ship that they constructed; instead, they comprise the crew.

A tiny number of this crew—that portion credulous enough to advocate socialism as originally conceived, i.e., state ownership of capital and the elimination of private capital formation—came to suspect that something had gone terribly wrong. The most famous of them was the principal academic Marxist of his generation, G. A. Cohen, the late Oxford University professor. Cohen, who

♦

was raised in Canada by two communist parents, explained in a book published in 2000 that he could not reconcile the membership of wealthy capitalists in the Communist Party with their alleged principles. Among the mostly poor communists he grew up with, there were some whose economic and social position, Cohen wrote, was anything but poor. One of them, "a wealthy and dedicated communist," recounted his recent visit to Soviet Russia, telling Cohen

> how wonderful it was to see efficient factories being run for the welfare of the people, with no capitalist in sight. This exchange occurred in David B.'s plush office in the plush office building that he owned in the Center of Montreal; David B. was a big man in real estate. Another dedicated communist was a big man in the garment industry, and reputed to be a pretty tough boss.
>
> Given all that I knew about them, and having strained the resources of my youthful imagination, I found that I could not attribute a consistent set of ideas to these comrades.[8]

In reality, there was and is nothing inconsistent: communism has been beset by such hypocrites from its inception, people who have designed a system in which they are willing to be the rulers, not the ruled. Karl Marx had a capitalist benefactor, Friedrich Engels. Engels, by his own definition, was an exploiter of the laborers whom he employed—and to whom, therefore, he should have transferred the ownership of his share of his partnership with the Erman & Engels textile factory at no cost to the factory workers.

He did no such thing. Instead, he sold his interest for a handsome amount that he multiplied by investing in the English stock market during one of its most prolific decades. As historian Tristram Hunt noted, the coauthor of *The Communist Manifesto* saw no contradiction between the principles in that document and his lifestyle. Responding to one critic, Engels retorted, "One can perfectly well be at one and the same time a stock exchange man and a socialist and therefore detest and despise the class of stock exchange men."[9] Elsewhere, he asked rhetorically, "Would it ever occur to me to apologize for the fact that I myself was once a partner in a firm of manufacturers? There's a fine reception waiting for anyone who tries to throw that in my teeth."[10] And when his capitalist friend, Friedrich von Eynern, pointed out the hypocrisy, Engels "showed no inclination to allow any limits to be placed on the basic freedom of his existence: to use his private earnings by himself as he saw fit."[11] Thus he moaned about the taxes he had to pay on his profits: "We poor *rentiers* are made to bleed."[12] As for charity for his exploited working class, he had no problems firing those he felt were inferior employees while handsomely subsidizing Karl Marx's upper-middle-class lifestyle.[13]

Economic equality has long been the leitmotif of socialists, progressives, and liberals, the achievement of which has long been used to justify and defend higher taxes—on income. And yet, during the Great Depression, Huey Long proposed to redistribute wealth—a proposal that was rejected, roundly denounced, and got nowhere (Roosevelt had the IRS investigate Long). Writing in 2006, Walter Benn Michaels, a progressive professor of literature at the University of Illinois at Chicago Circle, pondered the present-day implications of that episode. He noted that while current academic radicals were preoccupied with diversity and identity,

> the really radical idea of redistributing wealth becomes almost literally unthinkable. In the early 1930s, Senator Huey Long of Louisiana proposed a law making it illegal for anyone to earn more than a million dollars a year and for anyone to inherit more

than five million dollars. Imagine the response if—even suitably adjusted for inflation—any senator were to propose such a law today, cutting off incomes at, say, $15 million a year and inheritances at $75 million. It's not just the numbers that wouldn't fly; it's the whole concept. Such a restriction today would seem as outrageous and unnatural as interracial—not to mention gay—marriage seemed or would have seemed then.[14]

Among other clear-eyed Americans on the left such as David Callahan and Thomas Frank, the gradual capture of their political project and the Democratic Party, its instrument, has also sunk in. Callahan expressed a wan hope that such wealthy benefactors would be induced "to reduce inequality and diminish their own privilege."[15] Frank—author of *Listen, Liberal: Or, Whatever Happened to the Party of the People?*—was somewhat more realistic. "The Democrats have no interest in reforming themselves in a more egalitarian way," he wrote. "There is little the rest of us can do, given the current legal arrangements of this country, to build a vital third-party movement." Instead, he expressed the hope that by revealing the truth about "how starkly and how deliberately their political leaders contradict their values," the "smooth, seamless sense of liberal virtue" can be "cracked," and the "course of the party and the course of the country can both be changed."[16]

Frank and Callahan live in the same world that the late G. A. Cohen inhabited, a world seemingly controlled by their rich allies. In Cohen's case, it was the presence of wealthy Communist Party comrades who were only repeating the behavior of their predecessors, Engels and Marx.

In any case, wealthy "liberals" and their heirs are the captains of the progressive ship. Callahan, Frank, and legions of journalists and academics pull the oars in the galley.

◆

◆ ◆ ◆

Several decades ago, the late neo-Marxist sociologist Alvin W. Gouldner presented a striking overview of how today's elite class of governors emerged. "In all countries that have in the twentieth century become part of the emerging world socio-economic order," he wrote in 1979, "a New Class composed of intellectuals and technical intelligentsia—not the same—enter into contention with the groups already in control of the society's economy, whether these are businessmen or party leaders."[17]

To understand the historical evolution of this new class, Gouldner noted the decisive, and divisive, role in several European countries of secular public education during the 19th century. "On the one hand," he explained, "higher education in the public school becomes the institutional basis for the *mass* production of the New Class of intelligentsia and intellectuals. On the other hand, the expansion of primary and secondary public school teachers greatly increases the jobs available to the New Class."[18]

But especially at the lower levels, these public schools were part and parcel of a profound change in the self-defined role of educators: they came to understand themselves as representing "society as a *whole*" and not to have any "*obligation* to reproduce parental values in their children." In other words, "The socialization of the young by their families is now mediated by a *semi-autonomous* group of teachers. While growing public education limits family influence on education, it also increases the influence of the state on education."[19]

Meanwhile, Gouldner contended, with the spread of literacy the status "of humanistic intellectuals, *particularly in a technocratic and industrial society*, becomes more marginal and alienated than that of the technical intelligentsia."[20] Recall that Ladd and Lipset noted that "the university has become the great legitimizing

◆

and certifying institution of contemporary secular societies."[21] Through Gouldner's Marxist lens, this phenomenon meant that "the New Class is reproducing itself faster than any other class in society." From this observation, he predicted that this new class would supersede the existing ruling classes, "party officials and bureaucrats" in the communist societies and "propertied capitalists in the West."[22]

About this last prediction, however, Gouldner was not so prescient. He overlooked the realization of socialists such as Lenin, Mussolini, and Hitler that they could retain a one-party dictatorship while permitting the private ownership and use of property as a state-controlled privilege. Lenin called his party Communist while abandoning its adversarial relationship with capitalists; Mussolini and Hitler did the same, calling their parties Fascist and National Socialist. Working from the same playbook, China's post-Mao dictators Deng Xiaoping, Yun Jian Zemin, Hu Jintao, and Xi Jinping led a Communist Party but produced a fascist regime.

In the United States, where essentially personal income is the source of most government revenue and capital is not, this allowed any number of multimillionaires and billionaires—including the likes of Bezos, Bloomberg, Zuckerberg, Soros, and Buffett, as well as Callahan's wealthy "heirs of the sixties generation"—to forge alliances with, and ultimately regulate the affairs of—the left-wing Democratic Party. This party's long-lived pretext for power, the alleged exploitation of the working class by "Big Business," has been superseded by any pretext that seems handy—race, sex, climate, and a cluster of resentments promulgated by universities, the media, and internet companies.

From ancient times to the present day, the appetite for power among a class of "intellectuals" is so strong as to make most of them oblivious to those to whom power is ultimately ceded in the real world. Some intellectuals, however, have sought to satisfy their appetite by force rather than argument or propaganda. The Greek philosopher Plato, who conceived of a society regulated by intellectuals like himself, was not content with mere advocacy. His three attempts to persuade the tyrants governing Syracuse (the capital city of Sicily) to turn their power over to him and a Guardian class—his students—all failed. After these failures, Dion, a Syracuse aristocrat and a student of Plato, succeeded in seizing the city by force, murdering one of his allies, Heraclides, who was also a student of Plato. Dion was then murdered by Callipus, yet another student of Plato. So much for societal transformation through philosophical "discourse."[23]

The appetite of intellectuals to regulate the affairs of others led a generation of post–Civil War Americans, trained and inspired by Germany's academic socialists, to propose a society in which prestige, status, political influence, and even power would be ceded to them, their students, and their students' students. Unfortunately for the academic descendants of the original progressives, it is ultimately their wealthiest capitalist students who have assumed oligarchic control of their political vehicle, the Democratic Party.

CHAPTER 11

AMERICA'S SECOND CIVIL WAR

*One-party autocracy certainly has its drawbacks. But when it is led by
a reasonably enlightened group of people, as China is today,
it can also have great advantages. That one party can just impose
the politically difficult but critically important policies needed
to move a society forward in the 21st century.*
—THOMAS L. FRIEDMAN,
New York Times columnist, September 8, 2009

It is 141 years since Cornell University's Herbert Tuttle alerted readers of the *Atlantic Monthly* to the dangerous consequences that could stem from the many Americans who were being trained in German universities. Thanks to this largely unknown post–Civil War "scholastic pilgrimage," he wrote in 1883, American "higher education is rapidly becoming Germanized."[1] And that was the problem.

Why? As explained earlier in this book, Tuttle was a top historian of Germany with firsthand knowledge of its political and intellectual milieu. And the theory of government animating that country's professoriate, he explained, was the polar opposite of the one that inspired America's Founding. This theory "assumes as postulates the ignorance of the individual and the omniscience of the government" and a government "removed as far as possible from" the influence of elected legislatures and public opinion. If America's academic "pilgrims are faithful disciples of their masters," Tuttle warned, they will return as "advocates of a political system, which, if adopted and literally carried out, would wholly

◆

change the spirit of our institutions, and destroy all that is oldest and noblest in our national life."[2]

Tuttle's warning sums up, in a nutshell, what would actually play out, decade after decade, first in higher education, but spreading across America's institutional life—politics, government, law, journalism, and the economy. The first and foremost change was of course in higher education, where progressive academics trained in Germany (the term "progressive" having been taken directly from Germany's Progress Party) assumed the dominant position, in effect a monopoly, over the production of PhDs who would pass on their political and moral outlooks to students, including students who would go on to become teachers themselves, and so on. The fundamental political and moral outlooks pushed by this first generation of progressive academics were the opposite of those of America's Founders.

And so, by the beginning of the 20th century, political scientist Charles E. Merriam could write that the "individualistic ideas of the 'natural right' school of political theory, [e]ndorsed in the [American] Revolution," had been "discredited and repudiated."[3] Instead, the regnant political theory was that declared by Columbia University's John W. Burgess (who established the country's first major doctoral programs in political science, history, and economics): "The state is the source of individual liberty."[4] "No doubt a great deal of nonsense has been talked about the inalienable rights of the individual," Princeton University's then president Woodrow Wilson wrote in 1908. "Such theories are never 'law,' no matter what the name or the formal authority of the document in which they are embodied. Only that is 'law' which can be executed, and the abstract rights of man are singularly difficult of execution."[5]

This last argument—passed down through generations—remains the premise and default understanding today. Thus, Harvard law professor Cass Sunstein, President Obama's regulatory czar, wrote that because rights (including property rights) could not be protected without government-enacted law, it (allegedly) follows that they are not prelegal, intrinsically derived natural rights but instead are human conventions.[6] Yet this is like claiming that because murder and kidnapping must be defined by legislation in societies with governments, the rights that they protect are nothing but human conventions or inventions, i.e., arbitrary. That a right to be protected by a government (in contrast to self-protection) must be defined specifically by legislation, however, does not make this right an arbitrary convention. To be sure, governments may have varying definitions and standards of proof of a violation of natural rights. It surely does not follow that the rights themselves are human contrivances as opposed to the human discovery—by observation and abstraction—of a fact about themselves. Similarly, if something is produced by person A rather than person B, it is hardly just a convention to imagine that A rather than B is its creator and, hence, its owner. Sunstein ought to own the rights to the book he wrote, not anyone else, or "society" in general.

With natural rights repudiated by academic progressives in the late 19th century, so too was equality before the law—the ideal that inspired abolitionists, led to the Civil War, and resulted in the passage of the Thirteenth, Fourteenth, and Fifteenth Amendments. Thus Merriam would write that "liberty is not a right equally enjoyed by all. It is dependent upon the degree of civilization reached by the given people and increases as this advances." He added that "in a state composed of several nationalities, the Teutonic element should never surrender the balance of power to the others."[7]

His was not an isolated view among the professoriate; ethnocentrism and racism, as noted earlier, were common.[8] Progressive Albion W. Small (founder of the University of Chicago's sociology department), for example, "approvingly cited the actions of the Ku Klux Klan during the Reconstruction period," his biographer noted, "and the lynching in his own times as examples of 'moral' rebellion against arbitrary government."[9] After he was elected president, Woodrow Wilson proceeded to authorize the resegregation of the federal civil service.

Following World War II, the race- and ethnic-based theory of rights and equality held by progressives (who had renamed themselves "liberals") seemed to be replaced by a formal commitment to equality before the law—however, this would be contradicted by the practice of affirmative action in public universities. Yet even a formal commitment to equality before the law has been repudiated among the most recent generation of (newly rebranded) progressive academics by so-called antiracism, which is itself a blatantly racialist ideology—an ideology that is spreading throughout public schools, collegiate-level educational institutions, across professions from journalism to medicine, in government, indeed throughout the culture. Progressives now respond to dissenters and nonconformists as "racists" or "sexists" whose arguments do not have to be debated and can be ignored. And, by indoctrinating children that their race gives them criminally acquired and undeserved privileges, for which they (not their ancestors) are guilty, a new servile class is being created whose freedom of speech and dissent will be nullified through ad hominem intimidation and government coercion.

WHAT CAN BE DONE: EDUCATION, MEDIA, THE JUDICIARY, AND TAXATION

Treating academic disciplines that blended moral and political assumptions with empirical facts as the equals of disciplines employing only empirical and mathematical evidence for their conclusions was an error that cannot be retroactively repaired. Survey after survey, report after report, shows the overwhelming dominance of liberal (or more accurately, illiberal) political views in the social sciences and humanities, as well as the marginal position of conservative or libertarian scholars. This dominance is perpetuated by a climate of moral conformity and an academic caste system discussed earlier in this book. Private institutions at the collegiate level, including new ones, that maintain a true diversity of views among the social sciences and humanities—and drop any pretense that such disciplines are actually "scientific"—are surely welcome. But they will not change the culture. Seven generations of university humanities and social science disciplines dominated overwhelmingly by "progressives" make that virtually impossible.

Instead, all one can recommend now are political reforms that can impede the damage done over the past century and a half.

One such reform involves *public primary and secondary education*. The common presumption—that the state's educational values take precedence over those of parents—is unjustified. The values and preferences of a child's parents or guardians should instead come first, and the government monopoly on public education forcibly funded by the parents should be replaced by reform. There are already laws in some states now that allow parents to withdraw the percentage of a public school's per-child tax revenue and use it to pay for their children's education at a school of their choice. These laws should be adopted everywhere. If not, national legislation permitting such withdrawals should be passed. Columbia University law professor Philip Hamburger has argued that, with regard to minor children, the public education system violates parents' freedom of speech. "To be sure," he writes, "there is no formal requirement that parents must subject their children to government educational speech. But because education is mandatory, there is direct constraint. Parents must pay to opt out of government educational speech or they must accept such speech."[10]

Higher education, however, is another matter; the reform of today's colleges and universities is virtually impossible. They are dominated by progressive faculty—faculty who are over-whelmingly the intellectual descendants of Americans educated in Germany by state-socialist autocrats in the late 19th century. These men established this country's doctoral programs that churned out generations of professors who have taught, or rather indoctrinated, generations of students.

Today's universities have become secular churches, i.e., secular schools of a political ideology that propagate doctrines that are the antithesis of the ones upon which the country was founded. Asking them to change would be like asking a school of theology to hire either theologians of another religion or atheists. It will not happen because tenured faculty control all appointments.

Change, if any, will have to come from the outside, begin-ning with the elimination of federal subsidies and grants to all universities. The taxpayers who dissent from the ideology that dominates those institutions are having their First Amendment rights traduced.

One could also imagine the establishment of several major new universities with distinguished science and engineering fac-ulty, as well as, most significantly, social science and humanities faculties staffed by proponents of natural rights and the limited government established by the Constitution. They would certainly have a potential superb student body drawn from the rejected applicants of universities that now employ racial rather than intellectual qualifications for admission. Whether the Supreme Court decision forbidding racial discrimination in college admis-sions will be effective—when the administration and faculty oppose it—is a question yet to be answered. To be attractive to students, these new institutions would have to be tuition-free at the undergraduate and graduate student levels and also would likely have to offer three-year undergraduate degrees. But the bill for this enterprise would require tens of billions of dollars.

Still, there is a reform of public universities whereby state governors and legislators might undo the one-party universities that voters from other parties are currently compelled to finance. A state governor could make the presidents for each of the state's universities responsible for ideologically balancing its humanities and social science faculties. The university's president could be required to appoint chairs of all humanities and social science departments (without the consent of the faculty) with the views of the American Founders. In turn, these chairs would be required to fill all open seats in their departments with adherents of natural rights, libertarianism, classical liberalism, and/or limited-government conservatism—again without the consent of current faculty—until the faculty departments in the humanities and social sciences are ideologically balanced. Universities that failed to comply would not be abolished—but would lose all state funding for the humanities and the social sciences. After all, what we have demonstrated is that the taxpayers of one political party are compelled to finance the secular churches of the other party.

An alternative reform to achieve the same end would be to add a department, institute, or an entire college in public universities dedicated to the study of civil society based on the country's founding principles, as was recently instituted by the state of Ohio. The explicit goal would be to balance the ideological homogeneity of the rest of the faculty.

These measures could achieve the intellectual diversity that today's institutions are supposed to embody but never do. Without such changes, the philosophical genesis of today's social sciences and humanities will continue to place the United States on the same political trajectory as the European country from which they arose. To assure the security of that trajectory, universities have invented a vague pretext for censorship called Diversity, Equity, and Inclusion (DEI). The enforcement of DEI is assigned to administrators who have become Nazi-like prosecutors of intellectual conformity. Institutions that employ DEI policies should not receive public funds.

One chilling example of this dangerous political trajectory is Roscoe Pound, leader of the progressive "sociological jurisprudence" movement and dean of Harvard Law School from 1916 to 1937. Pound was an adamant opponent of natural rights and limited, constitutional government, as well as an enthusiastic supporter of Franklin D. Roosevelt's New Deal until 1937 (when he broke with FDR's court-packing scheme). Pound also boosted Nazi Germany, where he vacationed in the mid-1930s. He praised Hitler and Hitler's government in the *New York Herald Tribune*, denying that there was any persecution of the Jews, nor any Nazi restrictions on freedom of speech. Pound was awarded an honorary degree in September 1934 from the University of Berlin by Dr. Hans Luther, Nazi Germany's ambassador to the United States.[11]

Walter Lippmann, the author of *The Good Society* (1937), came to recognize the danger that his former progressive philosophy now posed for his country. Harvard Law dean Pound's contribution to this danger is illustrative of our present path toward an American National Socialist future.

Another reform that needs attention: *social media*. Throughout the 19th and 20th centuries, as Michigan State University law professor Adam Candeub has explained, legislation has provided certain companies—such as shippers or railroads—with limited immunity from certain kinds of traditional legal liability. In return for that special privilege, the proviso was that these companies had to serve the public, i.e., all customers, without discrimination. So too, communication companies such as telegraphs and telephones have been provided with limited immunity, in specified circumstances, against defamation. These companies also had a legal obligation to serve all customers.[12]

However, the 1996 Communications Decency Act provided social media platforms (such as X, formerly Twitter, and Facebook) with sweeping immunity from defamation posted by users[13]—but without any corresponding obligation to the public. Section 230(c) (2)(A) of this law also stated that these platforms can "restrict access to or availability of material that the provider or user considers to be obscene, lewd, lascivious, filthy, excessively violent, harassing, *or otherwise objectionable*, whether or not such material is constitutionally protected" (emphasis added). As consistently interpreted by federal courts, those three words, "or otherwise objectionable," have allowed these platforms to block anything or anyone that the company doesn't like for any reason, or no reason. Thus, legislation supposedly intended to unleash an unprecedented flow of free speech—except for narrowly defined cases such as pornography or criminal incitement (thus the word "Decency" in the title of the legislation)—has instead licensed these companies to be giant censors, shutting down or banning whomever they want. Moreover, thanks to the ever-present threat of antitrust lawsuits, politicians, government officials, and federal bureaucrats can pressure these giant companies to censor anyone whose views these government actors disfavor.

The reform? Strike the words "or otherwise objectionable" from the law—and make it explicit that—other than the kinds of material specifically named in the statute—these platforms must accommodate customers without discrimination if they wish to retain their immunity from defamatory posts by third parties.

The recent preliminary injunction by U.S. District Judge Terry A. Doughty of Louisiana has barred the White House and many federal agencies from coercing social media companies to suppress views with which they disagree. If successful, this decision will prevent the federal government from forcing the private sector to publish only views with which they agree.[14]

Next, appointments to the Supreme Court should be restricted to those who understand and accept that there are intrinsic, prelegal rights of self-ownership, liberty, and ownership of the fruits of one's labor. While the Constitution is the fundamental written law, it is constrained by those rights—rights that are also acknowledged in the document's first ten amendments (including the Ninth Amendment, which implicitly recognizes natural rights) and further spelled out in the Thirteenth and Fourteenth Amendments. Laws enacted by the federal or state governments that flout those rights should be struck down by the Supreme Court; so too must judicial precedents be overturned that conflict with these rights.

To understand the significance of this requirement for appointments to the Supreme Court, consider the answer given to an inquiry about her views on this matter from the candidate and now justice Ketanji Brown Jackson: "I do not hold a position on whether individuals possess natural rights." In other words, if asked if American slaves had a natural right of self-ownership, this black nominee would have no position. Frederick Douglass, the former slave and natural-rights defender, would have been appalled, as would his fellow abolitionists.

The most important and far-reaching political reform is taxation at the federal level. As explained earlier in this book, a tax on income is not morally justified by any of the criteria that its proponents (on the political left or right) have offered—and it should be eliminated. Income taxes are not a means of wealth redistribution, and income is not a measure of an individual's financial capacity. Nor is an income tax the appropriate measure for assessing the amount of property that a natural-rights republic should tax, since it is charged against only a portion of the property protected. In 2019, for example, the total household net worth in the United States was approximately $110 trillion,[15] while adjusted gross income was roughly $11.9 trillion. Of that $11.9 trillion, approximately $3.35 trillion, or about 3% of net worth, was collected by the federal government through income and payroll taxes, most of it collected from the middle class, not the rich.[16]

If one asks how government revenues *should* be raised in a natural-rights republic, the answer is that morally, only three sources are justified. The first would be a capitation tax that assesses an equal amount of money on every citizen for the protection of their person from crime. The second would be a wealth tax assessed proportionately on every person or family for the protection of their property from theft or damage done by someone. The third would be a sales tax assessed on every financial transaction to protect buyers of an entity or service from fraud and to protect sellers from nonpayment or fraudulent payment.

There are, however, problems with two of these morally justified taxes that make them unnecessary and, therefore, avoidable. A capitation tax at the federal level would be very small, as individuals are rarely protected from crime by the federal government as opposed to local government. The federal government's protections are chiefly needed in times of justifiable wars of defense, which are rare (e.g., World War II). Therefore, the practical insignificance of a capitation tax renders it unnecessary.

A second justifiable but unnecessary tax would be a proportional levy on the wealth of individuals or families. The practical problem associated with such a tax is that it would burden every individual with submitting to the government a list of all his or her assets and debts—yet it too would raise very little revenue, given the federal government's current expenditures.

◆

For example, Massachusetts's Democratic senator Elizabeth Warren has proposed a wealth tax that would assess a 2% levy on those whose net worth exceeds $50 million, and 6% on those whose wealth exceeds $1 billion. Her estimate of the federal revenues that would be raised by these taxes was $3.75 trillion for 10 years, i.e., $375 billion per year. That would raise less than 10% of the federal budget, which was approximately $4.7 trillion in 2019, $6.2 trillion in 2020, and $6.4 trillion in 2021. More likely, Warren's proposal would raise much less. The Wharton School of Finance, using its Penn Wharton Budget Model, found that "if implemented in 2021 [it] would raise between $2.3 trillion (including macroeconomic effects) and $2.7 trillion (not including macroeconomic effects) in additional revenues in the ten-year window 2021–2030 while reducing GDP in 2050 by about 1 to 2 percent, depending upon how the money is spent."[17] In other words, including its effects on the economy, Warren's wealth tax would raise about 5% or less than the federal budget.

However, a universal 1.13% sales tax on the purchase of all goods and services—including the hundreds of trillions of dollars in securities transactions—would be justified by the need to protect all exchanges of property from fraud. *This modest levy would have raised the funds necessary for the entire federal budget of 2019 without a deficit and would have allowed for the repeal of all existing federal taxes.* That is, the universal sales tax in 2019 would have raised $4.49 trillion[18] rather than the $3.35 trillion raised that year under the current federal tax regime.

The principal reason such a small tax can raise so much revenue is that 91% of that revenue would come from a currently untaxed source: the sale of a stock, bond, or derivative. For example, in 2019 there were $303.8 trillion in stock and bond sales and $49.9 trillion in the sales of derivatives (the sale of municipal bonds would be exempt from the sales tax proposed here). The

1.13% universal sales tax would also apply to all business purchases of goods and services as well as to the sales of their products to consumers or other businesses. The money raised would come from business output of $30.7 trillion a year, along with residential home sales of $3.5 trillion annually. In total, the tax base to which the 1.13% universal sales tax would have been applied in 2019 was $397.2 trillion and the application of the tax to that base would have raised the aforementioned $4.49 trillion, balancing the 2019 budget rather than permitting the $1.1 trillion federal deficit of 2019. (Further details and an analysis of the sales tax proposed here are presented in the appendix to this book.)

Should the universal sales tax raise a sum exceeding the federal budget, the legislation should include a requirement that the excess be applied to debt reduction.

Therefore, the United States should pass legislation to eliminate the taxation of personal and corporate income including capital gains, dividends, and interest. Estate tax and gift taxes, which raise a trivial sum but burden the upper-middle class more than the rich, should be eliminated as well. All of these would be replaced by the universal sales tax.

Finally, the current payroll tax for Social Security, Medicare, or federal taxes for unemployment insurance benefits would be eliminated for employers, wage earners, and the self-employed. The universal sales tax would raise more than enough to cover these programs. The seller of a product or service would pay the tax and transfer it to the federal government, except in the case of employment. In those transactions, the employer (the buyer of labor services) would both pay the tax and remit the money to the government, relieving employees of that obligation.[19]

This system would liberate employees and employers from the taxation of their personal and corporate incomes—and help undo the political dependency that results from today's slide into "collective ownership of the means of consumption."

To give average taxpayers some idea of what they would save under a universal sales tax that removed all personal and corporate income and payroll taxes, as well as estate and gift taxes, consider single filers with no dependents and taxable incomes of $30,000, $40,000, $50,000, $60,000, $70,000, $80,000, or $90,000.

First: These taxpayers face the current (2023) marginal tax rates on personal income (see table 11.1).

Table 11.1. Federal Tax Rates on Taxable Income, Single Filers

10%	$0–$11,000
12%	$11,000–$44,725
22%	$44,725–$95,375
24%	$95,375–$182,100
32%	$182,100–$231,100
35%	$231,250–$578,125
37%	$578,125 or more

Second: Assume that such an earner would spend 90% of his or her income with 70% on general expenditures, 20% on investments, 5% on cash savings, and 5% on state and local taxes. Finally: How much would he or she have to pay with the 1.13% universal sales tax and what would be the difference in taxes under the old and new systems—that is, how much of their income now stays in their pockets? The results are shown in table 11.2.

Would the replacement of federal income and payroll taxes with a 1.13% universal sales tax benefit the majority of taxpayers? The numbers in this table speak for themselves.

It should never be forgotten that today's "social democracies," welfare states, and fascist regimes (e.g., China) raise most of their revenues from taxes on the incomes of employees, not on the incomes or wealth of their employers. Yet the reduction in employee income provides the principal pretext for the govern-

Table 11.2. Higher Take-Home Pay when a Universal Sales Tax Replaces Federal Income and Payroll Taxes

ANNUAL EARNINGS*	INCOME AND PAYROLL TAXES ELIMINATED	90% OF EARNINGS	SALES TAX ON 90%	TAX SAVINGS
$30,000	$4,575.00	$27,000.00	$301.10	$4,273.90
$40,000	$6,640.00	$36,000.00	$406.80	$6,233.20
$50,000	$11,360.00	$45,000.00	$508.50	$10,852.00
$60,000	$13,097.50	$54,000.00	$610.20	$12,487.30
$70,000	$16,233.44	$63,000.00	$711.90	$15,521.54
$80,000	$19,027.50	$72,000.00	$813.60	$18,213.90
$90,000	$21,992.50	$81,000.00	$904.00	$21,088.00

*Single taxpayers with no qualifying children who earn more than $17,640 do not qualify for the EITC (Earned Income Tax Credit).

ment social programs needed to replace what has been extracted from workers by these very taxes on their incomes. The universal federal sales tax, which would leave all income with those who earn it, would deprive aspiring "progressive" autocrats of that pretext.

Individuals' access to their entire income (minus state and local taxes) would allow them to retain their earnings for savings or expenditures. As for its effect on the economy, the absence of a corporate income and payroll tax will attract capital investment from all over the globe, raising the standard of living for all Americans. The political party that favors and helps to pass this legislation will acquire majority control of the government for some time from citizens delighted by their relief from income and payroll taxes. Ultimately, the Sixteenth Amendment, enabling federal income taxation, could be repealed.

SOME FINAL WORDS

America's first civil war was ultimately the result of an irreconcilable disagreement about slavery—an institution completely contrary to every individual's natural right to self-ownership—that reached the boiling point after the 1860 election. I call it the

◆

first civil war because a second civil war emerged in 2016—when members of the outgoing administration, along with others inside and outside of the government, attempted to determine the results of the presidential election through a fabricated claim that the winner colluded with a foreign government. This behavior was ultimately a reflection of the actors' presumption that some people occupy a position of privilege analogous to past dictators and one-party governments.

Whether we have reached a point where a single party exercises sufficient autocratic power to impair the democratic political competition permitted by the Constitution is a question that remains unanswered. But it has become only too evident that opponents of natural rights have demonstrated their eagerness and ability to exercise such power.

We know that all too frequently people are surprised to learn of the capacity for evil in those whom they know or think they know. For example, the brother of the Unabomber recognized the possible culpability of his sibling only after the terrorist's long, anonymous, essay was published in prominent national newspapers.

Yet the inability to recognize threatening political circumstances is also striking. The German Jewish father of a friend of mine wrote that when Hitler became Germany's chancellor, he and the Jewish community generally failed to appreciate its implications for them: "Hitler took power in 1933," he wrote, "and unfortunately many Jews including ourselves lived under the misconception, that things would get better for the Jews once he had taken over the government." The author of this passage escaped Nazi Germany with his wife five days before Hitler touched off World War II by invading Poland in alliance with Stalinist Russia.

Nor was this man's misconception unusual. In his book *Einstein on the Run*, Andrew Robinson noted that "the German-Jewish reaction to the Nazi persecution was mostly one of paralysis, like 'a bird fascinated by a serpent,' according to Elsa Einstein's close friend Antonina Vallentin."[20]

On his trip to Nazi Germany in 1933, Joseph Kennedy Jr. (older brother of the future president John F. Kennedy) sent a letter to their father commenting on Hitler's political savvy. "He saw the need for a common enemy," he wrote. "Someone of whom to make the goat. Someone, by whose riddance the Germans would feel they had cast out the cause of their predicament. It was an excellent psychology and it was too bad that it had to be done to the Jews. This dislike of the Jews, however, was well founded."[21] In 1944, Kennedy, a Navy pilot, was killed in action during the war to defeat Nazism.

Political blindness can be a most dangerous malady.

◆ ◆ ◆

The accidental monopoly over higher education acquired by Americans trained in Germany in the late 19th century has— after generations of indoctrination masquerading as unbiased, disinterested teaching—replaced this country's original political philosophy with one that "assumes as postulates the ignorance of the individual and the omniscience of the government."[22] One can only hope that by recounting what happened since the first civil war, we can begin to recover universal human rights and the institutions founded to protect them.

◆

A UNIVERSAL SALES TAX

INTRODUCTION: HOW TO REPLACE FEDERAL, PERSONAL, AND CORPORATE INCOME AND PAYROLL TAXES, AS WELL AS GIFT AND ESTATE TAXES

Chapter II proposed changing the way the federal government raises revenue. The proposal: a universal tax on the sales of goods, services, and financial assets, which we call here a universal sales tax (UST).

The UST would replace nearly all existing federal taxes, including income taxes on individuals and businesses, along with the payroll taxes currently paid by both. The taxation of interest income, dividends, and capital gains, along with estate and gift taxes, would also cease. Instead, the sale of products and services sold by every business to consumers or other businesses would be taxed; so too would be the sale of owner-occupied housing. The tax would also apply to sales of stocks, bonds, derivatives, and other financial securities—which amount to hundreds of trillions of dollars—that are not taxed by the federal government. Excise taxes and customs duties would be the only remnants of the current federal regime.

The tax explored below is a uniform 1.13%—*although in practice, the various categories of transactions need not be taxed at the*

◆

same rate. In 2019, the UST would have raised the funds necessary to cover the federal government's annual spending, including expenditures on entitlement programs such as Social Security and Medicare. It could also have closed the deficit in that year.

The important preliminary research on the feasibility of a universal sales tax—determining the base and rate—was done by Gary Robbins, an economics research fellow of the Social Philosophy and Policy Foundation, a former Treasury economist and senior fellow at the Tax Foundation, and the president of Fiscal Associates. Robbins used 2019, the last non-pandemic year, as a representative period to establish the practicality of this tax.

In the following discussion, "Evaluation of a Universal Sales Tax," Jason DeBacker and Matthew Jensen build on Robbins's research to provide an analysis and commentary on how a universal sales tax would best be implemented, its effects on individuals and the economy, and the UST rate that would have covered the federal revenue actually raised in each year from 2011 through 2021. DeBacker is an associate professor of economics at the University of South Carolina, a nonresident fellow at the Urban-Brookings Tax Policy Center, and the vice president of research and cofounder of Open Research Group, Inc. (OpenRG). Jensen is a principal and cofounder of OpenRG. He was the founding director of the Open Source Policy Center at the American Enterprise Institute and a member of the advisory board of the Tax Policy Center's Synthetic Data Project.

◆　◆　◆

◆

Evaluation of a Universal Sales Tax

Jason DeBacker and Matthew Jensen

INTRODUCTION

The national sales tax outlined in chapter 11 of this book entails a comprehensive overhaul of the federal tax regime. It would replace individual and corporate income taxes, payroll taxes, the gift and estate tax, and other components of the current system with a universal sales tax (UST). The proposed rate of 1.13% would apply to the sale of all goods and services including consumer sales, business sales to other businesses, labor services, people's residences, and financial instruments. That rate would apply to all components of this wide base, and it was designed to cover all federal expenditures in 2019 and fill the budget deficit. The base is essentially equivalent to gross output and financial transactions, with financial transactions making up the lion's share.

In this analysis, we first qualitatively describe several notable implications of the proposed tax overhaul. Then we revisit the estimation of the tax base and conduct a static analysis to find the range of suitable initial rates. Next, we use a large-scale overlapping-generations model of the U.S. economy to analyze the proposal's macroeconomic effects and find general positive impacts on the economy. Finally, we consolidate and review recommendations from our analysis to improve how Americans experience the implementation of the new tax.

♦

QUALITATIVE DISCUSSION OF SIGNIFICANT EFFECTS

Eliminating the existing tax system will affect in numerous and significant ways how businesses arrange their productive activities and how individuals will arrange their financial, professional, and personal affairs. The new system would cause countervailing effects and others that influence behavior in unique directions. In this section, we qualitatively discuss several of the notable net effects.

- ◆ Simplification and transparency

Repealing most person-level taxes and replacing them with a sales tax will simplify tax filing for most individuals and families. They will no longer need to track the tax basis of their property, keep note of the gifts they give to loved ones, or record their itemizable expenses. For those who sell personal property or are involved in frequent transactions, paying taxes will likely be easier than under the current system, requiring only that they report how much they sold and keep copies of their receipts.

Similarly, a sales tax will simplify tax filing for most companies. Businesses of all types will continue to file taxes, but doing so will be much simpler. There will no longer be any need to keep track of expenses for corporate income tax deductions, but only for the universal sales tax. The challenge of distinguishing a business expense from an executive's personal expense is sidestepped by doing away with the deduction entirely. Companies will no longer need to meet the IRS record-keeping requirements associated with existing corporate tax credits, carve-outs, and the many deductions in the present tax code. Businesses will no longer need to track the depreciation or cost basis of assets. Tax collectors will not need to make the slippery distinction between business and personal consumption. There will no longer be a payroll tax levied on employers. The UST is likely to be a radical simplification for most firms, and reducing tax paperwork will relax one of the worst headaches of starting and running a small business.

Also, from the perspective of some hypothetical public tax educators, the tax system will be much simpler. The current system's multitude of rates, exemptions, credits, and deductions, each affecting the decisions of some subset of taxpayers, is not easy to understand or grasp even by tax professionals. In the case of the new system, there would be but one tax, albeit not an entirely transparent one, to educate the public about.

From the perspective of individual taxpayers, many may be happy not to think about taxes at all.

- Repealing gift and estate taxes will simplify long-term financial planning for individuals and families.

Many productive Americans, realizing they won't be able to or don't want to spend all of the money they've accumulated in their lifetimes, begin planning how to pass it on to their remaining spouse, children, charitable organizations, or others whom they'd like to benefit from their life's work. Under the current system, taxes play a major role in their planning. In the new system, that role would be much diminished. Under the current system, gift and estate taxes are responsible for likely millions of hours of extra planning and detours from preferred paths for the sake of tax avoidance. Under the new system, the transfer of assets across generations or between spouses would not be considered a transaction for tax purposes. Taxes would continue, however, to play a role in planning the liquidation of assets, including financial and residential assets.

◆

RETURNS TO LABOR AND CAPITAL

The reform will increase after-tax returns to both labor and capital held at the firm level, leading to increased output and a larger nonfinancial component of the tax base over time. We will quantify these changes and their impacts in the section on macroeconomic modeling below.

- Reducing the overall tax burden on labor will increase education and labor output.

The repeal of income and payroll taxes will dramatically increase workers' take-home pay. A higher return to labor will lead to greater work effort and workforce participation across the entire economy. It will lead workers to want to work more effectively and increase the compensation for self-improvement. More high-skilled workers will immigrate and more people of all kinds will develop new inventions and other innovations thanks to their overall greater focus on work. Within family units, it will increase the divide in take-home pay among spouses with different earnings and may encourage more specialization between work and family care.

- Reducing the overall tax burden on capital income at the firm level will increase capital accumulation and also increase returns to labor.

Higher after-tax returns on capital income at the firm level will encourage investors to move capital into American investments. The tax on financial transactions will mean the investments they pick will largely be those they plan to hold for some time. Increased capital in the United States will mean more machines and intellectual property to boost the productivity of American workers and increase their earnings.

♦

LOCATION DECISIONS FOR INDIVIDUALS AND FIRMS

The new system will have complex implications for the location decisions of individuals and firms, with the repeal of the corporate income tax and implementation of the universal sales tax each playing a role.

- ◆ Repealing the corporate income tax as well as the corporate payroll tax will increase the attractiveness of the United States as a location for corporate profit centers.

The elimination of the corporate income tax will lead to a boom of corporate-headquarters activity, including activities associated with creating and administering intellectual property, and other activities that determine the tax location of corporate profit.[1] The recent experience of nations like Ireland and other tax havens is instructive. Low corporate tax rates have helped their economies outperform in recent decades, and this reform will leave the United States with a much lower corporate income and payroll tax rate (0% for both) than any other advanced economy. It will make the U.S. a decisive winner in the recent corporate tax rate "race to the bottom" for multinationals and mobile corporate capital.

If other nations continue their collaboration under the auspices of the Organization for Economic Cooperation and Development to establish a harmonized minimum 15% rate on some corporate income, in addition to retaining their national corporate tax rates, then the United States under the UST will be that much more attractive.

◆

♦ The tax on financial transactions may make the United States less attractive as a location for financial exchanges, as well as firms and individuals that rely on frequent financial transactions.

Financial transaction taxes are common around the globe. In the United States, the Securities and Exchange Commission (SEC) already collects a small fee (0.00229%) from transactions on U.S. exchanges and over-the-counter trades by U.S. broker-dealers. The United Kingdom has administered a stamp duty since 1694. But the combination of the sales tax proposal's higher rate and broad base is unique in global policy. Many firms may be incentivized to cut ties with America if the transaction tax isn't implemented carefully, and some may do so even if it is. The specific details of how the base is defined will likely determine its success or failure in raising the revenue required to ensure the smooth funding and operations of the federal government and those the government supports through transfer payments, employment, and contracts.[2]

If the sales tax is levied based on the *location of the financial exchange* where a financial transaction takes place, then financial transactions will leave American exchanges, or the exchanges themselves will leave America. Sweden discovered painfully that a tax on financial transactions needs a stickier base than the location of an exchange. Their financial transaction tax on Swedish exchanges was enacted in 1984 and repealed in 1991 after precipitous declines in local financial activity.[3] To prevent a similar outcome, a sales tax on financial transactions as proposed here should be triggered when one or more of the counterparties is an American resident and/or citizen or company with American partners or shareholders.[4]

If the sales tax on financial transactions is *levied based on business residence*, it will incline firms that rely on high transaction volumes—such as those that work in market making, that rely on hedges needing frequent rebalancing, or that otherwise face and manage rapidly changing financial circumstances—to want to move themselves or critical components of their operations offshore. They'll merge with foreign companies in corporate inversions, use arrangements with foreign subsidiaries, and attempt other workarounds to the tax, taking on significant transition, administrative, and agency costs in the process. These perverse incentives to leave American jurisdiction could be countered to some extent through rules and regulations surrounding corporate inversions and subsidiary relationships. One of the rules would be that transactions involving a corporation with any American participation in ownership would be subject to the sales tax, no matter where the corporation or transaction was located. The corporate headquarters and its divisional components would have to be located in the United States to avoid paying corporate income taxes.

- ◆ **The UST will make America more attractive for high-skilled immigrants.**

Workers in America will face no personal income tax or payroll tax, and a low tax on their consumption. High-skilled foreign workers who face high taxes on their income and consumption (via value-added taxes) in their home countries will be motivated to immigrate here. The introduction of new high-skilled individuals to the American workforce should be expected to improve the productivity of American workers and benefit American capital owners in aggregate.

◆

OTHER NOTABLE BEHAVIORAL EFFECTS

◆ Firms will vertically integrate to remain competitive in their industries, leading to consolidation.

Taxing business-to-business sales of goods and services will add to a company's cost of production, with the amount determined by the number of transactions in the supply chains used in the production of the particular product or service. All active firms with American ownership and revenue will be affected, regardless of their other expenses. At each transaction in the supply chain, the tax will accumulate, so goods and services produced by vertically integrated firms will be at an advantage in the marketplace.

A report on the Washington State Business and Occupation tax hints at how much the tax burden can vary when intermediate production is included in the base. Using an input-output model of the state economy, the report found that the effective rate would differ across industries from 150% to 670% of the statutory rate.[5] The differences across individual goods and products and their unique supply chains would be even wider than industry averages.

Firms that can vertically integrate may do so, and when they do it may mean less competition. These effects are mitigated by the low statutory rate afforded by sharing the base with financial transactions. The sales tax revenue lost by such integration is likely to be offset by the number of new businesses created by the influx of capital from abroad and locally.

◆ States and local governments will adopt the new tax system or face significant challenges to administering an income tax system without federal support.

State tax administrators, especially those administering income and payroll taxes, benefit in many ways from the current federal tax infrastructure. States avoid substantial compliance labor on the

◆

part of their taxpayers when their tax computations overlap with the federal government's. Taxpayers can compute a figure once and have it affect their liability for both federal and state taxes. States also receive data from the federal government's federal tax returns to assist in forecasting revenues and enforcing compliance for their tax systems. For these reasons and others, it is easier for states to adopt tax systems that overlap the federal system. An expected outcome of the UST proposal will be for many states to relinquish their income taxes and adopt new taxes on universal sales. This is likely a positive outcome for plan designers, but it will create systemic contagion across federal, state, and local governments if the new tax doesn't collect enough revenue or has other unanticipated and deleterious effects.

- **There will be significant changes in the labor market as firms reorganize.**

The overhaul of federal taxes will shift how many firms are organized and the activities they pursue, both as a result of the introduction of the new tax and the elimination of the old taxes, including all the current system's many existing carve-outs. Relocating workers across firms and activities will be disruptive, as some workers lose their jobs and some leave for better offers, in both cases leaving behind firm-specific human capital. The disruption is unlikely to scar the economy or careers since job losers will be inclined to return to work quickly by higher after-tax returns to labor income as well as higher remuneration, thanks to increased capital accumulation and productivity.

- **Repealing revenue sources dedicated to government trust funds will change the political landscape for their uses.**

Social Security and Medicare, as well as highway and aviation infrastructure, are currently supported by dedicated revenue sources. With the new tax system, these dedicated revenue sources will no longer exist. However, the overall revenue raised by the UST is designed to cover all federal expenditures, including entitlements, which will mean dedicating federal revenues to the existing trust funds to cover their costs. If, as is proposed, the same proportion of revenues is dedicated to the trust funds under the new regime as under the current regime, then the trust funds will be better funded than they are now as more revenue will be raised overall.

- **It will be difficult to return to the old tax system after it is decommissioned.**

Taxpayers will pay dearly if their representatives don't like this new tax system or find it doesn't work well for some reason and then decide to reverse it shortly after enacting it. Taking the income tax rate immediately to zero and withdrawing the bureaucratic structures that collect and audit the current system will mean the rapid loss of institutional knowledge and ability, muscle memory so to speak, for administering the old system. Commercial providers of tax preparation software will change their offerings, and the officials at the IRS and other institutions will adopt new procedures, technologies, and habits for administering the new system. Taxpayers will reorient aspects of their professional and personal lives around the new system, responding to the new landscape. If the electorate or their representatives were to change their minds, the way back would be a difficult one. Some infrastructure may be dusted off or otherwise refurbished, but the bureaucracies of tax collection must be taken out for a regular spin like a performance chainsaw.

- **A transition plan for the UST would smooth out disruptions for Americans and their organizations.**

The short-term reshuffling of labor and capital markets, firms, and employers could be smoothed considerably through attention to transition planning. A simple approach would be to phase in and out the new and old rates, linearly, over a few years. One goes up, and the other goes down, steadily, until the new system is in place and the old is eliminated. A transition period would respect the work and planning of Americans who have built their lives around the structures and tradeoffs of the current system, and it would afford them time to rearrange their affairs deliberatively.

ESTIMATING THE UST BASE

The tax base in 2019 we estimate to be $397.2 trillion, composed of $30.7 trillion of gross sales, $9.3 trillion of wages and salaries, $303.8 trillion of securities transactions, including issuances, $49.9 trillion of payments resulting from derivatives contracts, and $3.5 trillion of sales of existing homes.

We review the estimates here:

◆ **Financial Transactions**

Securities transactions
Treasury securities: $149.6 trillion
Agency debt: $1.1 trillion
Equities: $81.1 trillion
Asset-backed securities and collateralized debt obligations, nonagency: $0.4 trillion
Corporate bonds: $8.6 trillion
Agency mortgage-backed securities: $62.7 trillion
Non-agency mortgage-backed securities: $0.4 trillion

Payments resulting from derivatives contracts
Exchange-traded futures: $23.1 trillion
Exchange-traded options: $8.0 trillion
Over-the-counter futures: $6.9 trillion
Over-the-counter interest-rate swaps: $11.9 trillion

◆

Total financial transactions base:
Securities: $303.8 trillion
Derivatives: $49.9 trillion
Total: $353.7 trillion

Estimates for securities transactions are from the Securities Industry and Financial Markets Association.[6] Limited data are available on annual flows of payment as a result of derivatives contracts. We assume that they amount to 2% of the notional value of derivatives transactions. This assumption appears broadly in line with those made by the Joint Committee on Taxation in their work for the related CBO Budget Option to impose a financial transaction tax where the derivatives base also consisted of payments made under the contracts.[7] Estimates for derivatives transactions are from the Bureau of International Settlements by location of the transaction, not accounting for the residence of counterparties.[8] We follow Pollin, Heintz, and Herndon (2018) in applying a 90% adjustment factor to North American exchange volume to estimate the U.S. base.[9]

The base of actual financial transactions will depend on how effectively over-the-counter transactions are captured, whether the American residence or citizenship of a single counterparty triggers the tax for the transaction regardless of exchange location, and the extent to which taxpayers reduce trading or move trading activity to non-U.S. entities.

◆ Other Transactions and the Total Tax Base

Apart from financial transactions, the sales tax base includes the gross sales of privately produced (nonfinancial) goods and services and sales of owner-occupied housing.[10] The sale of labor services would also be subject to the UST, including those by employees to employers. However, the burden of having to file sales tax collections can be shifted from employees to employers by having the latter send the sales tax revenue directly to the federal government. Employees would not have to file a separate return.[11]

Tax base:
Financial transactions: $353.7 trillion
Gross sales: $30.7 trillion
Employee labor services: $9.3 trillion
Sales of owner-occupied houses (approximated): $3.5 trillion
Total tax base: $397.2 trillion

◆ Estimating the initial tax rate

Forecasting revenues is a challenging endeavor even for small reforms, precisely defined, in certain economic times. This proposed reform is not small in any way, its base is not yet precisely defined by the legislative process, and economic times are by no means certain.

Our starting point, and indeed a natural starting point to understand any new tax system's revenue-raising potential, is to estimate how much the tax might raise if the rate is applied to the base without any further assumptions about how taxpayers might respond to the elimination of the old taxes and introduction of the new, a so-called "static" analysis. The static analysis doesn't attempt to predict the behavior of taxpayers or policymakers, positive or negative for revenue. Instead, it aims to set a reference point by calculating the amount of revenue that would be raised if behavior does not change at all.

We focus our analysis on 2019, the last "normal" year before the global pandemic. Focusing on just a single year is useful for estimating a practical starting point for the tax rate under the assumption that the new system makes it easier for politicians to react to changing circumstances year by year through fine-grained

◆

policy adjustments. Tax hikes (or cuts) may be easier thanks to the one simple tax instrument. This approach is less helpful for forecasting the potential impacts on economic output and its inputs, and so in the next section when estimating macroeconomic effects, we take a longer-term perspective.

◆ **Static estimation of the revenue and deficit-neutralizing rate, 2019**

A static analysis is simple thanks to the straightforwardness of the new tax system. We first solve for the tax rates that would collect enough revenue to offset existing revenue collection, which was $3.35 trillion in 2019.[12] The revenue-neutralizing rate would be 0.84%.

Next, we solve for the tax rate that would collect enough revenue to offset existing revenue collection and fill the deficit, which combined totaled $4.49 trillion in 2019. Using the same base, we see that the deficit-neutralizing rate would be 1.13%.

These estimates are imperfect because of the inherent uncertainty surrounding the size of the base. The base we have measured, for which data are available, is not precisely the base that will be taxed. The base might be broader in its design, for instance, by taxing financial transactions by the residence of a counterparty, and taxpayers meanwhile will rearrange their behavior to shrink the base, usually within the bounds of regulation and sometimes not.

◆ **Static estimation of the revenue-neutralizing rates, 2011–2021**

In table A.1 below, the key components of the UST base are presented alongside federal government revenues to be replaced from 2011 to 2021. From this, we derive the UST rate required to replace revenue in each of those years. This rate fluctuates between 0.67% in 2011 and 0.84% in 2021, peaking at 1.01% in 2017 during a year of strong economic growth and preceding the enactment of the Tax Cuts and Jobs Act.

◆

Table A.1. UST Base (in $trillions)

Year	Gross Sales[13]	Labor Services[14]	Securities[15]	Derivatives[16]	Owner Housing[17]	Total Base	Gov't. Revenue[18]	UST Rate to Replace Revenue
2011	$22.48	$6.63	$278.64	$25.93	$2.36	$336.04	$2.27	0.67%
2012	$23.53	$6.93	$264.49	$21.65	$2.43	$319.03	$2.39	0.75%
2013	$24.56	$7.11	$259.14	$24.07	$2.61	$317.49	$2.71	0.85%
2014	$25.81	$7.45	$246.99	$29.11	$2.73	$312.09	$2.90	0.93%
2015	$26.11	$7.86	$251.54	$30.19	$2.82	$318.52	$3.07	0.96%
2016	$26.58	$8.09	$262.33	$34.66	$3.01	$334.67	$3.10	0.93%
2017	$27.90	$8.47	$258.01	$38.84	$3.15	$336.37	$3.38	1.01%
2018	$29.65	$8.90	$292.74	$45.42	$3.32	$380.03	$3.21	0.84%
2019	$30.61	$9.32	$303.83	$49.69	$3.44	$396.89	$3.34	0.84%
2020	$29.30	$9.46	$358.30	$40.19	$3.70	$440.95	$3.39	0.77%
2021	$33.74	$10.29	$380.78	$40.76	$4.36	$469.93	$3.94	0.84%

MACROECONOMIC ANALYSIS

In this section, we estimate the macroeconomic impacts of the proposal, aiming to model economic activity in more detail as it evolves over time in response to tax changes, while also recognizing that we must take on more assumptions about how people, firms, and governments will behave in order to conduct such an analysis.

We use the open-source OG-USA model to forecast revenues and output under the new tax system. OG-USA is a dynamic, general equilibrium model with overlapping generations of heterogeneous households. We can't explicitly model all the effects discussed in the qualitative review above. Instead, our goal is to capture the principal influencers of aggregate productive capacity and economic output.

Overlapping-generations models cannot analyze situations in which structural deficits are left unattended over the long run, and so, in order to estimate the macroeconomic effects of the proposal, we make the assumption that the tax will be set initially to finance legislated future revenues, not just 2019 revenues, and

◆

that government spending will be decreased over time to eliminate long-run deficits.

◆ Description of Model

Simulated households make choices about how much to work and save based on current and future tax policy, their lifetime hourly earnings paths, and macroeconomic conditions. Model households are forward-looking and therefore their economic decisions are influenced by current and future policy and expected economic conditions. Model households face mortality risk, with rates of mortality, fertility, and immigration set to match U.S. demographics.

The supply side in OG-USA consists of firms that rent capital and employ labor to produce output that is purchased for private consumption, investment goods, or government expenditures. Firms face income taxes that are levied on corporate income, minus expenses for wages and depreciation.

The government can run budget deficits temporarily but must close the budget in the long run. Tax and spending policies can be modeled as transitory or permanent. OG-USA provides various policy tools to ensure that the budget is balanced in the long run, however, if tax and transfer policy results in unsustainable deficits, government spending is adjusted to close the gap and ensure a steady-state equilibrium can be obtained.

OG-USA offers parameterizations to consider closed economy, small open economy, and large open economy versions of the model.

Of importance for this analysis is how tax policy is modeled in OG-USA. Individual income and payroll taxes are modeled via parametric functions that allow for marginal and average tax rates to vary by income source (capital or labor income), total income, age, and tax year. The parameters of these functions are estimated on microdata produced from the open-source Tax-Calculator model.

◆

This model itself uses administrative or survey data on U.S. taxpayers and computes their tax liability, as well as their marginal tax rates under current law or proposed policy. In addition to income and payroll taxes on individuals, OG-USA can model sales taxes, wealth taxes, and corporate income taxes (including depreciation rules, investment tax credits, and other provisions).

♦ Model Calibration

The OG-USA model solves for the long-run steady state of the economy and the transition path from an initial period until that steady state is reached. We calibrate the household behavioral parameters of the OG-USA model to generate distributions of labor supply and wealth that are consistent with those observed in the U.S. in 2019. Demographics are set to match those in 2019 and then evolve in later years in accordance with recent trends in fertility, mortality, and immigration. Therefore, OG-USA exhibits population dynamics, with the population aging and its growth slowing according to observed trends until it reaches its long-run steady state.

Firm parameters, such as the capital-output ratio, are calibrated to match those observed in the United States. Government expenditures on goods and services are set as a fraction of GDP consistent with current policy, as are non–Social Security transfers. The Social Security system is modeled explicitly and uses current policy to determine benefit outlays. The parametric tax functions that represent the marginal and average tax rates on labor and capital income are estimated using Current Population Survey microdata in the Tax-Calculator model. We estimate these functions for each year from 2019 through 2031. This includes temporary provisions such as rate cuts that expire at the end of 2025. For model years 2031 and onward, we hold individual and payroll tax policy constant at its parameterization in 2031. We model the U.S. as a large

♦

open economy where government spending partially crowds out private investment.

To simulate the transactions tax, we zero out all federal taxes modeled by OG-USA: the corporate income tax, individual income taxes, and payroll taxes. We then levy taxes on consumption goods purchased by households, investment goods purchased by firms, and financial transactions. OG-USA does not include layers of intermediaries in the supply chain. To account for the cascading effect of the transactions tax through the supply chain, we use a factor estimated by Gary Robbins, 1.87, to scale up the transactions tax when applying it to final goods purchased by households. Thus, a 1% transaction tax will be represented by a 1.87% tax on consumption goods in the OG-USA model. We assume no cascading effect on the purchase of investment goods. OG-USA does not explicitly model the sale of assets; therefore we make the simplifying assumption that there is a fixed amount of turnover in asset portfolios and that the burden of the financial transaction tax is proportional to wealth.[19]

Because of the forward-looking nature of households and firms in OG-USA, a steady-state equilibrium must exist to enable one to solve for the transition path equilibrium from the present to the long-run steady state. A steady-state equilibrium cannot exist if government debt grows faster than GDP. Therefore, we need to assume that fiscal policy is implemented in such a way that eventually eliminates structural deficits. Our assumption is that this is done by adjusting government spending. To find the sales tax rate that results in the same revenue under current-law policy, we solve the model repeatedly with different sales tax rates until we find the one that generates the same revenue as current-law policy. The sales rate that generates equivalent revenue in OG-USA is higher than that under the static analysis because it includes an erosion of the transaction tax base from some behavior (e.g., from reduced household savings) that is not accounted for in the static analysis.[20] Note that the sales tax on financial transactions accounts for over 90% of the revenue raised.

MACROECONOMIC IMPACTS OF THE UNIVERSAL SALES TAX

Economic efficiency is increased with the removal of all income taxes and replacement with the proposed sales tax. *Employees are no longer directly taxed on their wages or salaries* (the tax on the sale of labor is borne by the buyer, that is, the employer); employees (and others) bear only a minor burden of the tax on financial transactions and consumer purchases. As a result, the long-run labor supply increases by 17%. GDP increases by 13% in the long run. Due to the tax on financial transactions—which increases tax rates on household savings—aggregate domestic savings increase by only about 4%. This is so despite the capital stock growing by about 5%. Thus, we see increases in the net inflows of capital from abroad as foreign investors seek higher after-tax returns from investing in U.S. companies.

◆ **Macroeconomic Effects**

	PERCENTAGE CHANGE
GDP	+13%
Capital stock	+5%
Savings	+4%
Labor supply	+17%
Consumption	+17%

◆ **Alternative Scenarios**

While OG-USA explicitly models behavior such as changes in labor supply, consumption, and savings, it does not explicitly

◆

model the turnover of assets in financial portfolios. The macro-economic effects above use the assumption that the ratio of asset sales to total assets remains constant. Because the tax on financial transactions represents such a high share of total revenue raised by the UST, this is a critical assumption. We, therefore, simulate the economy in the OG-USA model under alternative assumptions about how investors and traders would respond to the new system. These alternatives include a 10% reduction in financial asset turnover, a 25% reduction in turnover, and a 50% reduction in turnover. The results are presented in Table A.2.

Table A.2. Potential Responses to and Effects of Taxing Financial Transactions

REDUCTION IN ASSET TURNOVER	CHANGE IN GDP
0%	+13.05%
10%	+13.20%
25%	+13.47%
50%	+14.18%

As we assume lower asset turnover, the tax revenue raised by financial transactions shrinks and a higher rate is needed to match the long-run revenue under current-law policy. Despite this higher rate, GDP is not negatively affected because the lower turnover means that the tax burden on *holding* a unit of wealth declines, even though the cost of *selling* assets increases. Therefore, households' incentives to accumulate wealth increase in simulations with lower asset turnover. This results in a higher capital stock and higher GDP (though the effects are somewhat offset by countervailing effects of the higher rate on sales of consumption and investment goods).

Moreover, there is an alternative way of looking at the effect of a sales tax on asset turnover volume that could increase the volume of financial transactions. For example, the lure of tax-free realized capital gains, dividends, and interest will produce an incentive to purchase assets, thereby increasing revenue over the current tax regime.

These simulations do not capture any potential allocational efficiencies that are lost due to lower transaction volume. But they do show that behavior to avoid sales taxes by reducing financial transactions may not have significant effects on the main conclusions regarding the UST proposal.

◆ Review of Macroeconomic Findings

The proposal we've analyzed represents a feasible policy. The economy would expand under a universal sales tax. The tax on financial transactions generates the bulk of the revenue under the system, so a key question is to what extent it results in avoidance activities (such as lock-in effects on asset holdings) that could negatively affect the financial system. Modeling all of these precisely is outside the scope of the analysis here.

CONCLUSIONS AND RECOMMENDATIONS

The new federal tax system would have wide-ranging effects on the economy and the lives of Americans and others abroad. We have reviewed some of the more notable ones in a brief qualitative overview and a quantitative modeling analysis. Labor supply and capital will grow under the new system, increasing growth and opportunity.

Other effects will play a significant role in the lives of some individuals, families, and organizations, influencing their tax liabilities and reshaping the economies and markets in which they participate and interact with their fellows. Throughout the analysis, we included suggestions for the proposal designers to consider, and we consolidate those here:

◆

◆ **Define the financial transactions base carefully**

If it is too easy and remunerative for taxpayers to avoid the tax, they will do so, the base will erode, and the low rate envisaged here won't collect enough revenue. If the rate is dramatically higher than expected, its undesired behavioral effects will be more damaging, too. The offshoring of trading and trading firms, tax pyramiding, and tax-induced vertical integration will all be amplified at a higher rate. Carefully defining the base in the planning stages will allow the right starting rate to be estimated, and a broad and carefully protected base will be necessary to keep a low rate over the years.

◆ **Transition from the present tax system to the new one with care**

The UST proposal will likely benefit most American workers and businesses. Moving from the current system to the new system, however, will create meaningful short-term disruptions and be difficult to reverse if anything goes wrong. A transition plan will smooth the path considerably.

Careful planning to prevent undue erosion of the base of financial transactions will ensure a low tax rate and minimize tax distortions. A transition period, such as phasing in the new rates and phasing out the old rates linearly over a few years, would help to ensure that long-run benefits outweigh short-term disruptions.

◆

ACKNOWLEDGMENTS

Six people played a pivotal role in the writing of this book. The first of these, my old friend and colleague, philosopher Fred D. Miller, read several versions of its composition, and his help cannot be overstated. Political scientist Ronald J. Pestritto, the eminent scholar of American progressivism, read the original version of this book, which would never have been completed without his commentary and encouragement. Howard Dickman, a former editor at *Harper's*, *Reader's Digest*, the *Wall Street Journal*, and the Manhattan Institute for Policy Research, edited the book. His extraordinary talent made the writing and completion of this work possible.

The help provided by Gary Robbins, a retired economist from the Tax Foundation, was invaluable. The tax-reform proposal with which this book makes its closing arguments would not exist without his counsel. When I first suggested the reform, I was pleasantly surprised (perhaps "stunned" would be more accurate) when Gary, having investigated it, informed me of its feasibility.

Two other economists, Jason DeBacker and Matt Jensen, investigated the reform further and wrote the book's appendix in which they present their analysis of it.

Finally, my gratitude extends to my family, who encouraged me throughout the book's composition.

◆

ABOUT THE AUTHOR

Jeffrey E. Paul is a Research Professor in the Social Philosophy and Policy Center of the John Chambers College of Business and Economics at West Virginia University. He was previously a Research Professor at the Center for the Philosophy of Freedom at the University of Arizona from 2013 to 2022. Paul is Professor Emeritus at Bowling Green State University, where he served as Professor of Philosophy and as Associate Director of the Social Philosophy and Policy Center, formerly at Bowling Green. He played a pivotal role in the original founding and development of the Social Philosophy and Policy Center, where he led the center's highly successful fundraising campaign and also created and directed the center's influential resident scholar and conference programs. Professor Paul was a cofounder of *Social Philosophy & Policy,* published by Cambridge University Press, which has the largest circulation of any philosophical journal in the United States, the United Kingdom, and Canada. He continues in the role of Executive Editor of the journal. Paul has been a Visiting Scholar at the Hoover Institution of Stanford University.

◆

NOTES

CHAPTER 1

1 John Durham, Special Counsel, U.S. Department of Justice, "Report on Matters Related to Intelligence Activities and Investigations Arising Out of the 2016 Presidential Campaigns," May 12, 2023.

2 John Locke, *The Second Treatise of Government*, ch. 5, § 27. For the influence of Locke's natural-rights theory in America, see, e.g., Carl Lotus Becker, *The Declaration of Independence: A Study in the History of Political Ideas* (New York: Harcourt, Brace, 1922), chs. 2–3; Michael P. Zuckert, *Natural Rights and the New Republicanism* (Princeton, NJ: Princeton University Press, 1994); Zuckert, *The Natural Rights Republic: Studies in the Foundation of the American Political Tradition* (South Bend, IN: University of Notre Dame Press, 1996). More recently, C. Bradley Thompson has provided a comprehensive history of the Lockean foundation of the American Revolution. See his *America's Revolutionary Mind: A Moral History of the American Revolution and the Declaration That Defined It* (New York: Encounter Books, 2019).

3 James Otis, *The Rights of the British Colonies Asserted and Proved* (Boston and London: J. Almon, 1764), 30.

4 Ibid.

5 Ibid., 29.

6 Samuel Adams, "The Rights of Colonists," Report of the Committee of Correspondence to the Boston Town Meeting, November 20, 1772.

7 Moses Mather, *America's Appeal to the Impartial World* (Hartford, CT: Ebenezer Watson, 1775), 5, also quoted in Thompson, *America's Revolutionary Mind*, 162. A sermon preached after the Boston Massacre by Pastor John Lathrop—"Innocent Blood Crying to God from the Streets of Boston"—(reprinted in *Evans Early American Imprint Collection*) reflected the same perspective:

> BEFORE there was any such thing as civil government, which is founded on compact or the agreement of a number of people upon some plan to secure their general happiness, every individual had a perfect right to his own person, life, and limbs, and a clear sense of his duty and interest in preserving and defending them against the attacks of any one. These natural notions were planted in our breasts by the God who made us, and would for ever lead us to

determine that the life of man is sacred, and his blood not to be shed, unless forfeited by some atrocious crime.

Better known is the post–Revolutionary War short essay by James Madison, "Property," 1792, in Gaillard Hunt, ed., *The Writings of James Madison*, vol. 6 (1790–1802) (New York: G. P. Putnam's Sons, 1906), 101–3.

8 Among the "long Train of Abuses and Usurpations" laid at the feet of the king of Great Britain in the Declaration of Independence was "imposing Taxes on us without our Consent."

9 Vermont, Pennsylvania, Connecticut, Massachusetts, New Hampshire, and Rhode Island either banned slavery or instituted gradual emancipation by 1784. See Ira Berlin, *The Long Emancipation* (Cambridge, MA: Harvard University Press, 2015), 59–70.

10 "Declaration and Resolves of the First Continental Congress," in Jack N. Rakove, ed., *Founding America: Documents from the Revolution to the Bill of Rights* (New York: Barnes & Noble, 2006), 40.

11 Thomas Jefferson, "Notes of Proceedings in Congress [including Jefferson's draft of the Declaration of Independence with deletions and additions indicated]," in Rakove, *Founding America*, 124.

12 Ibid., 126–27.

13 Sean Wilentz, *No Property in Man: Slavery and Antislavery at the Nation's Founding* (Cambridge, MA: Harvard University Press, 2018).

14 See "Minutes of the Board of Visitors of the University of Virginia, Mar. 4, 1825," National Archives, Founders Online.

15 Theodore Dwight Weld, *The Power of Congress over the District of Columbia* (New York: John F. Trow, 1838), 43–44. "To abolish slavery," Weld went on, "is to take from no rightful owner his property; but to '*establish justice*' between two parties. To emancipate the slave, is to '*establish justice*' between him and his master—to throw around the person, character, conscience, liberty, and domestic relations of the one, the *same law* that secures and blesses the other. In other words, to prevent by *legal restraints* one class of men from seizing upon another class, and robbing them at pleasure of their earnings, their time, their liberty, their kindred, and the very use and ownership of their own persons."

16 See Francis Wayland, *Domestic Slavery Considered as a Scriptural Institution* (New York: Lewis Colby, 1845).

17 See "Slavery and Justice," Report of the Brown University Steering Committee on Slavery and Justice, 2006.

18 Francis Wayland, *The Elements of Moral Science*, ed. Joseph L. Blau (Cambridge, MA: Harvard University Press, 1963 [1835]), 311. This volume reprints the second (revised) edition, published in 1837.

19 Ibid., 183.

20 "A Friendly Word to Maryland: An Address Delivered in Baltimore, Maryland, on 17 November 1864," quoted in Peter C. Meyers, *Frederick Douglass: Race and the Rebirth of American Liberalism* (University of Kansas Press, 2008), 54.

◆

21 "Letter to Thomas Auld, September 3, 1848," quoted in David W. Blight, *Frederick Douglass: Prophet of Freedom* (New York: Simon & Schuster, 2018), 199.

22 Bills of rights were also a feature of several constitutions adopted by states in the Revolutionary War era; see William Clarence Webster, "Comparative Study of the State Constitutions of the American Revolution," *Annals of the American Academy of Political and Social Science* 9 (May 1897): 68–73.

23 "Speech on the Oregon Bill," June 27, 1848, in *Union and Liberty: The Political Philosophy of John C. Calhoun*, ed. Ross M. Lence (Indianapolis: Liberty Fund, 1992), 566.

24 Locke, *Second Treatise*, ch. 2, § 6.

25 "Speech on the Oregon Bill," *Union and Liberty*, 569. These views were repeated in Calhoun's famous *Disquisition on Government*, published posthumously in 1851; see *Union and Liberty*, 42–43 passim.

26 Ibid., 569–70.

27 John Fletcher, *Studies on Slavery in Easy Lessons* (Natchez, LA: Jackson Warner, 1852).

28 Wayland, *Domestic Slavery*; William Ellery Channing, *Slavery* (Boston: James Munroe, 1835).

29 Albert Taylor Bledsoe, *Essay on Liberty and Slavery* (Philadelphia: J. B. Lippincott, 1856), 36.

30 George Fitzhugh, *Sociology for the South: Or the Failure of Free Society* (Richmond, VA: A. Morris, 1854), 27–28.

31 Ibid., 69.

32 Ibid., 70.

33 Acknowledging these results, China's leadership began to transform its economic institutions after the death of Mao Zedong by restoring private property in capital. The effect of this change—lifting general standards of living—has been dramatic.

34 Ajay K. Mehrotra, *Making the Modern American Fiscal State: Law, Politics, and the Rise of Progressive Taxation 1877–1929* (New York: Cambridge University Press, 2013), 89. See also Angus Maddison, *Monitoring the World Economy 1820–1992* (Paris: OECD, 1995), 194–206; Maddison, *The World Economy* (Paris: OECD, 2001), 184; and Robert E. Gallman, "Economic Growth and Structural Change in the Long Nineteenth Century," in *The Cambridge History of the United States*, vol. 2: *The Long Nineteenth Century*, ed. Stanley L. Gallman and Robert E. Engerman (New York: Cambridge University Press, 2000).

35 Clarence D. Long, *Wages and Earnings in the United States, 1860–1890* (National Bureau of Economic Research) (Princeton, NJ: Princeton University Press, 1960), 109. Remarkably, these gains occurred during a period of substantial immigration and less than 10% of the labor force unionized in industry (116–17). Long served on President Eisenhower's Council of Economic Advisers and then served for two decades as a Democratic congressman from Maryland.

◆

36 Thomas C. Leonard, *Illiberal Reformers: Race, Eugenics, and American Economics in the Progressive Era* (Princeton, NJ: Princeton University Press, 2016), 3.

37 Werner Sombart, *Why Is There No Socialism in the United States?*, trans. Patricia M. Hockings and C. T. Husbands (New York: Macmillan, 1976 [1906]), 105.

38 Ibid., 65, has the table ("M" in the table represents German marks):

INDUSTRY	GERMANY	UNITED STATES
Clothing	621.4M	1323.0M – 2276.4M
Glass	724.9M	2154.6M
Pottery	772.2M	1701.0M
Brick and Tile	556.2M	1482.6M
Iron and Steel	792.5M–1014.2M	1642.2M–3074.4M
Chemicals	929.4M	2070.6M
Textiles	506.0M–776.5M	1129.8M–2192.4M
Paper	714.4M–765.9M	1318.8M–2087.4M
Leather	895.4M	1436.4M–1822.8M
Wood	698.8M–821.0M	1407.0M–1801.8M
Milling	743.0M	2007.6M
Sugar	496.0M	2045.4M–2326.8M
Tobacco	541.1M	1024.8M–1663.2M
Book-printing	893.7M	1747.2M–2234.4M

39 Ibid., 105.

40 The failure of Congress, the executive branch, and the judiciary to make good on the Fourteenth and Fifteenth Amendments during the Reconstruction era is well-known and the subject of a large literature. See, for example, Allen C. Guelzo, *Reconstruction: A Concise History* (New York: Oxford University Press, 2018) and Michael W. McConnell, "Originalism and the Desegregation Decisions," *Virginia Law Review* 81, no. 4 (May 1995): 947–1140. For a concise history of the failure to enforce the Second Amendment, see the concurring opinion of Justice Clarence Thomas in *McDonald v. Chicago*, 561 U.S. 742 (2010).

CHAPTER 2

1 Charles Edward Merriam, *A History of American Political Theories* (New York: August M. Kelley, 1969 [1903]), 307.

2 Ibid., 313.

3 Ibid., 313–14.

4 For an extended study of the ethnocentrism and racism of the early American progressives, see Thomas C. Leonard, *Illiberal Reformers: Race, Eugenics, and American Economics in the Progressive Era* (Princeton, NJ: Princeton University Press, 2016).

◆

5 Merriam, *History of American Political Theories*, 319.

6 Ibid., 320.

7 See Woodrow Wilson, *Constitutional Government in the United States* (New York: Columbia University Press, 1908), 16:

> No doubt a great deal of nonsense has been talked about the inalienable rights of the individual, and a great deal that was mere vague sentiment and pleasing speculation has been put forward as fundamental principle. The rights of man are easy to discourse of, may be very pleasingly magnified in the sentences of such constitutions as it used to satisfy the revolutionary ardor of French leaders to draw up and affect to put into operation; but they are infinitely hard to translate into practice. Such theories are never "law," no matter what the name or the formal authority of the document in which they are embodied. Only that is "law" which can be executed, and the abstract rights of man are singularly difficult of execution.

8 See Kathleen L. Wolgemuth, "Wilson and Federal Segregation," *Journal of Negro History* 44, no. 2 (April 1959): 158–73; Henry Blumenthal, "Woodrow Wilson and the Race Question," *Journal of Negro History* 48, no. 1 (January 1963): 1–21; A. Scott Berg, *Wilson* (New York: G. P. Putnam's Sons, 2013), 345–46. Ronald J. Pestritto, *Woodrow Wilson and the Roots of Modern Liberalism* (Lanham, MD: Rowman & Littlefield, 2005), 43–45, locates Wilson's racism not in his being raised in the South but in his political philosophy, heavily influenced by the German historicism discussed later in this book.

9 Berg, *Wilson*, 345–46.

10 Blumenthal, "Woodrow Wilson and the Race Question," 2.

11 Jean-Jacques Rousseau, "The Social Contract," 1762, in *The Social Contract and Discourse on the Origin of Inequality*, ed. Lester G. Crocker (New York: Washington Square, 1967), 17–18.

12 Ibid., 18–19.

13 Ibid., 19.

14 Ibid., 24.

15 Ibid., 27.

16 Ibid., 42–46.

17 Ibid., 44.

18 Ibid., 45.

19 See Adam Zamoyski, *Holy Madness: Romantics, Patriots, and Revolutionaries, 1776–1871* (New York: Penguin Books, 1999), 70.

20 Jeremy Bentham, "Review of the Declaration of Independence," *Scots Magazine* 39 (June 1777): 289.

21 Jeremy Bentham, "Anarchical Fallacies; Being an Examination of the Declarations of Rights during the French Revolution (c. 1795), in *Works of Jeremy Bentham*, vol. 2, ed. John Bowring (Edinburgh: William Tait, 1843), 501.

22 See Locke, *The Second Treatise of Government*, ch. 2, § 4: "To understand political power right, and derive it from its original, we must consider what state all men are naturally in, and that is, a *state of perfect freedom* to order their actions, and dispose of their possessions, and persons as they think fit, within the bounds of the law of nature, without asking leave, or depending upon the will of any other man."

23 Jeremy Bentham, *An Introduction to the Principles of Morals and Legislation* (London: Oxford at the Clarendon Press, 1823 [1780]), 1–2, 102.

24 John Stuart Mill, *Utilitarianism* (London: Parker, Son, & Bourn, 1863), 8–37.

25 Pestritto, *Woodrow Wilson*, 8–9, 18, 120.

26 Johann Kaspar Bluntschli, *The Theory of the State*, 3rd. ed. (London: Oxford at the Clarendon Press, 1895 [1885]), 67.

27 Ibid., 73.

28 Ibid.

29 Ibid., 91.

30 Ibid., 504.

31 Ibid., 84.

32 Andreas Dorpalen, *Heinrich von Treitschke* (Port Washington, NY: Kennikat, 1973 [1957]), 242.

33 Heinrich von Treitschke, *Politics*, vol. 2 (London: Constable, 1916), 271.

34 Friedrich Paulsen, *The German Universities and University Study*, trans. Frank Thilly and William W. Elwang (New York: Charles Scribner's Sons, 1906), 79–83.

35 Ibid.

36 Ibid., 80.

37 Ibid., 71.

38 R. Steven Turner, "The Prussian Universities and the Research Imperative, 1806 to 1848" (PhD diss., Princeton University, 1972), 366.

39 Ibid., 403.

40 James Axtell, *Wisdom's Workshop: The Rise of the Modern University* (Princeton, NJ: Princeton University Press, 2016), 267–68.

41 W. Carson Ryan, *Studies in Early Graduate Education* (Carnegie Foundation for the Advancement of Teaching, 1939), 32, 33.

42 Axtell, *Wisdom's Workshop*, 268.

43 Laurence R. Veysey, *The Emergence of the American University* (Chicago: University of Chicago Press, 1965), 130, 176.

44 F. W. Taussig, *Principles of Economics*, vol. 2, rev. ed. (New York: Macmillan, 1920), 251.

CHAPTER 3

1 John W. Burgess, *Reminiscences of an American Scholar: The Beginnings of Columbia University* (New York: AMS Press, 1966 [Columbia University Press, 1934]), 131.

◆

2   Ibid., 249.

3   Ibid., 252.

4   W. Elliott Brownlee, *Federal Taxation in America: A History*, 3rd ed. (Cambridge: Cambridge University Press, 2016), 51.

5   Fritz K. Ringer, *The Decline of the German Mandarins: The German Academic Community, 1890–1933* (Middletown, CT: Wesleyan University Press, 1990).

6   Paulsen, *The German Universities and University Study*, trans. Frank Thilly and William W. Elwang (New York: Charles Scribner's Sons, 1906), pp. 119–20. Ringer retranslated the passage from Paulsen; see *Decline of the German Mandarins*, 35.

7   E. R. A. Seligman, *Essays in Taxation* (Barcelona-Singapore: Athena University Press, 1915), 68.

8   Ibid.

9   E. R. A. Seligman, "Social Aspects of Economic Law," in *Essays in Economics* (New York: Macmillan, 1925), 310–11. This essay was Seligman's 1903 presidential address to the American Economic Association.

10 Seligman, *Essays in Taxation*, 71.

11 Ibid.

12 Ibid., 69.

13 Ibid., 69, 70.

14 Ibid., 71.

15 Ibid., 72.

16 Ibid., 27–30.

17 Kelly Phillips Erb, "Warren Buffett Gave Away 75% of Donald Trump's Net Worth in 2015, Offers Facts on Taxes," *Forbes*, October 10, 2016, forbes.com/profile/warren-buffett (as of February 14, 2023).

18 E. R. A. Seligman, *Progressive Taxation in Theory and Practice*, Publications of the American Economic Association, vol. 9, nos. 1 and 2 (January and March 1894) (Baltimore: Guggenheim, Weil, 1894), 190–200, 217. Seligman's justification for progressive taxation is not stated as precisely as my summary. And he thought, as well, that except for inheritance taxes, progressive taxation at the federal level in the U.S. was not at the time (1894) possible.

19 Edwin R. A. Seligman, *The Income Tax: A Study of the History, Theory, and Practice of Income Taxation at Home and Abroad*, 2nd ed. (New York: Macmillan, 1914), 633.

20 Ibid., 634.

21 Thomas Piketty, *Capital in the Twenty-First Century* (Cambridge: Belknap Press of Harvard University Press, 2014), 493–534.

22 Ibid., 525–26.

23 Ibid., 520–21.

24 Ibid., 522.

25 Quoted in Mark Leff, *The Limits of Symbolic Reform: The New Deal and Taxation, 1933–1939* (Cambridge: Cambridge University Press, 1984), 112. Leff

notes, paraphrasing La Follette, that this group of taxpayers pulled in "a whopping nine-tenths of the net income reported by taxpayers."

26 Ibid., 105–7.

27 Henry C. Simons, *Personal Income Taxation* (Chicago: University of Chicago Press, 1938), 219, also quoted in Leff, *Limits of Symbolic Reform*, 107.

28 John W. Burgess, *The Reconciliation of Government with Liberty* (New York: Charles Scribner's Sons, 1915), 369.

29 Ibid., 371.

30 John W. Burgess, *Recent Changes in American Constitutional Theory* (New York: Columbia University Press, 1923), 42–43, 50.

31 Frank Johnson Goodnow, *The American Conception of Liberty and Government* (Providence, RI: Standard Printing, 1916), 20–21.

32 Ibid., 19.

33 Ibid., 31.

34 Frank J. Goodnow, *Social Reform and the Constitution* (Norwood, MA: Norwood Press, 1911), 35–36.

35 Ibid., 221.

36 See Ronald J. Pestritto, *America Transformed: The Rise and Legacy of American Progressivism* (New York: Encounter Books, 2021), 181–82, 200–218. See also Pestritto, *Woodrow Wilson and the Roots of Modern Liberalism* (Lanham, MD: Rowman & Littlefield, 2005), 221–52; and Philip Hamburger, *Is Administrative Law Unlawful?* (Chicago: University of Chicago Press, 2014), ch. 24.

37 Hamburger, *Is Administrative Law Unlawful?*, 463.

38 Ibid., 114.

39 Burgess, *Reconciliation of Government with Liberty*, 380.

40 Ibid.

41 Nicholson was a fictional lead character in the Academy Award–winning World War II epic. In the movie, British POWs at a Japanese prison camp in Burma are ordered to construct a railway bridge to connect Bangkok and Rangoon, facilitating the Japanese war effort. The camp commander tells the POWs that their officers will work alongside them. Nicholson, the senior British officer, refuses, explaining that the Geneva Conventions exempt officers from manual labor—whereupon he and his officers are confined in metal boxes while their men labor under Japanese officers. Their efforts deliberately impede rather than facilitate the bridge's construction, so Nicholson and his officers are released, on condition that they will lead their men in the bridge construction. Citing the need for discipline among his troops to sustain their esprit de corps and sense of purpose, Nicholson succeeds in completing the bridge. Meanwhile, British commandos have made their way to the bridge in order to blow it up. On the threshold of succeeding in their plans, they are discovered by Nicholson, whose first instinct is to stop them. Then, as he slowly grasps the implications of what he has achieved for the enemy, he is hit by a bullet from the Japanese, who are aiming at the British commandos. Uttering the words "What have I done?"

◆

Nicholson falls involuntarily on the commandos' detonator, blowing up the bridge.

CHAPTER 4

1 Herbert Tuttle, "Academic Socialism," *Atlantic Monthly*, August 1883, 203, 208.

2 Herbert Baxter Adams, "The Historical Work of Professor Herbert Tuttle," in *Annual Report of the American Historical Association for 1894* (Washington, DC: Government Printing Office, 1896), 29.

3 Tuttle, "Academic Socialism," 204, 206.

4 Ibid., 207, 206.

5 Gilman to Reverdy Johnson, quoted in Hugh Hawkins, *Pioneers: A History of Johns Hopkins University 1874–1889* (Baltimore: Johns Hopkins University Press, 1996), 22.

6 Ibid., 33–78.

7 Ibid., 136.

8 Ibid., 137.

9 Loretta Marie Dunphy, *Simon Newcomb: His Contribution to Economic Thought* (Washington, DC: Catholic University of America Press, 1956), 9.

10 Joseph Dorfman, *The Economic Mind in American Civilization*, vol. 3: *1865–1918* (New York: Augustus M. Kelley, 1969 [1949]), 87.

11 Simon Newcomb, "The Let Alone Principle," *North American Review* 110, no. 226 (January 1870): 2; see also Albert E. Moyer, *A Scientist's Voice in American Culture: Simon Newcomb and the Rhetoric of Scientific Method* (Berkeley: University of California Press, 1992), 110.

12 See Richard T. Ely, *Ground under Our Feet* (New York: Macmillan, 1938), 41–45, 51–52.

13 On the historical school, see Daniel T. Rodgers, *Atlantic Crossings: Social Politics in a Progressive Era* (Cambridge, MA: Harvard University Press, 1998), 83–84, 89–91; Jurgen Herbst, *The German Historical School in American Scholarship* (Middletown, CT: Wesleyan University Press, 1965); Dorfman, *Economic Mind*, vol. 3, 87–98. See also Benjamin Rader, *The Academic Mind and Reform: The Influence of Richard T. Ely in American Life* (Lexington: University of Kentucky Press, 1966), 29–31.

14 Johann Kaspar Bluntschli, *The Theory of the State* (London: Oxford at the Clarendon Press, 1895 (1885), 67.

15 Ibid., 70.

16 Richard T. Ely, *Social Aspects of Christianity, and Other Essays* (New York: Thomas Y. Crowell, 1889), 119.

17 The attempt to reconcile these two objectives has been particularly well documented in two books: Peter Novick, *That Noble Dream: The "Objectivity Question" and the American Historical Profession* (New York: Cambridge University Press, 1988) and Mary O. Furner, *Advocacy and Objectivity: A Crisis in the Professionalization of American Social Science, 1865–1905* (New Brunswick, NJ: Transaction, 2011).

◆

18 Richard T. Ely, *The Past and Present of Political Economy*, Johns Hopkins University Studies in Historical and Political Science, Second Series III (Baltimore: Johns Hopkins University, 1884), 49–50.

19 Ibid., 52–53.

20 Rodgers, *Atlantic Crossings*, 91.

21 Ibid.

22 Ely, *Past and Present*, 62–63.

23 Richard T. Ely, *Hard Times: The Way In and the Way Out* (New York: Macmillan, 1931), quoted in Rodgers, *Atlantic Crossings*, 90.

24 Evalyn A. Clark, "Adolph Wagner: From National Economist to National Socialist," *Political Science Quarterly* 55, no. 3 (September 1940): 378.

25 Rodgers, *Atlantic Crossings*, 89.

26 Richard T. Ely, "Fundamental Beliefs in My Social Philosophy," *Forum* 18, no. 2 (October 1894): 183.

27 See Furner, *Advocacy and Objectivity*, esp. pp. 59–142.

28 Ibid., 63, 65.

29 Edmund J. James, "Newcomb's Political Economy," *Science* 6, no. 147 (November 27, 1885): 470. See also Moyer, *A Scientist's Voice*, 106, and Furner, *Advocacy and Objectivity*, 81–84.

30 Simon Newcomb, "The Two Schools of Political Economy," *Princeton Review* 60 (July–December 1884): 299; see also Moyer, *A Scientist's Voice*, 117.

31 Moyer, *A Scientist's Voice*, 116.

32 Furner, *Advocacy and Objectivity*, 69. The expression "men of the Sumner type" is from a letter by Ely to E. R. A. Seligman.

33 Rodgers, *Atlantic Crossings*, 82–83.

34 "Report of the Organization of the American Economic Association," *Publications of the American Economic Association* 1, no. 1 (March 1886): 6, 7.

35 Simon Newcomb, "Review of Richard T. Ely, *An Introduction to Political Economy* and *Outlines of Economics*," *Journal of Political Economy* 3 (December 1894): 106; also quoted in Furner, *Advocacy and Objectivity*, 73.

36 See Furner, *Advocacy and Objectivity*, 77, and 68–80 generally for an account of the formation of the AEA based on primary sources.

37 E. R. A. Seligman, "Changes in the Tenets of Political Economy with Time," *Science*, vol. 7, supplement, April 23, 1886, reprinted as "Continuity of Economic Thought," in *Science Economic Discussion* (New York: Science Company, 1886), 22–23. See also Furner, *Advocacy and Objectivity*, 98–99.

38 Furner, *Advocacy and Objectivity*, 144.

39 Rader, *Influence of Richard T. Ely*, 111.

40 Ely's successful endeavors echo on a state scale what Gustav Schmoller (Adolph Wagner's successor as the most influential state-socialist economist) pulled off on a national scale in Germany. Because all faculty appointments were made by the Prussian state, Schmoller was able to get himself, by "his close ties to the Prussian Ministry of Education into a position as the most

◆

powerful 'professor-maker' in late-nineteenth-century Germany; by the turn of the century, despite the emperor's efforts to dilute Schmoller's influence, economics chairs and government offices throughout Germany were filled with his pupils." See Rodgers, *Atlantic Crossings*, 92–93.

41 Joseph Dorfman, *The Economic Mind in American Civilization 1865–1918*, vol. 3 (New York: Augustus M. Kelley, 1969), p. 277.

42 John R. Commons, *Races and Immigrants in America* (New York: Macmillan, 1907), 41, also quoted in Leonard, *Illiberal Reformers: Race, Eugenics, and American Economics in the Progressive Era* (Princeton, NJ: Princeton University Press, 2016), 50.

43 Edward A. Ross, *Changing America: Studies in Contemporary Society* (New York: Century, 1912), 4–5, partially quoted in Leonard, *Illiberal Reformers*, 50. See Ross's comment on black suffrage in *Social Psychology: An Outline and Source Book* (New York: Macmillan, 1913), 361–62.

44 Leonard, *Illiberal Reformers*, 40.

45 Frederic C. Howe, *Wisconsin: An Experiment in Democracy* (New York: Charles Scribner's Sons, 1912), vii.

46 Ibid., 42. Another progressive cheerleader claimed that Wisconsin's accomplishments could be attributed to its people's Teutonic racial origins: see Leonard, *Illiberal Reformers*, 41.

47 Emmanuel Saez and Gabriel Zucman, *The Triumph of Injustice: How the Rich Dodge Taxes and How to Make Them Pay* (New York: Norton , 2019), 130–31.

48 Westel Woodbury Willoughby, *An Examination of the Nature of the State* (New York: Macmillan, 1896), 108–10.

49 Ibid., 123, 124.

50 Ibid., 126.

51 Ibid., 130.

52 Ibid., 134.

53 Ibid., 346.

54 Ibid.

55 Westel Woodbury Willoughby, *Social Justice: A Critical Essay* (New York: Macmillan, 1900), 315.

56 Ibid., 268.

57 Westel Woodbury Willoughby, *Prussian Political Philosophy: Its Principles and Implications* (New York: D. Appleton, 1918), p. 3.

58 Ibid., 18.

59 Willoughby, *Nature of the State*, 132.

60 Willoughby, *Prussian Political Philosophy*, 47.

CHAPTER 5

1 Susan Zlotnick, "Contextualizing David Levy's *How the Dismal Science Got Its Name*; or Revisiting the Victorian Context of David Levy's History of Race and Economics," in *Race, Liberalism, and Economics*, ed. David Colander,

◆

Robert E. Prasch, and Falguni A. Sheth (Ann Arbor: University of Michigan Press, 2007), 88, 89.

2 John Ruskin, *Unto This Last* (New York: Cosimo Classics, 2006 [1862]), 48.

3 Mary Ritter Beard, *The Making of Charles A. Beard: An Interpretation* (1955), quoted in Richard Drake, "Charles Beard & the English Historians," *Constitutional Commentary* 29, no. 3 (Summer 2014): 314. While he was at Oxford, Beard helped establish Ruskin Hall in his hero's honor.

4 Ellen Nore, *Charles A. Beard: An Intellectual Biography* (Carbondale: Southern Illinois University Press, 1983), 24–25, citing Charles A. Beard, "A Living Empire I," *Young Oxford*, October 1901, and "A Living Empire II," November 1901; see also Drake, "Charles Beard," 316–17.

5 See Nore, *Charles A. Beard*, 30–34.

6 Edwin Seligman, *The Economic Interpretation of History* (New York: Columbia University Press, 1907 [1902]), 155. On Seligman and Beard, see Richard Hofstadter, *The Progressive Historians* (New York: Alfred A. Knopf, 1968), 196–200.

7 Nore, *Charles A. Beard*, 56, quoting from a 2016 letter that Beard wrote to his then student, Raymond Moley.

8 Robert E. Brown, *Charles Beard and the Constitution: A Critical Analysis of "An Economic Interpretation of the Constitution"* (Princeton, NJ: Princeton University Press, 1956), 3.

9 Ibid., 197. Two years after Brown's book came out, historian Forrest McDonald published another, independently researched critique of Beard: *We the People: The Economic Origins of the Constitution* (Chicago: University of Chicago Press, 1958).

10 Charles A. Beard, "That Noble Dream," *American Historical Review* 41, no. 1 (October 1935): 74.

11 Carl Lotus Becker, *The Declaration of Independence: A Study in the History of Political Ideas* (New York: Harcourt, Brace, 1922), 134.

12 Ibid., 74.

13 Ibid., 99 (Becker quoting from a letter to Dennys De Berdt, January 12, 1768); see *Writings of Samuel Adams*, ed. Harry Alonzo Cushing (New York: G. P. Putnam's Sons, 1904), 135.

14 Ibid., 108 (quoting from James Wilson, *Considerations on the Nature and Extent of the Legislative Authority of the British Parliament* [1774]).

15 Ibid.

16 Ibid., 122.

17 Ibid., 225.

18 Ronald D. Rotunda, *The Politics of Language: Liberalism as Word and Symbol* (Iowa City: University of Iowa Press, 1986), 39.

19 See Butler's introductory remarks to "The Great Political Superstition," in Herbert Spencer, *The Man versus the State*, ed. Truxton Beale (New York: Mitchell Kennerly, 1916 [1884]), 177–81.

20 Rotunda, *Politics of Language*, 45, 46.

◆

21 "Homeless Liberals," *New York Times*, September 28, 1924, quoted in Rotunda, *Politics of Language*, 49.

22 "That Blessed Word 'Liberal,'" *New York Times*, February 6, 1930, quoted in Rotunda, *Politics of Language*, 49.

23 Herbert Spencer, "The New Toryism," in *The Man versus the State* (Caldwell, ID: Caxton Printers, 1940 [1884]), 8.

24 L. T. Hobhouse, *Liberalism* (Cambridge, UK: Cambridge University Press, 1911).

25 John Dewey, *Liberalism and Social Action* (New York: Capricorn Books, 1963 [1935]), 3–6.

26 Ibid., 19.

27 Ibid., 21.

28 Ibid., 90.

29 Burton Folsom Jr., *New Deal or Raw Deal? How F.D.R.'s Legacy Has Damaged America* (New York: Threshold Editions, 2008), 43.

30 John T. Flynn, *Country Squire in the White House* (New York: Doubleday, Doran, 1940), 79.

31 Ibid., 80–81.

32 *Schechter Poultry Corp. v. United States*, 295 U.S. 495 (1935). Two contemporary economists have presented the case that the collusive, anticompetitive arrangements established by the NRA not only retarded a recovery, but they lived on for several years *after* the law was struck down, wreaking additional damage on the economy. See Harold L. Cole and Lee E. Ohanion, "How Government Prolonged the Depression," *Wall Street Journal*, February 2, 2009; Lee E. Ohanion, "Lessons from the New Deal," testimony before the U.S. Senate Committee on Banking, Housing, and Urban Affairs, April 4, 2009.

33 Flynn, *Country Squire*, 81.

34 Walter Lippmann, *The Good Society* (New Brunswick, NJ: Transaction, 2005 [1937: Boston: Little, Brown]), 106–30.

35 Ibid., 123.

36 Louis Hartz, *The Liberal Tradition in America: An Interpretation of American Political Thought since the Revolution* (New York: Harcourt, Brace & World, 1955), 4.

37 Lippmann, *Good Society*, 5.

38 Gene Smiley, *Rethinking the Great Depression* (Chicago: Ivan R. Dee, 2002).

39 Milton Friedman and Anna Jacobson Schwartz, *The Great Contraction* (Princeton, NJ: Princeton University Press, 1965).

40 Thomas E. Hall and J. David Ferguson, *The Great Depression: An International Disaster of Perverse Economic Policies* (Ann Arbor: University of Michigan Press, 1998).

41 Ibid., 148–51.

42 Robert Higgs, *Depression, War, and Cold War: Challenging the Myths of Conflict and Prosperity* (New York: Oxford University Press, 2006), 81.

◆

43 Ibid., 81, 82.

44 Ibid., 82.

45 Ibid., 91.

46 Alice Schroeder, *The Snowball: Warren Buffett and the Business of Life* (New York: Bantam Books, 2008), 77–78.

47 Russell Kirk, *The Conservative Mind* (New York: BN, 2008 [1953]), 24.

48 Ibid.

49 Ibid., 44.

50 Jean-Jacques Rousseau, *The Social Contract and Discourse on Inequality*, ed. Lester G. Crocker (New York: Washington Square, 1967), 36.

51 Kirk, *Conservative Mind*, 158.

52 Gordon Keith Chalmers, "Goodwill Is Not Enough," *New York Times*, May 17, 1953; "Generation to Generation," *Time*, July 6, 1953.

53 Clinton Rossiter, *Conservatism in America: The Thankless Persuasion*, 2nd ed., rev. (New York: Vintage Books, 1962), 80. When he was not in the process of inventing a history to suit his political inclinations and creating a fictitious conservative and liberal tradition before the terms were in use in America, Rossiter, in his more serious and scholarly work, did carefully explicate the natural-rights theory of the revolution and attributes to Locke a principal role in informing the views of the Founders: see *The Political Thought of the American Revolution* (New York: Harcourt, Brace & World, 1963), 68–70.

54 Gordon S. Wood, *The Creation of the American Republic 1776–1787* (Chapel Hill: University of North Carolina Press, 1969), 68.

55 Michael P. Zuckert, *Natural Rights and the New Republicanism* (Princeton, NJ: Princeton University Press, 1994), 157. See also 155–59 and notes, which draws on historians' critique of Wood's thesis. Zuckert, 159–75, also discusses J. G. A. Pocock, whose 1975 book *The Machiavellian Moment* made yet another attempt to submerge Locke's influence.

56 Garry Wills, *Inventing America* (New York: Doubleday, 1978).

57 Kenneth S. Lynn, "Falsifying Jefferson," *Commentary*, October 1978. A year later, historian Ronald Hamowy published a meticulous, devastating critique of Wills: "Jefferson and the Scottish Enlightenment: A Critique of Garry Wills's *Inventing America: Jefferson's Declaration of Independence*," *William and Mary Quarterly* 36, no. 4 (October 1979): 503–23. See also Zuckert, *Natural Rights*, 19–23.

58 John Rawls, *A Theory of Justice* (Cambridge, MA: Belknap Press of Harvard University Press, 1971), 101.

59 Michael J. Sandel, *Liberalism as the Limits of Justice* (New York: Cambridge University Press, 1982), 78.

60 Ibid.

61 "Remarks by the President at Presentation of the National Medal of the Arts and the National Humanities Medal," the White House, Office of the Press Secretary, September 29, 1999.

◆

CHAPTER 6

1 William F. Buckley Jr., *God and Man at Yale: The Superstitions of Academic Freedom* (Washington, DC: Regnery, 1951), ch. 2: "Individualism at Yale."

2 McGeorge Bundy, "The Attack on Yale," *Atlantic Monthly*, November 1951. Bundy would go on to be national security adviser to Presidents John F. Kennedy and Lyndon Johnson, and president of the Ford Foundation.

3 See David M. Levy and Sandra J. Peart, *Towards an Economics of Natural Equals: A Documentary History of the Early Virginia School* (New York: Cambridge University Press, 2020).

4 Ibid., 48–49.

5 Ibid., 91.

6 Ibid., 255–57.

7 Paul A. Samuelson and William D. Nordhaus, *Economics*, 13th ed. (New York: McGraw Hill, 1989), 837.

8 Paul F. Lazarsfeld and Wagner Thielens Jr., *The Academic Mind* (New York: Free Press, 1958).

9 Everett Carll Ladd and Seymour Martin Lipset, *The Divided Academy: Professors and Politics* (New York: McGraw Hill, 1975).

10 Ibid., 1, 2, 3.

11 Ibid., 26. In the authors' smaller 1972 survey, 49% of faculty described themselves as Left or Liberal, while 25% classified themselves as moderately or extremely conservative (27).

12 Ibid., 60.

13 Carnegie Foundation for the Advancement of Teaching, *The Condition of the Professoriate: Attitudes and Trends, 1989* (Princeton, NJ: Princeton University Press, 1989), 143. The survey reported the responses of more than 5,000 faculty members.

For a number of years, the Higher Education Research Institute at the University of California at Los Angeles conducted large national surveys of faculty members at hundreds of private and public colleges and universities. Among many other questions, those surveyed were asked to identify themselves politically, and the results consistently showed an imbalance. For example, the 2004–05 survey of 40,670 faculty members at 421 colleges and universities showed that in public universities, 9.5% identified as "Far Left" and 49.5% as "Liberal," while 14.3% were "Conservative" and 0.4% were "Far Right" (26% were "Middle of the Road"). In private universities, 9.8% were "Far Left" and 49.6% were "Liberal," while 14.2% were "Conservative" and 0.3% were "Far Right" (26.2% identified as "Middle of the Road"). See "The Nation: Opinions and Attitudes of Full-Time Faculty Members," *Chronicle of Higher Education* 54, no. 1 (August 31, 2007).

The political tilt was apparent, but the problem with this survey, as with the others (such as in 1989–90, 1998–99, or 2000–02), is that it reported the aggregate results across *all disciplines*—they did not break out the social sciences and humanities. Surveys that did focus on

◆

these crucial disciplines have consistently shown a far greater political imbalance.

14 *Colorado Review* 1, no. 3 (1987): 24.

15 See, for example, *Delaware Spectator*, October 6, 1993 (University of Delaware); *Stanford Review*, November 14, 1994; Kenneth Lee, "Our Monotone Universities," *American Enterprise*, September/October 1995, 7–8 (Cornell and Stanford).

16 "The Shame of America's One-Party Campuses," *American Enterprise*, September 2002, 19–25.

17 Daniel B. Klein and Charlotta Stern, "Political Diversity in Six Disciplines," *Academic Questions* 18, no. 1 (Winter 2004–05): 40–52. The authors received 1,678 responses to the 5,486 surveys mailed.

18 Daniel B. Klein, Charlotta Stern, and Andrew Western, "Voter Registration of Berkeley and Stanford Faculty," 53–65. See also Stanley Rothman, S. Robert Lichter, and Neil Nevitte, "Politics and Professional Advancement among College Faculty," *The Forum* 3, no. 1 (2005): 1–16, which discussed the stark contrasts over the years between faculty self-descriptions of their political leanings and those of the general public. Another study, a few years later—Bruce L. R. Smith, Jeremy D. Mayer, and A. Lee Fritschler, *Closed Minds? Politics and Ideology in American Universities* (Washington, DC: Brookings Institution Press, 2008)—also showed a political/ideological imbalance. In that study, however, the number of faculty queried in the pivotal social sciences and humanities—the disciplines in which normative views affect conclusions—was tiny.

19 Klein, Stern, and Western, "Voter Registration," 60.

20 Ibid., 48. The quoted material by Robert George was taken from a column by David Brooks, "Lonely Campus Voices," *New York Times*, September 27, 2003.

21 Richard Hofstadter and Walter P. Metzger, *The Development of Academic Freedom in the United States* (New York: Columbia University Press, 1955), 419–24 passim.

22 Ibid., 418.

23 Ibid., 485.

24 See, for example, Robert P. George, "Free Speech and Due Process at Princeton: The Case of Joshua Katz," *Quillette*, June 10, 2022.

25 Mitchell Langbert, Anthony J. Quain, and Daniel B. Klein, "Faculty Voter Registration in Economics, History, Journalism, Law, and Psychology," *Econ Journal Watch* 13, no. 2 (September 2016): 422–51.

26 Ibid., 425.

27 Ibid., 427.

28 Ibid., 428.

29 Mitchell Langbert, "Republicans Need Not Apply: An Investigation of the American Economic Association Using Voter Registration and Political Contributions," *Econ Journal Watch* 17, no. 2 (September 2020): 392–404.

30 Ibid., 397.

◆

31 John Cochrane, "Political Diversity at the AEA," *The Grumpy Economist* (blog), October 1, 2020.

32 Philip Hamburger, "Intolerant Lawyers Shouldn't Be Judges," *Wall Street Journal*, February 9, 2022.

33 Mitchell Langbert, "Homogeneous: The Political Affiliations of Elite Liberal Arts Colleges," *Academic Questions* 31, no. 2 (Summer 2018): 186–97.

34 Ibid., 192.

35 John Tierney, "Where Cronies Dwell," *New York Times*, October 11, 2005. His column referenced a report of political imbalance by David Horowitz and Joseph Light, "Representation of Political Perspectives in Law and Journalism Faculties," Center for the Study of Popular Culture, October 2005.

36 John Tierney, "Why Righties Can't Teach," *New York Times*, October 15, 2005.

37 Neil Gross and Solon Simmons, "The Social and Political Views of American Professors," working paper, September 24, 2007.

38 Summers quoted in David Glenn, "Few Conservatives but Many Centrists Found in American Academe," *Chronicle of Higher Education*, October 8, 2007.

39 Neil Gross, *Why Are Professors Liberal and Why Do Conservatives Care?* (Cambridge, MA: Harvard University Press, 2013).

40 "Jordan Peterson: Why I Am No Longer a Tenured Professor at the University of Toronto," *National Post*, January 19, 2022.

41 Meimei Xu, "More than 80 Percent of Surveyed Harvard Faculty Identify as Liberal," *Harvard Crimson*, July 13, 2022. See also Phillip W. Magness and David Waugh, "The Hyperpoliticization of Higher Ed: Trends in Faculty Political Ideology, 1969–Present," *Independent Review* 27, no. 3 (Winter 2022/23): 359–69.

42 "UNC vs. the Echo Chamber," *Wall Street Journal*, January 27, 2023. For the voter data, see Gigi De La Torre, "Democrats Outnumber Republican Professors 16 to 1 at UNC," *The College Fix*, August 24, 2022.

43 Magness and Waugh, "Hyperpoliticization of Higher Ed," 364.

44 Quoted in Robert B. Westbrook, *John Dewey and American Democracy* (Ithaca, NY: Cornell University Press, 1991), 441.

45 Robert Nozick, *Anarchy, State, and Utopia* (New York: Basic Books, 1974).

46 Thomas Nagel, "Libertarianism without Foundations," in *Reading Nozick: Essays on Anarchy, State, and Utopia*, edited and with an introduction by Jeffrey E. Paul (Lanham, MD: Rowman & Littlefield, 1981), 193.

CHAPTER 7

1 Everett Carll Ladd and Seymour Martin Lipset, *The Divided Academy: Professors and Politics* (New York: McGraw Hill, 1975), 2.

2 Ibid., 2–3. The report they quoted from was A. James Reichley, "Our Critical Shortage of Leadership," *Fortune*, September 1971.

3 Quoted in Janet Maslin, "'The War Room': Behind the Scenes of Clinton's Campaign," *New York Times*, November 3, 1993.

◆

4 S. Robert Lichter, Stanley Rothman, and Linda S. Lichter, *The Media Elite: America's New Power Brokers* (New York: Adler & Adler, 1986), 20–21. (The interviews were conducted by a survey research team in 1979 and 1980.)

5 Ibid., 30.

6 Ibid., 39.

7 Ibid., 40.

8 Ibid., 41.

9 Ibid., 51, quoting Daniel Patrick Moynihan, "The Presidency & the Press," *Commentary*, March 1971.

10 Kenneth Dautrich and Jennifer Necci Dineen, "Media Bias: What Journalists and the Public Say about It," Roper Center, *The Public Perspective*, October/November 1996, 7.

11 Quoted in Bernard Goldberg, *Bias: A CBS Insider Exposes How the Media Distort the News* (New York: HarperCollins, 2003 [Regnery, 2002]), 130.

12 Ibid., 130–31. A study published in 2019 by David H. Weaver, Lars Willnat, and G. Cleveland Wilhoit found that only 7.1% of 1,080 full-time journalists consider themselves Republican, with 38.8% leaning left, 43.8% middle-of-the-road, and 12.9% leaning right. However, their survey included *all* types of journalists (political and others) from all over the country. See "The American Journalist in the Digital Age: Another Look at U.S. News People," *Journalism and Mass Communication Quarterly* 96, no. 1 (2019): 11.

13 Thomas E. Patterson, "News Coverage of Donald Trump's First 100 Days," Shorenstein Center on Media, Politics and Public Policy, Kennedy School, Harvard University, May 18, 2017. The report also surveyed London's *Financial Times*, as well as two public broadcasters—Britain's BBC and Germany's ARD—whose coverage was also unfavorable.

14 Ibid.

15 Edith Efron, *The News Twisters* (Los Angeles: Nash, 1971).

16 Efron, *How CBS Tried to Kill a Book* (Los Angeles: Nash, 1972).

17 William McGowan, *Gray Lady Down: What the Decline and Fall of the* New York Times *Means for America* (New York: Encounter Books, 2010).

18 Paul Matzko, *The Radio Right: How a Band of Broadcasters Took on the Federal Government and Built the Modern Conservative Movement* (New York: Oxford University Press, 2020), 18.

19 See Paul Matzko, "'Do Something about Life Line': The Kennedy Administration's Campaign to Silence the Radio Right," *Presidential Studies Quarterly* 48, no. 4 (December 2018): 4, for estimates.

20 Matzko, *Radio Right*, 5, 76. The Reuther Memorandum was eventually leaked to the public. A complete text is in Victor G. Reuther, *The Brothers Reuther and the Story of the UAW/A Memoir* (Boston: Houghton Mifflin, 1976), 491–500.

21 Reuther, *Brothers Reuther*, 497–98.

22 Matzko, *Radio Right*, 97–98. David Burnham, a longtime investigative reporter for the *New York Times*, concluded in "Misuse of the I.R.S: The

Abuse of Power," September 3, 1989, that "although Nixon was notorious for treating the I.R.S. as though it were his private domain, the records show that Franklin Delano Roosevelt may have set the stage for the use of the tax agency for political purposes by most subsequent Presidents."

There is a long, sordid history of American presidents (of both parties) misusing the IRS to punish critics and political enemies. Matzko touches on this history; but see also David Burnham, *A Law unto Itself: Power, Politics and the IRS* (New York: Random House, 1989), 226–90; Gail Russell Chaddock, "Playing the IRS Card: Six Presidents Who Used the IRS to Bash Political Foes," *Christian Science Monitor*, May 17, 2013; Ben Shapiro, *The People vs. Barack Obama* (New York: Threshold Editions, 2014), 85–117; and Tom Fitton, *Clean House: Exposing Our Government's Secrets and Lies* (New York: Threshold Editions, 2016), 163–79.

23 Reuther, *Brothers Reuther*, 498.

24 Matzko, *Radio Right*, 98.

25 Ibid., 104.

26 Ibid., 112–13.

27 Matzko, "Silence the Radio Right," 13; see also Matzko, *Radio Right*, 194–224.

28 Fitton, *Clean House*, 177–78. Fitton is president of Judicial Watch. See also Juliet Eilperin and Zachary A. Goldfarb, "IRS Officials in Washington Were Involved in Targeting of Conservative Groups," *Washington Post*, May 13, 2013; Treasury Inspector General for Tax Administration, "Inappropriate Criteria Were Used to Identify Tax-Exempt Applications for Review," Department of the Treasury, Washington, DC, May 14, 2013.

29 Jeff Gerth, "The Press versus the President," *Columbia Journalism Review*, January 30, 2023, part 1.

30 Ibid., part 4.

31 Ibid.

32 Kyle Pope, "Looking Back on the Coverage of Trump," *Columbia Journalism Review*, January 30, 2023.

CHAPTER 8

1 Richard Pipes, *The Russian Revolution* (New York: Vintage Books, 1991 [1990]), 672.

2 Ibid., 673.

3 Mikhail Geller and Alexsandr Nekrich, *Utopia in Power: The History of the Soviet Union from 1917 to the Present*, trans. Phyllis B. Carlus (New York: Summit Books, 1986), 118, 120. See also Pipes, *Russian Revolution*, 695–99, and Jack Hirshleifer, "Disaster and Recovery: A Historical Survey," RAND Corporation, April 1963, 15–31.

4 Pipes, *Russian Revolution*, 687.

5 Ibid., 701.

6 Geller and Nekrich, *Utopia in Power*, 120. According to H. H. Fisher, *The Famine in Soviet Russia 1919–1923* (New York: Macmillan, 1927), 553, the total expenditure to Russia administered through the ARA was $61,566,231. This

◆

included congressional appropriations, private U.S. philanthropy, and funds from Russian republics and the Soviet government.

7 Pipes, *Russian Revolution*, 703. Compulsory labor—organizing workers as in the military—was an article of faith in the original 1848 *Communist Manifesto*: "8. Equal liability of all to labour. Establishment of industrial armies, especially for agriculture."

8 Ibid., 708.

9 Ibid., 711.

10 Ibid., 793 (citing I. Steinberg, *Gewalt und Terror in der Revolution*).

11 Ibid.

12 V. I. Lenin, "The New Economic Policy and the Tasks of the Political Education Departments," October 17, 2021, in *V. I. Lenin Collected Works*, vol. 33, translated from the Russian, edited by David Skvirsky and George Hanna (Moscow: Progress Publishers, 1973), 60–79.

13 Ibid., "The Role and Functions of the Trade Unions under the New Economic Policy," January 12, 1922, 184–96.

14 Ibid., 184–85.

15 Pipes, *Russian Revolution*, 671–72.

16 Ibid.; Pipes also quotes Trotsky and another communist authority that the measures undertaken during the war were means to implement the planned economy that followed from Marxist theory.

17 Edward Jay Epstein, *Dossier: The Secret History of Armand Hammer* (New York: Random House, 1996), 59, quoting from a speech by Aleksandr Solzhenitsyn in Carl Gershman, "Selling Them the Rope," *Commentary*, April 1979. The speech was delivered in 1975 to the AFL-CIO.

18 Epstein, *Dossier*, 61.

19 See Antony C. Sutton, *Western Technology and Soviet Economic Development, 1917–1930* (Stanford, CA: Hoover Institution Press, 1968), 4, 327–40.

20 F. L. Carsten, *The Rise of Fascism*, 2nd ed. (Berkeley: University of California Press, 1982), 73.

21 Ibid., 75.

22 Robert Gellately, *Hitler's True Believers: How Ordinary People Became Nazis* (New York: Oxford University Press, 2020), 19–20.

23 Ibid., 24.

24 Ibid.

25 Ibid., 2.

26 Ibid., 75, quoting from Otto Strasser, *Hitler and I* (Boston: Houghton Mifflin, 1940), 81.

27 Ibid., 83.

28 Henry Ashby Turner Jr., *German Big Business and the Rise of Hitler* (New York: Oxford University Press, 1985), 89–96.

29 Ibid., 233–34.

30 Ibid., 238–39.

◆

31 Quoted in Epstein, *Dossier*, 324.

32 Steven W. Mosher, "China's New 'Social Credit System' Is a Dystopian Nightmare," *New York Post*, May 18, 2019. See also Isabelle Qian, Muyi Xiao, Paul Mozur, and Alexander Cardia, "Four Takeaways from a *Times* Investigation into China's Expanding Surveillance State," *New York Times*, July 26, 2022.

CHAPTER 9

1 Edwin R. A. Seligman, *The Income Tax: A Study of the History, Theory, and Practice of Income Taxation at Home and Abroad*, 2nd ed. (New York: Macmillan, 1914), 633: "So far as national taxation is concerned, it will scarcely be doubted that the income tax is not needed—at all events not for purposes of normal revenue."

2 Thomas Piketty, *Capital in the Twenty-First Century* (Cambridge: Belknap Press of Harvard University Press, 2014), 493–534.

3 Ibid., 525–26.

4 Emmanuel Saez and Gabriel Zucman, *The Triumph of Injustice: How the Rich Dodge Taxes and How to Make Them Pay* (New York: Norton, 2019), 146.

5 Thomas Piketty, *A Brief History of Equality* (Cambridge, MA: Belknap Press of Harvard University Press, 2022 [2021]), 149–79.

6 *Internal Revenue Service Data Book*, 2022, 3.

7 OECD.org, Revenue Statistics—OECD countries: Comparative tables, 4300: Estate, Inheritance, and Gift Taxes.

8 Michael T. Kaufman, *Soros: The Life and Times of a Messianic Billionaire* (New York: Vintage Books, 2003), 170. For another wealth-protecting device, the grantor retained annuity trust (GRAT), see the discussion of Mark Zuckerberg and Dustin Moskovitz in Steven C. Hartnett, "Facebook Founders Provide an Excellent Estate Planning Example," American Academy of Estate Planning Attorneys, May 16, 2012.

9 Quoted in David Cay Johnston, "Dozens of Rich Americans Join in Fight to Retain the Estate Tax," *New York Times*, February 14, 2001.

10 Jeff Ernsthausen, James Bandler, Justin Elliott, and Patricia Callahan, "More than Half of America's 100 Richest People Exploit Special Trusts to Avoid Estate Taxes," ProPublica, September 28, 2021.

11 For some of these would-be egalitarians, David Callahan, *Fortunes of Change: The Rise of the Liberal Rich and the Remaking of America* (New York: John Wiley & Sons, 2010), 125–42.

12 See ch. 3

13 Jesse Eisinger, Jeff Ernsthausen, and Paul Kiel, "The Secret IRS Files: Trove of Never-Before-Seen Records Reveal How the Wealthiest Avoid Income Tax," ProPublica, June 8, 2021.

14 "Historical Income Tax Rates and Brackets, 1862–2021," Tax Foundation, August 24, 2001.

15 Amity Shlaes, *Great Society: A New History* (New York: HarperCollins, 2019), 11.

◆

16 Ibid.

17 See also Michael Janofsky, "Pessimism Retains Grip on Appalachian Poor," *New York Times*, February 9, 1998.

18 Shlaes, *Great Society*, 11.

19 *Internal Revenue Service Databook*, 2019, table 1: Collections and Refunds, by Type of Tax, FY 2018 and 2019, p. 3.

20 Ajay K. Mehrotra, *Making the Modern American Fiscal State: Law, Politics, and the Rise of Progressive Taxation 1877–1929* (New York: Cambridge University Press, 2013), 388.

21 PriceWaterhouse Worldwide Tax Summaries, 2022.

22 Ibid.

23 See Ronald Hamowy, "Failure to Provide: Healthcare at the Veterans Administration," Independent Institute, March 2010; Michael Pearson, "The VA's Troubled History," CNN, May 23, 2014.

24 John Ubaldi, "VA Still in Disarray Four Years after Veterans Wait-List Death Scandal," Ubaldi Reports, April 12, 2018.

25 "Statement of Dr. Minu Aghevli, Coordinator, Opioid Agonist Treatment Program at VA Maryland Health Care System before the Subcommittee on Oversight and Investigations, United States House of Representatives, June 25, 2019"; see also Karma Allen and Stephanie Ebbs, "Veterans Affairs Whistleblowers Call for End to Culture of Retaliation: The Employee Received a Letter the Day She Was Set to Testify," ABC News, June 25, 2019.

26 See "More VA Documents Expose Wait-Time Manipulation and Denial of Care," Concerned Veterans for America, March 30, 2022; John Byrnes, "Veterans Affairs Bureaucrats Are Keeping Vets from Using Health Care outside Its Troubled System," *New York Post*, December 1, 2021; Leo Shane III, "VA Has a 'Broken Culture' regarding Patient Safety, Watchdog Warns," *Military Times*, October 27, 2021.

27 Charles Blahous, "Even Doubling Taxes Wouldn't Pay for 'Medicare for All,'" *Wall Street Journal*, August 1, 2018, and "The Costs of a National Single-Payer Healthcare System," Mercatus Center, George Mason University, July 30, 2018.

28 Chris Jacobs, *The Case against Single Payer* (Alexandria, VA: Republic, 2019), 121.

29 Ibid., 122.

30 Ibid., 148.

31 "Waiting Your Turn: Wait Times for Health Care in Canada, 2022 Report," Fraser Institute, December 8, 2022.

32 Jacobs, *Case against Single Payer*, 152–58.

33 David Luhnow and Max Colchester, "The U.K.'s Government-Run Healthcare Service Is in Crisis," *Wall Street Journal*, February 6, 2023.

34 Jacobs, *Case against Single Payer*, 25–43, 239–40.

CHAPTER 10

1 David Callahan, *Fortunes of Change: The Rise of the Liberal Rich and the Remaking of America* (New York: John Wiley & Sons, 2010), 2.

2 Ibid., 3.

3 Ibid., 266.

4 Ibid., 251–67.

5 Ibid., 266.

6 Ibid.

7 Ibid., 280.

8 G. A. Cohen, *If You're an Egalitarian, How Come You're So Rich?* (Cambridge, MA: Harvard University Press, 2000), 154.

9 Engels quoted in Tristram Hunt, *Marx's General: The Revolutionary Life of Friedrich Engels* (New York: Metropolitan Books, 2009), 263.

10 Ibid.

11 Ibid., 189.

12 Ibid., 263.

13 Ibid., 189–92.

14 Walter Benn Michaels, *The Trouble with Diversity: How We Learned to Love Identity and Ignore Inequality* (New York: Metropolitan Books, 2006), 15–16.

15 Callahan, *Fortunes of Change*, 284.

16 Thomas Frank, *Listen, Liberal: Or, Whatever Happened to the Party of the People?* (New York: Metropolitan Books, 2016), 256–57.

17 Alvin W. Gouldner, *The Future of the Intellectuals and the Rise of the New Class: The Frame of Reference, Theses, Conjectures, Arguments, and an Historical Perspective on the Role of Intellectuals and Intelligentsia in the International Class Contest of the Modern Era* (New York: Seabury Press, 1979), 1.

18 Ibid., 3.

19 Ibid.

20 Ibid., 4.

21 Everett Carll Ladd and Seymour Martin Lipset, *The Divided Academy: Professors and Politics* (New York: McGraw Hill, 1975), 2.

22 Gouldner, *Rise of the New Class*, 90–91.

23 Alvin W. Gouldner, *The Hellenic World: A Sociological Analysis* (New York: Harper & Row, 1965), 156–58.

CHAPTER 11

1 Herbert Tuttle, "Academic Socialism," *Atlantic Monthly* 52, no. 310 (August 1883): 200–210.

2 Ibid.

3 Charles Edward Merriam, *A History of American Political Theories* (New York: August M. Kelley, 1969 [1903]), 307.

4 Ibid., 313.

◆

5 Woodrow Wilson, *Constitutional Government in the United States* (New York: Columbia University Press, 1908), 16.

6 Cass Sunstein, *The Second Bill of Rights: FDR's Unfinished Revolution and Why We Need It More than Ever* (New York: Basic Books, 2004), 26–27; see also Liam Murphy and Thomas Nagel, *The Myth of Ownership: Taxes and Justice* (New York: Oxford University Press, 2002), 74–75.

7 Merriam, *History of American Political Theories*, 313, 314.

8 See Thomas C. Leonard, *Illiberal Reformers: Race, Eugenics, and American Economics in the Progressive Era* (Princeton, NJ: Princeton University Press, 2016).

9 George Christakes, *Albion W. Small* (Boston: Twayne, 1978), 81; see also Albion Small, *General Sociology* (Chicago: University of Chicago Press, 1905), 296:

> Morality is observance of a certain code recognized by the group as suitable. So long as government and laws are not recognized as suitable, conduct regardless of government, or subversion of government, may count merely as physical resistance of superior force trying to maintain itself in the place of rightful government. Such conduct may be denounced as crime by the *de facto* government, but it will not be so rated by the State as a whole, nor will it be classed as immorality. It is not violation, but observance of the order regarded as fit (e.g., the Boers, November, 1901, resisting the British government in spite of Lord Kitchener's proclamation declaring them traitors; the Ku Klux Klan under negro domination in the reconstruction period; this is doubtless the psychology of much of the lynching in the United States today).

10 Philip Hamburger, "Education Is Speech: Parental Free Speech in Education," *Texas Law Review* 101, no. 2 (2022): 471.

11 Stephen H. Norword, *The Third Reich in the Ivory Tower: Complicity and Conflict on American Campuses* (New York: Cambridge University Press, 2009), 56–57.

12 Adam Candeub, "Bargaining for Free Speech: Common Carriage, Network Neutrality, and Section 230," *Yale Journal of Law & Technology* 22 (1920): 391–433.

13 47 U.S. Code § 230(c)(1): "No provider or user of an interactive computer service shall be treated as the publisher or speaker of any information provided by another information content provider."

14 *Missouri v. Biden Jr.*, 2023.

15 Board of Governors of the Federal Reserve System, Federal Reserve Economic Data (FRED), Federal Reserve Bank of St. Louis.

16 *Internal Revenue Service 2019 Data Book*, 3.

17 University of Pennsylvania, Wharton School of Finance, Penn Wharton Budget Model, "Senator Elizabeth Warren's Wealth Tax: Budgeting and Economic Effects," December 12, 2019.

◆

18 The sources for the dollar figures in this paragraph are discussed in the appendix.

19 Employees would need to file a simple statement of their annual earnings to the IRS (as documented by their employer) in order to be included in Social Security, Medicare, etc.

20 Andrew Robinson, *Einstein on the Run: How Britain Saved the World's Greatest Scientists* (New Haven, CT: Yale University Press, 2019), 226.

21 David Nasaw, *The Patriarch: The Remarkable Life and Turbulent Times of Joseph P. Kennedy* (New York: Penguin Books, 2012), 200.

22 Tuttle, "Academic Socialism," 207.

APPENDIX

1 For a discussion of the impact of statutory rates on location decisions, see Michael P. Devereux and Rachel Griffith, "Evaluating Tax Policy for Location Decisions," *International Tax and Public Finance* 10, no. 2 (March 2003): 107–26.

2 For a useful discussion of bases and base erosion for financial transaction taxes, see Thomas Matheson, "Security Transaction Taxes: Issues and Evidence," *International Tax and Public Finance* 19, no. 6 (December 2012): 884–912.

3 Steven R. Umlauf, "Transaction Taxes and the Behavior of the Swedish Stock Market," *Journal of Financial Economics* 33, no. 2 (April 1993): 227–40.

4 See a discussion of similar considerations by European Commission planners of a proposed European Union Financial Transactions Tax in Thomas Hemmelgarn et al., "Financial Transaction Taxes in the European Union," *National Tax Journal* 69, no. 1 (March 2016): 217–40.

5 Washington State Tax Structure Study Committee, table 9-7, "A Measure of Pyramiding of the B&O Tax," in "Tax Alternatives for Washington State: A Report to the Legislature," vol. 1, November 2002, 112.

6 Securities Industry and Financial Markets Association, "Statistics," 2022.

7 Congressional Budget Office, "Options for Reducing the Deficit 2019 to 2028," 2018.

8 Bureau of International Settlements, "Exchange-Traded Futures and Options, by Location of Exchange," "OTC Foreign Exchange Turnover by Country and Instrument in 2019, 'net-gross' basis," "OTC Single Currency Interest Rate Derivatives Turnover by Country and Instrument in 2019, 'net-gross' basis."

9 Robert Pollin, James Heintz, and Thomas Herndon, "The Revenue Potential of a Financial Transaction Tax for US Financial Markets," *International Review of Applied Economics* 32, no. 6 (2018): 772–806.

10 The gross sales come from the U.S. Bureau of Economic Analysis, "Gross Output by Industry," 2019. In his research, Gary Robbins adjusted the BEA numbers—used here—by deducting the sales of services by Federal Reserve banks, owner-occupied housing, services provided by nonprofits, religious, grantmaking, civic, professional, and similar organizations, and output

◆

produced from within private households. Robbins derived the average annual sales revenue of owner-occupied housing from the Commerce Department and the Census Bureau's housing survey. Housing sales were estimated at one-sixth of the Commerce Department's estimate of owner-occupied residential capital.

11 Wages and salaries come from the U.S. Bureau of Economic Analysis, "2019 Personal Income and Its Dispositions," 2023, and includes both private and public sectors.

12 Estimates for 2019 revenue collection and deficits are derived from the U.S. Bureau of Economic Analysis, table 3.2, "Federal Government Receipts and Expenditures" (accessed August 25, 2022). They exclude excise taxes and duties, which will be kept and whose revenues do not need to be replaced.

13 U.S. Bureau of Economic Analysis (BEA), "U.S. Gross Output by Industry" (accessed June 14, 2023). Includes private-industries output less Federal Reserve banks, credit intermediation, and related activities; owner-occupied housing; religious, grantmaking, civic, professional, and similar organizations; and private households' production.

14 BEA, "Table 2.1. Personal Income and Its Disposition" (accessed June 14, 2023). Includes private industry and government wages and salaries.

15 SIFMA (Securities Industry and Financial Markets Association), "U.S. Statistics Database" (accessed June 14, 2023). Includes annualized transactions volumes, including issuances, for the following asset types: Treasury securities; agency debt; equities; nonagency asset-backed securities and collateralized debt obligations; agency mortgage-backed securities, non-agency mortgage-backed securities, and corporate bonds.

16 Bureau of International Settlements, "Exchange-Traded Futures and Options, by Location of Exchange," "OTC Foreign Exchange Turnover by Country and Instrument, 'net-gross' basis," "OTC Single Currency Interest Rate Derivatives Turnover by Country and Instrument, 'net-gross' basis." We apply a 90% adjustment factor to North American exchange volume to estimate the U.S. base and, following the Joint Committee on Taxation, assume that the annual flows of payment as a result of derivatives contracts amount to 2% of the notional value of derivatives transactions.

17 BEA, "Table 5.1. Current-Cost Net Stock of Residential Fixed Assets by Type of Owner, Legal Form of Organization, and Tenure Group" (accessed June 14, 2023). The volume of residential sales is estimated as one-sixth of the BEA's estimate of owner-occupied residential capital.

18 BEA, "Table 3.2. Federal Government Current Receipts and Expenditures" (accessed June 14, 2023). Includes personal current taxes, taxes on corporate income, contributions for government social insurance, and capital transfer receipts.

19 Due to this modeling choice, the statutory burden of the tax on financial transactions only falls on domestic savers in OG-USA. Depending on the details of the proposal and potential avoidance, this tax may directly affect foreign savers who own U.S. assets.

◆

20 Certain potential responses, such as changes in the composition of investment portfolios or changes in the duration securities are held are not directly modeled in OG-USA. However, in the next section we do provide an analysis of the macroeconomic effects of reduced turnover of financial assets using an exogenous change in the duration assets are held.

INDEX

◆

◆

◆

◆

Index